The

E R O S

of

E V E R Y D A Y

L I F E

Susan Griffin

ANCHOR BOOKS
DOUBLEDAY
NEW YORK   LONDON   TORONTO   SYDNEY   AUCKLAND

The

EROS

of

EVERYDAY

LIFE

Essays on Ecology, Gender and Society

AN ANCHOR BOOK
PUBLISHED BY DOUBLEDAY
a division of Bantam Doubleday Dell Publishing Group, Inc.
1540 Broadway, New York, New York 10036

ANCHOR BOOKS, DOUBLEDAY, and the portrayal of an anchor
are trademarks of Doubleday, a division of Bantam Doubleday Dell
Publishing Group, Inc.

The Eros of Everyday Life was originally published in hardcover by Doubleday in 1995.

The Library of Congress has cataloged the Doubleday edition as follows:

Griffin, Susan.
The eros of everyday life : essays on ecology, gender and society
/ Susan Griffin.
p.   cm.
1. Sex role.   2. Women—Social conditions.   3. Nature.
4. Feminism.   I. Title.
HQ1075.G74   1995
305.42—dc20   95-5871
                                                          CIP

ISBN 0-385-47399-0
Copyright © 1995 by Susan Griffin
All Rights Reserved
Printed in the United States of America
First Anchor Books Edition: September 1996

5   7   9   10   8   6   4

Contents

II

OCTOBER 1, 1930

BUT MAYBE I HAVE THE SOLUTION——WHY OTHERS FIND SEX
IN MY WORK AND I DO NOT: IT CAME FROM AN ARTIST . . .
WHO CALLED ON ME RECENTLY. . . . HE SAID, IN EFFECT,
THAT I HAD SEEN . . . NATURAL FORMS . . . WITH SUCH
INTENSITY, WITH SUCH DIRECT HONESTY, THAT A TREMENDOUS
FORCE LIKE SEX, WHICH ENTERS INTO, PERMEATES ALL NATURE,
COULD NOT BUT BE REVEALED.

—Edward Weston, *The Daybooks*

I

THE EROS OF
EVERYDAY
LIFE

1
Sometimes It Is Named

So this is how the world was made flesh,
though surely the word came after
the sublime idea, after the sea's
withdrawal and the island's emergence
with first birds and giant lizards
carrying their young into the pampas.

—LYNN MCMAHON,
"Poems at Christmastime"

Clever, but schoolteacher beat him anyway to show him
that definitions belonged to the definers—not the defined.

—TONI MORRISON,
Beloved

Sometimes it is named. Sometimes not. A movement, a ripple moving through the social body, a new shape in the shared thought of a society. This time it is a meeting. Distinct visions are coming together: the understanding that nature is a source of meaning encounters the hope for a just society. There is no simple name for what is occurring. But certainly a familiar habit of mind, already frayed, is dissolving.

To describe this shift in consciousness, a phenomenon which is still unraveling, one must include the presence of the less defined too, that which one cannot easily discern from what we mistakenly call background. Because to know the texture, the full complexity, or the wanderings of this latest form of social change, is to witness a phenomenon that cannot be found in one place alone. Its genesis, as with the genesis of any authentic movement in thought, is not located in any single book, essay, or even conversation. It arrived as if in a congregation, in a confluence of events, thoughts, words. The union took place, and is still taking place, through meetings between social forces, ideas of spirit, gender, equality, empire, progress, democracy, events such as the building of factories, the invention of machineries and technologies in cooperation or collision with natural existence, great bodies of water or the needs of the mammalian body, forests or the earth's atmosphere, the life cycle of salmon, the hieroglyphs of DNA.

The change proceeds in so many directions I cannot be its narrator. I am instead immersed in the atmosphere of this motion myself, my own thought changing even as I write. But I can speak of a philosophical shift I am witnessing in my thinking, a shift that is beginning to occur in the political, social and religious assumptions which I have inherited and which persist in Western culture today.

These old assumptions are as much the focus of this essay as is another kind of thought just emerging. Because the assumptions that belong to a culture are often invisible in their fullest dimensions and consequences, one must make them visible before discerning change. The very process of seeing the structure of thought *is* itself a crucial kind of change and genesis.

Much of what I write about here, the fragmented identities which also divide society by injustice and conflict, an equally divisive and hence alienated approach to knowledge, the spoiling of nature, the building of empires, warfare, has been written about before. But there is a thread that connects all these, a psychology and a sad destructive logic common among them which one senses yet has remained in many ways unrevealed.

I would like to report that the growth of another way of thinking is inevitable, an approach that posits consciousness as part of nature, an experience of knowledge as intimacy rather than power. But there is no foregone conclusion. The domination of Western thought expands even now throughout the world. Because the subject of this work is thought, the mood may be reflective. Yet this is the reflection of an intelligent animal, searching for solutions to what may be a catastrophe in the making. I write with a sense of urgency. If my thought is part of a larger and continual evolution of thought that is still partly incipient, at the same time that it is cracked open here and there by a few words, it is also a response to a crisis that is yet unfolding too, and still unrevealed in its full dimension.

The activities of highly industrialized human society threaten the ability of the earth to sustain life. This is a staggering observation, difficult to take in: human society is destroying life on earth. Yet the condition is palpable. Air grows thinner, and death becomes more common among species. Here where I live, the last stand of the oldest redwoods on the face of the earth is threatened. I was born in California. I know the feel of the bark, have watched so much of the old terrain vanish.

And yet another terrain seems to vanish too, if not the fact of land, of a certain orientation, a map of the world, stories of creation, histories, and, along with this, ways in which the world made sense and heaven and earth were connected into one pattern of meaning. If somewhere a shift in consciousness occurs which promises to open up new possibilities to the imagination, this is not the pervasive mood. One senses instead a kind of disintegration, a fragmentation of meaning as an older order which once unified and explained experience fails.

Even the popularity of fundamentalism, which on the surface might belie meaninglessness, can be read as a symptom of a fundamental lack of meaning. The grasp seems too tenacious, as if the intent were to rescue something that has already been lost.

The very rigidity of belief signals an inward collapse, as if any fuller vision might reveal faults in the vision. What is no longer present in these doctrines is that quality of motion which identifies life. If the appearance of stability is the principal virtue of such a philosophy, still such an inflexibility has a quality close to death. And this can only bring despair, the kind of desperation that leads to violence.

But at this moment desperation has a wider provenance. One feels it at the core of contemporary sensibility. Coming of age as I did after two world wars, one is wary of belief. The difficulty deepens, as so many utopias fail, and ideals are betrayed even by their own achievements. At times the only meaning that seems possible is meaningless itself. That over the last two decades deconstruction has permeated almost every form of inquiry with doubt is only part of this larger mood of unraveling. In *Race Matters,* Cornel West writes about the "cultural decay and moral disintegration of poor black communities." This is a disintegration one encounters everywhere, among the most and least privileged. Children murdered, or murdering each other, a panoply of violence, warfare, rape, abuse, and the widening gap between rich and poor, hunger, deprivation etched in too many human lives. This is our social landscape.

It is in this atmosphere that I write. My thought, shaped by this particular place in time, California near the end of the twentieth century, resonates to these crises, both social and environmental. To an old, and perhaps not entirely perceptible, habit of mind, these two deteriorations, that of nature and society, are scarcely related. For centuries the European culture into which I was born has pitted the necessities of nature against the requirements of society. In this culture, the guiding paradigm of action has as its goal a mastery of nature. And one still thinks along these old lines. If there are not enough jobs, if there is not enough food on the table, not enough money for schools and medicine, society cannot afford to worry about preserving a forest, or one species of owl, a certain kind of fish. Instead, the habitual response has been to extend the length and breadth of human control over natural process.

Yet, writing now, I do not find the loss of forests, the loss of a way to make a living, and a sense of meaninglessness unconnected. There is a resemblance in the look and feel of a field that has been polluted with chemical waste, a neighborhood devastated by poverty and injustice, a battlefield. And this resemblance is not coincidental. The alienation of human society from nature has led to many different kinds of destruction, not the least of which has been the fragmentation of consciousness.

Still, at this moment, many different movements come together in my mind. In the small city where I live a protest continues against the careless storage of radioactive waste in the green hills that I see even now out my window to the east, a region seasonally threatened by fire, prone to earthquake. In my thoughts this protest mingles with stories I hear from a friend about successful efforts to clean the Ganges River in India, and these mingle with what I know of movements for the survival of first peoples, the Sami of Scandinavia, the Mbuti Pygmies of Zaire, the Karen of Thailand. And I do not separate any of these movements from efforts to democratize American society, to understand the consequences of rape and abuse, the causes of war, prejudice, injustice.

I am not alone as I try here to trace these attempts at change to a shift in the deepest levels of meaning we share. An early, still fragile meeting in consciousness between the care for nature and a care for human society offers a glimpse of a possibility redolent with promise. If human consciousness can be rejoined not only with the human body but with the body of earth, what seems incipient in the reunion is the recovery of meaning within existence that will infuse every kind of meeting between self and the universe, even in the most daily acts, with an eros, a palpable love, that is also sacred.

But this is not an easy juncture; it requires more than simple addition. By the science of ecology it has been established that all phenomena in nature, including human beings, are interconnected. And in the modern social world the interdependency of human beings and human societies with each other as well as with nature is in some ways beginning to be better understood now. Yet to act in concert with these insights or, even more crucial, to cultivate states of being and ways of living which are located in this knowledge is not simple.

When fundamentalists say that the problem of contemporary society is that no one believes in anything anymore, this is only partly true. The problem lies also with what is believed. Underneath almost every identifiable social problem we share, a powerful way of ordering the world can be detected, one we have inherited from European culture and that alienates consciousness both from nature and from being. Even as I write, the progression of words, sentences, ideas are social, and arise from history, a history that burdens perception at the same time that it enables vision. In my own life, whenever I have sought change I have had to reexamine certain assumptions in my thought. And even if I have come to see again and again that when I strip away the old structure it is not simply chaos that I find but another order of meaning, implicit in my own experience and in the life of the earth, this is a fearsome process.

Since my earliest childhood, I have witnessed a slow and complex process of change, sometimes hardly visible, often contradictory, by which an old idea of the cosmos disintegrates and another vision emerges. Though the collaboration has often been subterranean and has involved far-flung, disparate, even divergent minds, the effort is social. "History," as John Edgar Wideman has written, "is driven by mind in the same sense a flock of migratory birds, its configuration, destination, purpose, destiny, are propelled, guided by the collective mind of the immediate flock and also the species, all kindred birds past and present inhabiting Great Time." The motion of this change does not have that air of historical inevitability that has been claimed by other social movements in this century. It is filled instead with conflicts, reversals, ambiguities, ambivalences, false paths, and above all that abiding fear which, however great the need and hope for transformation, must of necessity accompany a shift that is so deep and momentous in its potential, a fear that at times makes consciousness appear to be rigid and unchanging even in the midst of motion.

I came of age in a time of intellectual confinement. These were the middle years of the twentieth century which followed in the wake of terrifying violence. The Second World War ended eight months after my third birthday. This history has shaped my moral imagination. Good had won over bad; democracy had triumphed, or so it seemed. But the celebration was shadowed. Almost immediately, a war of a different kind began, one with atomic bombs, then missiles, then nuclear warheads that were tested, paraded, stockpiled, or used to threaten. And the intellectual atmosphere was mobilized, too. One was schooled in a new wartime rhetoric. The enemy was close. Certain ideas entered the realm of the forbidden.

Although my grandfather was a Republican who sat on the edge of his seat while he watched the televised Senate hearings, cheering as Joseph McCarthy conducted his interrogations, by the time I reached fifteen years of age, I was a radical. In my second year in college, I was even investigated by the FBI for my own activities in a growing student movement. I had attended meetings of a Marxist discussion group. Members of the Communist Party were there, perhaps hoping to find new recruits. They were what my father would have called nice guys, but I slept through the meetings. A few years earlier I had read my first socialist literature, including Marx, and been strongly influenced. I believed in economic equality, and the Marxist insistence on the material causes of history was crucial to the development of my own thought. But for reasons which were only vague to me then, I found this talk of the proletariat class and the means of production somehow fusty.

It would take me years to understand my boredom. The Cold War had divided thought by the most rigid moral categories. From the establishment's perspective one was either an anti-Communist or un-American. Radicals and liberals who defended free speech were publicly shamed, marginalized, informed and spied upon, hounded from jobs, forced into unemployment and poverty, driven to despair and even suicide. And the Rosenbergs had been executed.

The ambience of the divide was stifling. The effect was to polarize the social imagination. Dissident thinkers of every kind found it difficult to criticize either China, the Soviet Union, or Marxist theory for fear of being used in any fashion to aid or abet the witch hunt. One way or another rigidity came to characterize thought on both sides of the partition.

I was not aware then how much my own thinking had been foreshortened by the habits of this polemic. In a decade captivated by a false grin, what was crucial was simply to be able to speak the unspeakable, to break the silence. Families praying together on billboards, shiny new cars, dozens of housing tracts, built just yesterday, but all for tomorrow. *Progress is our most important product,* was the slogan, uttered before a yawning refrigerator door, a metaphor beamed by electronic waves into millions of homes across the country.

I was born in the City of Angels Hospital in a Los Angeles already so filled with asphalt and highways that the shape of the place, a wide bowl between several ranges of mountains, skirted by the Pacific Ocean, was scarcely visible any longer. That my mother was anesthetized during my delivery, or that she fed me according to her doctor's instructions, by a statistically devised schedule, instead of my own hunger, seemed somehow to be part of this altered landscape. As I grew up the city increased its sprawl with tracts of boxlike structures. Here was an architecture based on efficiency that yielded to no other human or natural impulse. Taken together, the look of the city ran against the grain of consciousness, of any connectedness between one person and another, to place or history.

I went to high school in the San Fernando Valley. When I lived there before as a five-year-old child, in a small tract house, we were situated at the end of the block, near an orchard where my sister and I spent hours together. In my mind this is still a rich, almost mythic place. At the other end of the block there was an open field with an old barn at its center. I liked to go there simply to stand and gaze at the field. At six I moved back to the city. By the time I returned several years later, there was hardly any sign of such places having existed. One evening when my friends and I were gathered together drinking a few cans of forbidden beer one of our group appeared to announce that he had something amazing to show us. Eight of us crowded into his small car. He drove us on an intricate route out to and through the latest housing developments. We were not headed in the direction of Topanga Canyon, or the Hollywood Hills, but to a little patch in the center of the valley, wedged between developments that had somehow survived. It was a small hollow, intensely green after a new rain. At the bottom of it, where we got out of the car, all you could see was green. No wires, no houses, no other cars. And you could feel the wet, dark soil. It was nothing more than that, a small valley. I had seen the dramatic mountains of Yosemite, camped in the High Sierras, driven with my father along the steep cliffs of the Northern coast, walked in the desert as it began to bloom, but for years I remembered this valley and the astonishing contrast it offered to the larger valley where it was hidden, that flat, unredeemed place with its quietly deadening ground.

In that time I would not have associated this spiritless terrain with the manner of my birth and first nourishment. One was divided in so many ways from the ground of being, from the sources of sustenance, food and water, and what we call nature. America is a country of immigrants. But by mid-century we were all in another kind of exile. The changes of the last century had been severe. Though Los Angeles was a city that had lost even the memory of earth, many of its inhabitants, including my grandparents, had once lived on farms. This was a sign of the future. After 1940, the proportion of Americans living on farms went from almost one out of every three to two out of every hundred. Increasingly across the country the attitude and architecture of L.A. was being replicated. The exigencies of agriculture, seasons, the demands of soil, of growing things and animals that once shaped the life of a family and the culture of surrounding towns were vanishing.

What replaced this old way of life lived in nature was a rational *idea* of nature. If in European culture religion had once made sense of the world, and connected one to a larger cosmos, the reigning perspective of the modern age was scientific. No one in my immediate family, including my grandparents, really went to church. Having been taken in my eighth year to Sunday school, I entered a period of intense and mystical belief. But by my twelfth year I had stopped going to church and at fifteen I had declared myself an agnostic.

In my thinking, as with many of my generation, I connected modernity and the scientific world view with justice, equality, and freedom. I loved visiting the farm where my grandmother had been born, drinking milk warm from the cow, picking berries, walking through yellow wheat fields that grew taller than I. But then there was the small farming town where my sister was raised after the family divorce that separated us. They still went to church there. My sister was ostracized when she arrived because she wore lipstick and a blouse with a low neckline. One fled from this narrowness to cities and a rational frame of mind.

Yet there was a subtle undertow. Though while still young I was thrilled by a group of essays by J. Robert Oppenheimer on the philosophical implications of nuclear physics, I found the science which we were all encouraged, prodded, and even forced to study unbearably flat and, though I could not have articulated it as such then, I found the scientific world view uninhabitable. I preferred poetry. The motion was entirely intuitive, almost a tropism. My friends and I would sit together reading *The Love Song of J. Alfred Prufrock* aloud. One of my favorite phrases was "like a patient etherized upon a table."

But these words which compelled me so were oddly unanchored in my mind. I connected them neither to my own birth nor to the scientific world view I had inherited. I knew little of the history of science. Though I had certainly sensed it, I did not know that in the reigning paradigm of Western science the material world was considered dead. That the implications of high-energy physics had challenged this assumption hardly changed the mood and manner either of perception or of decision making which had evolved over centuries from a premise of superiority over earthly existence. Very young I was taught that science was objective and that subjective response had no value in describing reality.

Though I had no enthusiasm for technology, I never questioned the notion of progress. I assumed it was a mandate of equality and justice to spread the improvement of life by machine and medicine all over the world. If forests were being swallowed by a modern world that replaced rivers and valleys with reservoirs and shopping malls, I explained this to myself within the polemic of the Cold War, as a product of greed, an uncaring marketplace, heedless of any concern but profit.

The silence imposed on public discourse regarding socialism and most forms of radical thought had in the end the opposite effect on me and many of my generation than intended. Whatever dissatisfied us became loosely associated in our minds with the fact of this censorship and the polemic behind it. It was not that one believed the Soviet Union to be environmentally more aware. Rather the range of critical thinking about the problem of ecology stopped on the other side of a wall, an invisible one erected by the censors, but just as formidable as its twin in Berlin.

Yet, by another logic, there was also a way in which ecology escaped the confines of Cold War thought. Among the many reasons why this issue had an uncommon vibrancy was that it fell outside the parameters of the debate. Here was an immediate issue, urgent, three-dimensional, and not so thoroughly encased in ideological terms. The same was true of perhaps the most profound and formative issues of the student movement: civil rights. Thinking about the existence of racism brought North American society into a new focus. It was true that a largely white, Marxist viewpoint regarded racism as a subordinate effect of economic oppression, and not as a phenomenon with causes of its own. When I first read stories that anti-Semitism, as well as racism toward a number of ethnic minorities, still existed in the Soviet Union, I looked on these reports with a jaundiced eye. So many lies were part of the Cold War rhetoric. But despite my distrust of this news, I did not experience racism as something that would be automatically solved by a more egalitarian economic system. What I witnessed, and my own sense of life in a racist society, was different. Though I could not have said how, I knew racism to be somehow at the core of the trouble in our lives.

Above all it was my encounter with African-American, Hispanic, and Asian activists and thinkers about the issue of civil rights which refined my social and political perceptions and allowed me, in my late twenties, to delineate my own social condition first as a woman and, later, as a lesbian. Through this education I began to understand how I had been put at a remove from myself in my own mind. I had lived within another kind of segregation. Books that I read, films, paintings I studied, even the very grammar I used took a man and a man's body as the defining center, the touchstone of meaning. If a woman was pictured, she was seen from a man's point of view. Rarely did one enter the life of a woman as she lived and felt it. It would be several years later, and after I had come to understand that the issues of social justice and ecology are intimately connected, before I would come to see that the idea of a universal human being, generically masculine and white, is analogous to the idea of objectivity in Western science.

By the time I had this insight, I had also had the first glimpse of a different political orientation, an approach by which one could understand that, despite Cold War rhetoric, the two superpowers, the Soviet Union and the United States, were alike. This was not a middle ground I had found but a territory outside the old geography. A ground reconceived.

One could say that from this perspective the similarity between the capitalist world and the Communist world is more significant than the difference. The resemblance is profound, the fundamental approach of both societies the same. In ideology as well as practice, capitalism and Communism together have followed an older path, well established in Western culture, which has as its unobtainable end the mastery of nature.

By this longer view, what once appeared to be a polemic in the Cold War seems instead a competition between two societies for greater and greater control over material existence. The Soviet Union, the countries of the Eastern bloc, Europe, and the United States all assumed that life could only be bettered through scientific progress, first by industrialization and then through technology. Yet beneath this apparently rational assumption on both sides of the polemic, the same ancient alienation from nature shaped these efforts into a nearly insane and hubristic duel for power.

Just now one is beginning to see that the Stalinist purges and McCarthyism bore an ironic resemblance to one another. But what is perhaps still less obvious is that in both societies these attempts to silence dissent were part of a zealous commitment to scientific progress. In the Soviet Union, Stalin pushed the nation beyond human and natural capacity toward industrialization, over and over setting goals physically impossible to achieve, and ruthlessly punishing those who failed his demands. In part his purges answered the dissatisfaction and rebellion this effort caused. But this was not, as has been argued, anomalous to the ideology he practiced. The persecution of dissidents was justified even before Stalin by the idea that Marxism was scientific, that social justice was tied to industrialization, and that progress through both means was inevitable.

With McCarthyism the connection between censorship and the mastery of nature is clearest in the case of the Rosenbergs, who were accused of giving technological knowledge to the other side.

And to submit the Rosenbergs or J. Robert Oppenheimer and countless other scientists and intellectuals to scrutiny, placing them on trial in the public eye, diverted attention from another question which was never asked in the public arena: "Should we be developing nuclear technology at all?"

As the polemic of the Cold War is peeled away, one can begin to interpret the mood of mid-century America in a different light. There was more than one sign of inner conflict. In popular culture, the brooding, injured anger of James Dean was preceded by *film noir,* a style which surrounded every image in shadow. Nothing presented in these films turned out to be the way it looked. No one could be trusted. If the atom bomb was developed to win the war and thus to protect us all from a German or Japanese invasion, still it was created in great secrecy, shrouded by lies, and nuclear diplomacy continued the habit of deception. If the bomb did end the war, in the peace that followed, the world was endangered as never before. This knowledge and the awful memory of the technologically efficient massacres of the Holocaust shadowed every bright and smiling evocation of the future wonders of progress. In such an ambivalent atmosphere, it becomes necessary to invent an enemy. The inner conflict was resolved with red-baiting.

It is not surprising then that perhaps the most memorable rallying cry of the student movement against McCarthyist repression for freedom of speech were Mario Savio's famous words: "There's a time when the operation of the machine becomes so odious, makes you so sick at heart, that you can't take part, you can't even tacitly take part. And you've got to put your body upon the gears and the wheels, upon the levers, upon all the apparatus, and you've got to make it stop." A large part of the enormous appeal of his words was the feeling students had that life was becoming mechanized, that we were all cogs in a larger, heedless machine, and that the society which used us thus somehow valued a dead and therefore ultimately controllable mechanical world more than the living world.

Other visions did exist. There were the nightmare dystopia of Orwell, Huxley, Ray Bradbury, critical of progress and thus, by implication, pointing to other possibilities. And the very science that invented the atomic bomb also produced a different portrait of the universe through which one might imagine the human spirit as part of nature rather than imprisoned by matter. If first theology and then science divided the spirit, or energy (the scientific analogue of spirit) from corporeality, Marie Curie, Einstein, Heisenberg, Born, Bohr discovered that energy itself, which is to say spirit itself, is incarnate. By the light of the new physics, existence has a double nature as both particle and wave, matter *is* energy at its core, and the inspiriting force of existence has mass. The cosmological, ethical, and social implications of this new insight are profound. But this philosophical shift did not take place. Rather the specter of this change persisted and persists almost as an unconscious doubt.

And after the war there were other threats. Another radical transformation presented itself at the periphery of the old way of thinking. Gender, sexual identity, the certainty of a social and political distinction between men and women had been challenged. During the war masses of women had gone to work in factories, taken over businesses and positions in government. Now women were exhorted to return home, take on the role of wife and mother again. But the smoothly pliant image of a June Allyson in film or a Donna Reed on television was too thin to be believed. And somewhere in the popular imagination, as uncertainty or nightmare, one had to guess at the truth: James Dean was gay.

At the same time, by the end of the Second World War another major transformation was taking place. If European culture had turned a blind eye to the atrocities of colonialism, the horrific consequences of the idea of a pure white race had been unavoidably displayed within Europe's boundaries, played out in the Holocaust to a murderous conclusion. Now the African-American movements against lynching, Jim Crow laws, segregation, and discrimination of all kinds, forms of resistance that had existed since the first days of slavery, gained strength.

Underneath this tension about gender and race lurked an earlier divide. The idea of masculinity and femininity, and a complementary heterosexuality, served to symbolize a separation between spirit and matter, mind and body and make this schism seem, even to a small degree, real. By a similar logic the idea of the superiority of the white race was another way European culture had been able to imagine itself as elevated above nature. Both the movement of women away from the traditional feminine role and the shattering of a myth of race endangered the stability of the entire system.

But if on the surface the valence was to resist change, still, even before the student movements of the sixties, a deep transformation of consciousness was taking place. Ecology was not yet a large movement, nor had an alternative ecological philosophy been articulated. But a new attitude was emerging through the arts that preceded and predicted a philosophical metamorphosis. Trotsky once wrote about this process in a letter to Frida Kahlo. When she lamented to him that she regretted her art was not political enough, he wrote back saying that her art gave the world a vision of the politics of a future which present political prejudices had obscured.

I liked abstract art, modern music, experimental forms in literature, theater, film, but it would be a number of years before I came to understand what this aesthetic meant for me as politics. Here was a realm not paralyzed by the polemics of the Cold War. All the old forms were being shifted. There was movement. Fresh air. Open space.

In this new topography experience itself was being looked at as if for the first time. The notion of beginner's mind had been imported from Asia with Buddhism by John Cage or Gary Snyder (as it was earlier by Thoreau and Emerson). Was this desire for the unpredictable and the innovative a response to a tired system of thought grinding itself to a halt?

Perhaps Matisse, Dufy, Diebenkorn kept painting open windows because that was the direction that consciousness sought. An opening. But there was more: the discovery of what was there all along, yet hidden from a mind acculturated to a twentieth-century European perspective in North America. From impressionism through abstract art, the epistemological distrust of sensual experience was being countered by an art that celebrated the perplexity and the very diversity of sensual knowledge. Even if the theory was idealist, the practice rediscovered material existence. Modern music slipped away from certain constructed scales which had been confused with the whole range of possible sound. Literature also crossed the lines of old forms, as well as, through the work of Woolf, Joyce, Faulkner, presenting a multiplicity of views in place of a single perspective. Consciousness was being reimagined. And place too, where the foot falls, earth envisioned as responding with its own intelligence. While a hand dashed paint over surface, or sound resonated as if accidentally off surfaces, records of this seemingly random disorder became art, revealing a deeper, unexpected order and beauty intrinsic to existence.

There was so much then that was moving in the same direction. Yet one would not have said this at the time. Like their predecessors in the Harlem Renaissance, the Beat poets began to read out loud and sometimes to the accompaniment of jazz. In San Francisco, Ornette Coleman, John Coltrane, Carmen McRae, Charles Mingus played in clubs around the corner from City Lights Books (which had published the first edition of Allen Ginsberg's *Howl*). Over several decades, through the work of the jazz masters, and Langston Hughes, Gertrude Stein, W. C. Williams, Zora Neale Hurston, as well as Isadora Duncan and Katherine Dunham, the principle of spontaneity in art, so much a part of African traditions, made its way into American art.

The work was not without its own political issues. Just as jazz

in an earlier decade had been maligned as "jungle music," Ginsberg or Robert Duncan or Peter Orlofsky outraged mid-century
America by being gay. And this poetry with images of sexuality
outside the boundaries of gender did constitute a challenge in the
same way that jazz as an art form had its own subversive meanings,
carrying within it the memory of African cultures, the horrors of
the middle passage and of slavery. And at the same time all this
was connected to history and place, the great forests, plains,
rivers, seas, and that meeting which had occurred roughly four
hundred years ago between European culture and the New World.
Speaking of the Beat movement, Michael McClure remembers a
first reading, at the Six Gallery in San Francisco. ". . . Ginsberg
read *Howl,* which has as its basis—in my thinking—consciousness
itself. . . . Snyder read his poem, "A Berry Feast," which is a
celebration of nature, especially as seen through American Indian
rites. And I read my poems, almost all of which were inclined
toward nature. Including "The Death of Whales," which in 1955
was an early poem against biocide by governments." Looking
back, he could see how deeply this poetics was connected to a
passionate engagement with nature.

I was fifteen when I first heard a Beat poem. I was at a party
and had grown heady and wild because, for the first time in my
life, I had just met contemporaries (other than my sister) who
shared something of a world view, *insolite,* interested in art, writing, film, and in reclaiming our bodies from an era of prudery.
The poem was read from a collection, brought from the north of
the state, almost as if contraband, like the *samizdhat,* illegal, mim-
eographed manuscripts circulated in the Soviet Union. The emis-
saries had gone upstate for their first year at the university. They
told us that this was a movement that would change everything.
We formed a circle around them. Later the same night, after
sampling a series of different kinds of alcohol, my head swimming,
I let my friend Harvey put his hands over my vagina and felt an
intense and overwhelming pleasure. Though I wanted the feeling
to continue, he stopped. I would have gone on toward more

prohibited acts, yet all the time I was vaguely aware that I was not in love with him. I hid from myself an even more forbidden desire, my heated attraction to someone I had just met that night, a girl a year older than I.

Looking back, I can see the events at that party as part of a transformation in consciousness which was to unfold with greater drama in the next two decades. By now the changes are famous. At the same time that a new poetics came into being, there would be what was called a sexual revolution. These were not unrelated. Both the form and content of this new work reflected a changing knowledge of the body. To speak directly of the sexual body in literature, saying the names vagina, vulva, penis awakened a sharper and more intense bodily consciousness.

For women this was the beginning of a radical departure. As Joyce Johnson writes in her memoir of the fifties, "Experience, adventure—these were not for young women. Everyone knew they would involve exposure to sex. Sex was for men. For women it was as dangerous as Russian roulette. . . ." But the women who rebelled in this period "did not want to be our mothers or our spinster schoolteachers or the hardboiled career women depicted on the screen." By leaving home they became "a bridge to the next generation, who in the 1960's when a young woman's right to leave home was no longer an issue, would question every assumption that limited women's lives. . . ."

The questioning was in time to go beyond the boundaries of the sexual revolution of the sixties. A revolution that still circumscribed the body with old definitions of masculinity and femininity and an eros trapped by these categories. In various experimental literary and artistic movements women existed in a bardo-like state, still partly passive, half object, recognized as artists only in a minor way. And this prejudice continued in the left and hippie movements of the sixties.

Yet subterranean motion persisted. It was a change that had begun earlier. One could see it in women's lives. Though my mother wanted to study design, she had no schooling after high school. I went to a university and completed my degree. But the change was even closer to the core. A different way of being in the flesh, of standing, talking, moving was evident between one generation and the next. Writing now, if I were to try to characterize this change I would begin by saying that as one generation followed another, even in my own family, women became more natural in our bodies and less confined by mannerisms prescribed as feminine. And one might also say in that case that we became more intimate with our own nature. Which was also a greater intimacy with nature itself.

The use of the word "nature" associated with a woman's body has a complex history in European culture. In 1949 the first Gallimard edition of Simone de Beauvoir's great work, *Le Deuxième Sexe,* was published. "Woman?" the book's first sentence read. "Very simple, say the fanciers of simple formulas: she is a womb, an ovary; she is a female—this word is sufficient to define her." At least since Aristotle, the dimensions of female existence had been reduced to biology, and even simply reproduction. And if modernity produced the image of a liberated woman, hair bobbed, free of Victorian restraints and domesticity, it also created the modern homemaker whose duties as a wife and mother were scientifically justified even as they were technologically streamlined.

Yet beneath this rhetoric there was another dense layer of meaning. Underlying the thought and imagery of both traditional and modern European society lies a habit of mind which takes woman as a symbol of material existence. "In woman are incarnated the disturbing mysteries of nature," De Beauvoir wrote, "and man escapes her hold when he frees himself from nature." One might add that, in the imagination of European culture, the reverse is also true; when a man controls a woman, he masters nature.

At the same time, the old association between woman and nature was taking on still another shade of meaning in public

discourse. In 1950, just one year after the Fr...
The Second Sex, and three years before its publica\
States, Rachel Carson was to open *The Sea Aro\
words, "Beginnings are often shadowy, and so\
beginnings of the great mother of life, the sea."]
here was not of dark and dangerous mysteries, but o\ ...mys-
teries, of a knowledge that, like divine wisdom, is at times larger
than the capacity of the human mind to know.

If the sea was described here as a woman who has given birth to
life, this description was intended neither to foreshorten the proportions of female existence nor to diminish nature but instead,
through the ancestral lineage between natural and human existence, to express reverence and respect. And though on the surface the language carries with it all the baggage of older prejudicial
ways of thought, including a symbolic duality between masculine
and feminine, something else existed in this usage in nascent
form. In the paucity left by the end of religious traditions, the
possibility of another orientation which might connect the universe into one whole again was arising.

Unspoken as it was, this possibility was part of the atmosphere of
the times. It existed almost as a counterweight in the imagination
to what was the dominant tendency. As I was coming of age,
everything was increasingly fragmented. A twentieth-century education in America had become an almost clinical affair, with neat
categories for the student to absorb (and on which she or he
would be efficiently tested). But seldom did one category have any
connection with another. One learned American history as if it
did not take place within world history. Science as if it had no
history. Mathematics apart from philosophy. Philosophy not at all.
But in the universities and colleges the fragmentation within each
discipline was far worse. The higher one moved in education, the
more an extreme specialization was expected. One might do a
study, for example, on cotton production in Mississippi from
1870 to 1880 with no reference to a history beyond those years,

vents elsewhere, as if this were an isolated shard of time and
pace belonging nowhere.

Certainly this was dull reading. But beyond that I can remember a feeling of inward panic, as if my mind were being enticed into a small windowless place, while the larger world I was so excited to enter slowly disappeared from sight. I resisted this confinement. But all around me another disappearance was occurring. The sense of a terrain—the shape of a watershed system, for instance, mountain snow melting into rivers traversing a distance their bodies remember and know—was decomposing in the mind. The mountains and the valley were still there, but one scarcely saw these shapes. What in turn were coming to delineate the landscape were steel and concrete structures, and superhighways, signs of the speed of a progress that seemed as implacable as the onrush of traffic.

Cities have always had structures as landmarks. Notre Dame in Paris, the Duomo in Florence, the Brooklyn Bridge in New York. Architecturally what occurred was partly just a matter of degree as increasingly countryside gave over to cities and housing tracts. But this hasty architecture also mirrored a lack of a center, of a sense of placement, and of any unifying grace. Paradoxically, the strict utilitarian shape of this future one found oneself inhabiting produced a feeling of uselessness. *Why is it I exist?*

This was particularly so because oddly this time of fragmentation was also a period of conformity. Perhaps lacking a center, idiosyncrasies became too threatening. Instead of a unifying grace, there were monolithic designs. One witnessed the proliferation of chain stores, generic apartment houses, and hundreds of thousands of cheap plastic replicas of things which before had been crafted by hand. Objects descended as if from nowhere to a once familiar earth. But it was not only things. It was also thought and experience. From television, film, advertisements, mass-produced images of all kinds, a golem arose, a two-dimensional imitation of life which nevertheless threatened to replace one's own living experience. The nightmare was of a machine-made mind controlled by distant, uncaring manipulators, whose minds were the same.

But on the other side of this nightmare a reverie was being formed. And when I look back to find the earliest sources I can remember of this movement that is yet unnamed, it is here that my memory settles. On the back side of Cold War politics, an unarticulated dream, often sentimental or naive, expressed itself still, sometimes in the idea of mother earth, at other times in the desire to empower idealized feminine values of nurturance, relation, kindness, or an attempt at a communal and hand-made life, giving the movement for social justice a hidden chiaroscuro, a perspective that stretched beyond the articulated boundaries of politics. A wish for a meaning that might weave oneself and the world together. Not dictated from above the earth but palpable, embedded and experienced in daily life.

The seeds of this deeper meaning, one that does not spring from an opposition to nature but instead takes nature as a source, have existed throughout the history of European culture, and if sometimes it has not been fully revealed, this may have been the only way it could have survived. Not every vestige of meaning is recognizable as thought. Ways of life lived on the land by peasant cultures which have not only retained traces of older religions but have also remained embedded in earthly process. An iconography which contradicts the orthodoxy it is supposed to express, beautiful or terrifying images, the carnality of a saint's ecstasy, a face blended by light and shadow into landscape. Domestic rituals. Another shape to a street. An atmosphere in a gathering place, another kind of medicine, emotional exchanges between women, a once forbidden act openly revealed, all these can express another avenue of significance.

And this other consciousness has also been spoken. Throughout the history of European culture, dissident philosophical and literary movements have existed which defined human existence, and even the human spirit more as part of nature than opposed to it. Elements of such a dissent can be found in the thought of William

Godwin, Mary Wollstonecraft, and her daughter Mary Shelley, together with other early Romantics, Shelley, Wordsworth, Keats, George Sand, who criticized modern industrialism even as they saw it unfold. If in many ways the Romantics preserved the old duality between spirit and nature, they chose nature as the place of inspiration and took natural experience as the literal stuff of thought. And a passion for social justice among the early English Romantics was part of the same breath that expressed a passion for natural beauty. In a single letter, for instance, written from Norway in the late eighteenth century, Mary Wollstonecraft describes with great beauty an "undulated valley" surrounded by "pine-covered mountains," regrets a technology which has discolored the stone in this soil, leaving "an image of human industry in the shape of destruction . . ." and descries an example of "the cloven foot of despotism" which she has encountered in the region.

A similar intermingling can be found in the writing of Henry David Thoreau. In parallel works he advocates civil disobedience as a protest against slavery and argues for a simpler life lived closer to nature. One finds the same sensibility in both texts. As in the work of Whitman, his is a voice which enfolds politics, society, and nature into one meaning.

But these voices had too little effect on history as it unfolded in the mid-twentieth century. Though the curriculum in American literature that I studied as a child nearly enshrined Thoreau and Whitman, reading this work was like visiting Yosemite National Park. A beautiful place, yet a landscape for vacations, isolated from everyday life, not really relevant to practical reality. If within this work the chrysalis of a less divided vision has been preserved, this vision has remained at the periphery.

Now if consciousness is to migrate further toward the eros embedded in daily and practical life, certain histories must be told and habits of mind revealed. So much is at stake: identity, years of study, of training, of experience, economic sustenance, social acceptance, a way of life. For what I suspect is that a metamorphosis is required. Profound changes are incipient in the culture of my birth, even affecting the way one delineates a self, certainly the way one understands the world and aims toward the discovery of truth at all.

For if this metamorphosis promises unexpected answers to what is after all a crisis of meaning, it also threatens an old and familiar structure of mind that has in many ways become synonymous with meaning.

The awareness grows that something is terribly wrong with practices of European culture that have led to both human suffering and environmental disaster. Patterns of destruction which are neither random nor accidental have arisen from a consciousness that fragments existence. The problem is philosophical. Not the dry, seemingly irrelevant, obscure or academic subject known by the name of philosophy. But philosophy as a structure of the mind that shapes all our days, all our perceptions. Within the particular culture to which I was born, a European culture transplanted to North America, and which has grown into an oddly ephemeral kind of giant, an electronic behemoth, busily feeding on the world, the prevailing habit of mind for over two thousand years, to consider human existence and above all consciousness and spirit as independent from and above nature, still dominates the public imagination, even now withering the very source of our own sustenance. And although the shape of social systems, or the shape of gender, the fear of homosexuality, the argument over abortion, or what Edward Said calls hierarchies of race, the prevalence of violence, the idea of technological progress, the problem of failing economies have been understood separately from ecological issues, they are all part of the same philosophical attitude which presently threatens the survival of life on earth.

A history of empires and regencies, of warfare, injustice, inequity, slavery, has shaped the modern vision. Everything one sees, not only what one would leave behind, but also what one treasures has been touched by this inheritance. The whole is like a fresco, appealing in its own way, but also disappointing, somehow blunted, and even hopeless in the way the form turns back on itself in irony and despair, but through which here and there one can see a slightly different coloration, places where the paint is peeling, to reveal another, more interesting layer. To see underneath one must pare away the more recent layer, and perhaps even a second or third layer, which obscure the reach of vision.

As one searches history for the causes of present crises the fear is of the forfeiture of continuity and tradition. But this history is also filled with imprisoned wishes, unrealized dreams, for democracy, a good life, a just society which one can reclaim only by rereading the past. And in the end it is only by the light of continued reflection that continuity and tradition are kept alive.

2

A Collaborative
Intelligence

*Yes, poor Louis, Death has found thee. No palace walls or
life-guards, gorgeous tapestries or gilt buckram of stiffest
ceremonial could keep him out; but he is here, here at thy
very life-breath, and will extinguish it. Thou, whose whole
existence hitherto was a chimera and scenic show, at length
becomest a reality: sumptuous Versailles bursts asunder, like
a dream into void Immensity; Time is done and all the
scaffolding of time falls wrecked with hideous clangor round
thy soul: the pale Kingdoms yawn open: there must thou
enter, naked, all unking'd. . . .*

—THOMAS CARLYLE,
The French Revolution

These were the words Thomas Carlyle used in the nineteenth
century to describe the death by smallpox in 1774 of Louis
XV, the last king of France to reign before the ensuing French
Revolution. Carlyle's language about the end of the king's life
prophesied the prince's demise too. Not quite twenty years
later, in 1793, Louis XVI would be sent to his death by the
Reign of Terror. This death signaled the end of a way of life.
But it was also the end of a way of ordering the earth, and of

a particular sense of meaning, the ghost of which has not been laid to rest.

In Carlyle's ambivalent portrait of a king's death one feels a mourning for the protective walls of a philosophy that gave not only kings but commoners a sense of safety. The old structure had housed human society within the cosmos. God gave kings the right to rule; social authority *was* divine authority; monarchy was part of God's plan for creation. To serve a king was to have a clearly defined place in the universe, and this role was imbued with the same meaning that defined heaven and earth. Because that system was failing, when Louis was unkinged, so were his subjects.

Now if by mortality, the great leveler, every subject eventually felt the scaffolding of time destroyed, what pale kingdom yawned beyond? Not only the divine right of kings but divinity itself was waning in the European mind. By the same subtle process through which the English monarchy was to become an anachronistic symbol of a vestigial order still cherished in the imagination, in European culture what had once been an encompassing religious system of thought slowly diminished to peripheral, largely irrelevant beliefs. By the death of this system, one was left in the void of immensity without even a day of judgment to anticipate. It appeared that in the modern view of reality there would no longer be any way to draw the world into one composition.

What this new vision of reality offered instead was the idea that all of natural existence might finally be explained and charted in the human mind. And with this a corollary dream was born, the plan to remake the world according to human need and desire. One was to hear the breath of this hope in Marx's words, "Religion is the opiate of the people." But though reason replaced divine transmission, the opiate remained at the fringes, and obscured by its very presence an otherwise unavoidable chasm. Science had left a void. In the domain of reason, no cohesive vision, no reason for one's own existence, or existence at all, remained.

·   ·   ·

In a sense the erasure of coherence was the ingenious solution European culture posed to the conflict between a growing body of scientific knowledge and religious doctrine. By separating science and theology, scientists won the right to make assertions which otherwise would contradict religious descriptions of the universe. That Copernicus had shifted the center of the solar system from the earth to the sun, or that Galileo had observed the gravitational pull of the earth eventually became irrelevant to religious inquiry. In this way, modern science began to exist alongside theology as a parallel system which ceased to engage with any knowledge of the experience which for centuries had been called spiritual.

The rupture was at first liberating. By this separation a new territory was created where the authority to know no longer belonged exclusively to church and state. This was a profound move toward democratization. In this freer space, anyone could conjecture and try to prove a theory. Truth was to depend less on old texts than on what was observed. And through the method of experimentation physical life, nature, appeared again, and became the touchstone of reality.

Yet, by this division, separate spheres of meaning came into being. Even if science had not yet replaced the old mythos, it had done something even more consequential. It had invented a world. From the scientific practice of studying material existence apart from any consideration of spirit, or intrinsic meaning, unwittingly a world of matter apart from spirit, of function without significance, was created. Now as science has come to replace divine authority, instead of a meaning that unifies the universe, one is left with the seemingly raw forces of nature.

And where is this world? Does it really exist? That nature is without intrinsic meaning or that soil, rock, water, sky are dead may be only ideas. But through human agency these ideas have taken physical shape: the word made flesh. Though it is increasingly uninhabitable, we dwell within the confines of a world made after the idea of meaninglessness. Cities exist, machines, technologies, even institutions, about which the best description one can make is that they seem lifeless; every natural phenomenon that falls under this gaze seems to lack spirit.

I grew up believing that this cold, dry approach to existence was a necessary component of intellectual freedom, that the courageous mind could look at a universe stripped of all myth with a clear, unblinking eye. I thought somehow that meaninglessness presented the mind with an open field. Only later did I come to sense that underneath this idea of freedom an older way of ordering the world remained.

If at one time in European history science seemed to present an opening, a way to escape a religious system of thought that had become too confining, what appeared to be an escape has in its own way kept European thought imprisoned in the same assumptions. Because an earlier habit of mind, one that is as invisible as it is unconsidered, and which determines a divided relationship to nature, lies underneath both science and religion as we know them.

Just like the former enemies of the Cold War, the religious idealism of Western civilization and mechanistic materialism are as alike as they are different. Yet, one born to this culture has difficulty perceiving the similarity between these two philosophies. I was educated by conventional histories of European culture to believe that materialism and idealism were opposite visions of the universe. This history was preceded by and surrounded with a received wisdom. The world was divided in twos and one line neatly divided the field. There was heaven and earth, and accompanying this pair were other couplings, man and wife, masculinity and femininity, and of course, mind and body, spirit and nature. Heaven was a masculine province, and spirit had a masculine character, transcendent, abstract, literally free of gravitational fields and the more sensual pulls of earth. Earth was familiar and feminine, heavy with the corruption of sensual knowledge and emotion. Through every possible means, not only religion, but also the implied meanings of words, written and unwritten laws of intellectual discourse, social forms, manners, gestures, one learned that the division of these pairs included a hierarchy. Even if the existence of heaven was subject to scientific doubt, intellect and abstract principle were assigned to a territory of mind superior to the material, sensual, emotional realm of the body.

By a linear process of mind that cannot ultimately be separated from the desire for dominion by both church and state, a nearly invisible idea of hierarchy in science has determined both its epistemology and its methodology. What was once divine authority has been replaced by the myth of objectivity, an imagined position which, like the Christian idea of the divine, is not embedded in nature, and from which alone truth can be perceived. The absolute truth of religion has been replaced by the abstract principles of science, and as if numbers or statistics were intrinsically beyond doubt, even by quantification. And just as religious doctrine placed the sacred above the profane, scientific theory has been placed above experience itself, while socially the scientific establishment has come to occupy the same position of authority once held by the church.

Not only do abstract principles partake of the rarefied, immortal climate of heaven, but the idea of transcendence over earthly life, the life cycle, and death continues in science in another guise, and that is the notion of technological progress. Continuously since the eighteenth century new inventions, whether they be locomotives, electric lights, or computers, have been taken as signs of a coming transformation not only of life on earth but of consciousness itself. Science promises a kind of heaven on earth, a brave new world made ever better through technology. And if by Western religion meaning is deferred to a future afterlife in which accounts will be not only taken but also understood, science also defers ultimate meaning to a future not only happier in material fulfillment but one in which a unified theory has revealed the true nature of the universe.

Just as science and religion have shared a vision that rends experience into two unequal fragments, despite the great political and economic differences between capitalist and communist theory, a single orientation to existence unites both philosophies. If in the political history of this century certain systems within Western culture have called themselves materialist, others idealist, some "under God," some claiming the inspiration of the gods, at the same time that they claim themselves to be scientific, they too have shared an underlying paradigm: the idea of a hierarchy that places human consciousness above nature. This is perhaps most obvious with fascism, which asserts both a superior knowledge of nature and a superiority over nature as the defining quality of the *Übermensch*. Capitalism differs only by degree. The notion of the survival of the fittest, misinterpreted as ruthless combat for possession of goods or territory, and taken out of the context of an ecosystem in which evolution favors diversity, has within it another more subtle version of a superman, the one who conquers both nature and society for his own gain.

But the Marxist vision of economic equality also conceals a hierarchy, for it too places human existence in conflict with nature. Taking the ownership of the means of production as its goal, communism has assumed that it is only by mastering nature that life can be bettered. And hierarchy is also implicit in both the manner and end of the Marxist idea of an almost Darwinian struggle in which the stronger, those who are larger in number and whose labor is necessary, achieve dominance over those who once dominated. Nature conceived as property simply changes ownership, and the idea of domination continues.

On the surface this dedication to dominance might appear to conflict with another approach that these modern systems share— that each ideology claims itself as an inevitable and necessary expression of nature. The Nazi reverence for "blood and soil," and the capitalist's concept that a state of limitless freedom is everyone's birthright, as well as the idea of the survival of the fittest mirror the Marxist invocation of class struggle as the natural course of history. But in all these systems, nature remains only the dumb stuff of life, potentially powerful, even dangerous, but awaiting the destiny of human intelligence to mobilize and direct it toward a more perfect realization which is also almost always a scientific achievement.

An unquestioning belief in technological progress has been shared across the warring ideologies of capitalism, fascism, and Communism. Today technological advance is the *ultima ratio regum* of capitalism, its justification, substance, and force all at once. Despite glorified portraits of a Teutonic or Roman past, fascism embraced technology with an obsessive eroticism that celebrated Panzer tanks and airplanes. In another mood, Heinrich Himmler, who developed a crude precursor to a computer, a mechanical way of sorting index cards that allowed the SS to carry out mass arrests, was famous for his fastidious obsession with efficiency.

And that ecological disasters were part of the inheritance of socialism in Russia and Central Europe should come as no surprise. The sky dark from coal in much of Poland, water so heavily polluted most of it is undrinkable; until a few years ago, DDT still in wide use in Azerbaijan; waterways diverted in Kazakhstan, arable land in Czechoslovakia destroyed by chemicals and overuse. The devastation of forests throughout Russia. Burial of radioactive waste in the North Sea near Siberia. Describing collectivization in Czechoslovakia, Vaclav Havel writes, ". . . it raged through the countryside thirty years ago, leaving not a stone in place. Among its consequences were . . . tens of thousands of lives devastated by prison, sacrificed on the altar of a scientific Utopia about brighter tomorrows. . . . [T]hirty years after . . . scientists are amazed to discover what even a semi-literate farmer previously knew—that human beings must pay a heavy price for every attempt to abolish, radically, once for all and without trace, that humbly respected boundary of the natural world. . . . People thought they could explain and conquer nature—yet the outcome is that they destroyed it and disinherited themselves from it." In fact collectivization, with its geometric and large fields unbroken by woods and hedges, led to the death of wild birds, hence the proliferation of insects, destroyed in a matter of years topsoil that had accumulated over centuries, poisoned land, water, and air with pesticides.

One might argue that this ecological destruction occurred simply from ignorance and a desire to make life better for masses of people who had suffered terrible poverty. As a young woman raised in the midst of the Cold War, I looked toward socialism as a means to social justice and a more egalitarian society. Yet, in the process, I did not see another aspect to Marxist thought, an ambivalence toward nature which at the same time subtly diminished human nature. This was the attitude that shaped scientific and enlightened thought in the nineteenth century. If in 1840, describing the French Revolution of the previous century, Carlyle wrote admiringly, "Your mob is a genuine outburst of Nature . . . here once more, if nowhere else, is a Sincerity and Reality," he also described this manifestation of nature as wildly unpredictable, a blind, ignorant force. "The thing they will do is known to no man; least of all to themselves. It is the inflammablest immeasurable Fire-work, generating, consuming itself." Though in his early work Marx departed from a mechanistic idea of human existence, he also describes class struggle as having an inevitable end, as if natural forces within masses of laborers operate without any amplitude of intelligence. That Marxist theory did not give birth to democratic forms cannot be separated from Marxism's claim to a scientific view of human nature, a view that limits the power of knowledge to a privileged few.

Yet from the same direction another portrait of both nature and knowledge is emerging. If with the modern scientific sensibility we have inherited a reductive idea of existence, science has also revealed a glimpse of a different vision. Through zoology, and biology, and genetics evidence has been produced for a different view of nature, not as raw force but as intelligent. The intricate structure and memory of DNA, the geometry of the honeycomb, the refined acoustical abilities of birds indicate a universe in which human intelligence is neither unique nor superior. And in the twentieth century relativity and quantum theory have made it clear that no place of objectivity exists in nature. Perception, measurement, every experience of space and time are affected by location and circumstance. Contemplating the nature of reality, science has had to accept two apparently conflicting theoretical descriptions of matter, both as wave and as particle.

The implications of these insights are great. Referring to recently what he calls the humanlike quality of birds and other animals, Theodore Barber writes that "humanity's philosophy of life will turn around along with cultural institutions." If human beings are no longer considered above nature, one's relationship with the earth, other life forms, ecological process, and especially with one's own body and mind radically changes. And at the same time new answers to old problems appear. In the intellectual milieu of my childhood, one was forced to choose between two unsatisfying descriptions of how the universe operates. I was schooled in both alternatives, one during the week and the other on Sundays. During the week I was educated in the modern idea that the natural universe consists of random forces without consciousness or meaning. On Sunday I learned that God created and still rules a universe constructed with meaning and a moral order. But as the intelligence of material existence begins to be evident, a third description of how the universe acts arises. Instead of the image of one God controlling creation, or the picture of existence as random and mindless, it is possible to imagine a collaborative intelligence shaping form, event, circumstance, consequence, life. By this shift in perception one is no longer placed in an alien environment. Instead, in and through existence one enters community.

Such an ontological shift away from hierarchy is implicit in ecology. The ecologist views the forest as a collaborative creation, the leaves of trees making soil and oxygen for animals; animals making compost that feeds the soil; insects pollinating plants; the evolution and continuation of each species, and the shape of soil, weather, or watershed dependent on the work-

ings of the whole. In the ecological view, instead of one cre-
ator there are a multitude of creators. And the many different
kinds of creative consciousness that exist are all equally significant to the whole.

But though ecology is generally embraced as a cause, no astonishing transformation in the way we think has occurred. Nor have
the insights of theoretical physics, astrophysics or molecular biology, the new geometry of fractals, or the ideas of fuzzy logic
reshaped the paradigmatic thinking of science as it is widely practiced both in science and society today. And, just as important,
the idea of truth that shapes most of modern political and social
discourse retains a religious and scientific attitude which is opposed to nature. In the European mind the universe is still ordered
in a hierarchy of masters and objects, despite many revolutions,
the bone structure of Louis's reign still exists.

This intransigence should not be surprising, for a shift in a way of
thought requires more than simple knowledge or intellectual understanding. In European culture, the idea of logic, reason, even
the capacity for insight, thought, or clear-mindedness have been
situated so firmly in the duality between intellect and emotion,
mind and body, spirit and matter that to challenge this duality
must seem like a threat to consciousness itself.

This dividedness is rooted deeply, in childhood memory, in a
sense of self, as if written into the body. In the child's mind, self
and the world become distinct simultaneously. All the dualities
that structure the social order also become powerful ways of
ordering experience. The arguments for a new way of thinking
that an ecologist may make after years of observing life in a rain
forest, or that a quantum physicist can suggest through mathematical equation, fail to address this level of existence, through which
one grows up, receives a name, and finds one's place in the social
order. All this, the very boundaries and definitions of one's life,
are attached by countless threads of culture to an old
epistemology. To sever them would seem like erasing the

very facts of one's own existence. To change how one sees the world is to change the self.

Very early in life, I learned that I was a girl. This was more than a code of behavior or a social role. In my permeable and developing psyche, it was an identity that became inextricable from the central fact of my existence. No one spoke about gender; the word was not even in our family vocabulary. This is just the way things were. And because sexuality was one of the first means by which I learned to make distinctions at all, gender was confused in my mind with difference itself.

But the difference is not neutral. With distinctions of gender, one ingests an intricate system of significance through which differences determine position on a scale of value. One learns to connect one life with another by ligaments of power. And by these same ligaments, experience itself is divided into separate worlds, not only masculine and feminine, but also public and private, sacred and profane, intellectual and emotional.

And there were other partitions that I learned unwittingly. In the symbolic life of the language I learned, words like "light" and "dark" were freighted with an implicit exclusion that also situated me in the world and gave me, willingly or not, definition as "white." A geography of being became part of the landscape of my consciousness, one that was in many ways more vivid to me than the range of mountains so seldom visible past the smog in Los Angeles. I knew that other worlds existed at the periphery of my own; the worlds of those with darker skins, seemingly exotic or dangerous, that formed the boundaries by which I located myself.

Yet at the same time I felt these distinctions inside myself. They were enveloped by the shame I was taught about my body: what part of myself I must not touch or reveal to men, what words about the body not to use. And suffering, too, belonged to this netherworld. I was a child of divorce, frequently abandoned, filled with a sorrow that could not be told because in the sunny climate of mid-century America there were few I encountered who would listen to such sadness. A sadness that did not fit the pattern.

If very early I was able to name the ambiguities, exceptions, and rebellions that existed within this implicit order, it was because as a child I was an outsider. My existence offered living evidence that things were not as they were supposed to be. And there was visible suffering around me, the cruel effects of differences in power that, however they were explained and justified by this system of identities, were so consequential and in many lives so disheartening that a child could almost touch them.

Ironically, these divisions encoded a strange and perseverating longing for an ideal world, impervious to suffering and change that was also nearly palpable. One cannot separate a culture's way of ordering reality, its cosmology, its epistemology, from the social structures it contains. Modes of consciousness have a psychology and a mental atmosphere in common. With the same motion by which the European mind has divested itself of nature it has also created the category of the Other. In this system of mind, the role of the other is to contain nature. Throughout the history of European culture, in various ways the Other has acted as a receptacle for the experience of nature the European mind would wish to deny. The way we come into being, from conception to birth, is so clearly physical. And it is the same with how we keep alive. We eat of the earth, we take shelter in the earth, our bodies respond with sleep, blood, semen to the rhythms of the material universe. How then can a transcendence that requires independence from earthly life be claimed by human consciousness, except through the creation of a separate human realm, a realm of Otherness, that symbolically contains both mortality and human immersion in earthly process. In this way, through the various categories of identity that fragment society, the psyche has been provided with an escape from the obvious fact of immersion in a transitory, material existence.

But of course this containment is not only symbolic. The illusion of transcendence over nature which is so central to the European mind is wholly dependent on a social structure which relegates physical labor to the other. According to traditional divisions of labor within Western culture, women have most often performed the labor of sustenance, the labor that makes human contingency on the earth obvious. Preparing meals, raising children, cleaning house, washing clothes, all these activities are indivisible from material existence. But when this work is placed into the feminine realm, both physical need and dependency vanish from the realm of masculinity. Even in economic theory, since domestic labor is not included in the measurement of Gross National Product, this work literally disappears.

The higher a man rises on the social and political ladder the more he is shielded from evidence of human embeddedness in the earth. Under slavery, the gentile plantation owner not only protected himself from physical labor but even passed on the overseeing of this work to other men. And the mark of the highest class of man has traditionally been the possession of a wife who does not work herself, even in the home. The trivialization of the lives and pursuits of aristocratic women has acted as a kind of foot binding which signifies the great distance between nature and the aristocratic men who are their husbands. Through wealth and power, such men acquire still a second buffer against the truth of domestic existence, which is the truth of survival. Their wives provide this second layer of protection by managing a household but refraining from manual labor themselves. In this way, an upper-class man can nearly avoid any intimacy with the understanding which comes from such labor (though the extremity of this exclusion may explain that erotic longing felt by upper-class men for a woman or a man of a "lower" class, that is, a class closer to the ground of existence).

What is lost is not just a quantifiable knowledge. It is also an understanding that can only develop from an emotional confrontation with the requirements of survival. Though domestic culture as well as all cultures of physical labor are often sentimentalized, a deeper understanding does belong to these worlds. When a daily immersion in a world of need and dependency, reciprocity, and natural exigencies is avoided at all costs, something of inestimable value is sacrificed.

Paradoxically, it is the system of denial which threatens life on earth today that has helped to fabricate a feeling of safety in the European psyche. When the physical experience of survival is isolated in the domestic realm, it is severed from public consciousness. What is lost to public awareness is a strong visceral reaction to environmental disaster, the bodily intelligence necessary to survival. And if the severance of self from nature has created a fragmentation of experience and a sense of dislocation, another geography has been layered over any sense of loss and conflict one might feel, a map of the cosmos that *appears* to piece together the fragments of existence. As both mortality and nature recede into the domestic world of women and servants, what steps into the foreground is a cultural construction of reality. Through custom, law, habit, and language, theory is layered over the body, as over the body of earth. A certain shape of eros, for instance, has taken on a gloss of inevitability: woman as unthinking backdrop, passive, pursued, possession and object, ground of being rather than being, man as subject, thinker, actor, initiator, hunter, victor. Sensual experience is subsumed and controlled by these categories. Ideas of what is masculine and feminine are woven into desire, passion, impulse, feeling, need, and so too become inextricably linked in the psyche with love, relatedness, family, and even the generation of life itself. Similarly ideas of race are forged to the body, so that, strangely, the American mind perceives a person with one African-American grandparent, or even a great-grandparent or a great-great-grandparent, as definitively non-white. Like the fundamentalist's frantic attempts to maintain an order that is no longer viable, the racist's obsessive insistence on purity of blood and the misogynist's worried effort to preserve sexual difference can be read as a nearly hysterical desire to separate simultaneously his own existence from and assert his power over nature.

In a world that seems increasingly chaotic, masculinity and whiteness do provide definition, significance, and orientation for the European psyche. The intrinsic meaningfulness of experience may have vanished. But meaning is manufactured in another way, as a realm of exclusion. Not only does the color of skin, called whiteness, the shape of a body, called masculinity, situate the "white" man in an elevated place, above the natural landscape, but these identities come to stand for meaning itself. If all that is *different* recedes into the background, a terrain of labor and resource which has no meaning of its own, this terrain of meaninglessness creates through contrast a frame. Significance not only resides with but becomes human, white, male.

Changes in this way of ordering existence are taking place now. With ecology, one might say the ground we walk upon reappears. In some minds, nature has become a source of meaning again. With this shift in perspective the environment is no longer simply what surrounds us. It is no different from us. We are environment. Because what was in the background has come forward, there is no longer any foreground or background. Nothing can be called surrounding. There is no center, no above, no below. And when no perspective is valued above any other, the old orientation dissolves.

This shift alone is momentous. Just as Copernicus challenged the idea that the earth was the center of the universe, ecology has challenged the concept that human consciousness is central and unique in the universe. By this turn matter and spirit are not separate. Spirit and significance, numinosity and revelation are no longer evidences of a realm above nature, impervious to change and mortality. Intelligence exists in all of nature, not just the human mind, but throughout the entire human body, in the bodies of plants, animals alike, soil, water, sky.

But within society, too, what was once the background also moves into the foreground. Different voices are beginning to be audible. Those who were silenced, ignored, pushed to the periphery are telling their own stories. Meaning no longer belongs exclusively to any single tradition or identity. And because all that is defined as meaningful in the European mind depends on the exclusion of a corollary world of insignificance, European culture stands at the edge of a major transformation.

What changes have occurred are small and inadequate. Practices of pollution, the destruction of irreplaceable forests, the disregard for other species, watershed systems, even human health, along with social injustice, hatred, and violence continue. One can elect a woman as Prime Minister, or an ecologist as Vice-President, allow women to attend West Point, legislate civil rights, eat organic food, but by themselves these changes evaporate. The behemoth continues at the same pace. What remains to be changed now is an attitude, a psychological orientation to existence. The European psyche is profoundly attached to an old order of mind. The same mental structures which render identity, definition, the outlines of the body, a relationship with a large social order and even the very meaning of existence are also meant to provide protection from anarchy, chaos, and an inhospitable wilderness.

If one would create an egalitarian society, nature must be restored as the common ground of existence. Yet this common ground cannot be reclaimed without the transformation of an unjust social order. And every aspect of this transformation demands reflection. The task is to study the nightmare that has driven us to self-destruction. The process of such a profound change may not be easy. Yet old ideas of self, familiar maps of existence which have come to feel like life itself, are already dissolving. One feels oneself even now on an unsteady footing. And beneath familiar ideas of reality there lives perhaps an older sense of self tied to an older connection to the cosmos, a sense of being and place that hold a coherence one has all along desired.

3

Being

Why is there being rather than nothing?
That is the question.

—MARTIN HEIDEGGER,

An Introduction to Metaphysics

All night I could not sleep
because of the moonlight on my bed.
I kept on hearing a voice calling:
Out of Nowhere, Nothing answered "yes."

ZI YE (6TH–3RD C.B.C.E.)

Who am I? There are moments when I glimpse another self swimming as if in a great watery world beneath all the definitions I have been given. It may be in movement, or meditation, wakefulness, or near sleep, and suddenly a door has opened as if into a vast room. I discover dimensions in myself I had not known before and yet recognize with some sorrow as if I had been separated from an old friend for too long.

The sense that I have at these moments is that I have broken through a wall into another world than the one I was raised to believe existed. In this world sensual experience has a significance beyond the narrow boundaries I learned as a child. I feel no division between what I call self and world. At these times I have felt everything in my own life and all of existence to be brilliant with a kind of lucidity.

Because this clarity is inseparable from experience itself, it does not reveal a meaning that can be formulated through any logical system of words or numbers. Yet the experience can be evoked. Thoreau speaks of the spring thaw at Walden Pond: "It is glorious to behold this ribbon of water sparkling in the sun, the bare face of the pond full of glee and youth, as if it spoke the joy of the fishes within it, and of the sands on its shore,—a silvery sheen as from the scales of a leuciscus, as if it were all one active fish. . . ."

If at such moments nothing in life seems random or without purpose, it is easy to forget this feeling as I enter another mood, becoming part of the atmosphere which predominates in late twentieth-century America. There is too much to do and too little time. One hardly notices that in the rush something is left behind, that I am not present to my own life.

And a kind of vicious cycle starts here. Unknowingly separated from the full amplitude of my own existence, I begin to hunger for something I cannot name. A kind of greed for experience and objects overtakes me. And in the effort to take in more, I become even more divorced from myself.

Though even at this moment my mind leans toward what the Buddhists call beginner's mind, wanting to listen, to see freshly, to reclaim the expansiveness of my own existence, I cannot settle in this state of being without loosening the strictures of a system of thinking and being that seems now to diminish rather than deepen perception. A habit of mind obscures vision. Unexamined assumptions together with a submerged psychology carry older assumptions into the present even in ideas that declare themselves to be from the "New Age" or revolutionary.

Though it is the nature of mind to create and delineate forms, and though forms are never perfectly consonant with reality, still there is a crucial difference between a form which closes off experience and a form which evokes and opens it. I am thinking of a painting by Richard Diebenkorn. The subject matter is simple. One sees a wall inside a room and in the wall an open window and out the window the ocean. But nothing in the images is perfunctory. Every surface, every color is alive with nuance. Looking, one is pulled in further and further, as if into an infinitely expanding dimension of awareness. I grew up near the Pacific Ocean, swimming there often when I was younger, and have lived near that sea all of my life. Seeing that ocean, I cannot help but feel the blue of the water in my body, and it is this feeling Diebenkorn's water captures for me.

The small patch of blue in this painting seems more real than countless supposedly realistic paintings I have seen of the sea which predictably follow an idea of the ocean, yet seem to me as if those who painted them had not really looked at water for years. Though formally it may be realistic, such an image seems far more abstract to me than a painting with no recognizable subject but rendered as if the artist were alive to all the nuances of color, brush stroke, the physical presence of the work.

The effect that a deadening form has on a human life is more complex if only because a living, complex being still exists beneath any assumed identity, hiding behind and yet contradicting and rebelling against the mask. I have written elsewhere about my grandfather. How at times he seemed hollow. He lived his life with a rigid repetitiveness, always dressing perfectly, straying in no way from an almost Victorian idea of manhood, which included earlier affairs and drinking, and a later reticence to speak of these affairs. I came into his life after he had retired. He had a few simple household tasks. He hung up the laundry on washdays and after every meal he dried the dishes. Otherwise he had not much to do but read his mysteries and in later years watch television.

When I was very young and alone with him he would play with me in a tender and almost impish way. He would tell me stories from his own childhood which made him laugh with excitement. At these times he came to life, almost as if he were a different person. That he would be enlivened in the company of a small child, or while telling me stories of his own childhood, makes sense to me now. It was only as a child that he had been able to express the full range of his being. But in the company of other adults he seemed dull, especially compared to women. On that level of emotional exchange between people which is so often lightning quick and subtle, he seemed preternaturally ignorant. Sensually he also had a limited repertoire, at least when it came to food. He liked meat and potatoes, bread dipped in gravy, and was not much interested in trying anything new. If the culture that shaped him dictated that men should be less emotionally and sensually aware, he played his part well.

My grandmother's rebellion was more evident. Though in one way she loved to cook, bake, can, garden, nearly all the domestic work she did was infused with resentment. She had wanted to be an actress. But she would not have named this as the cause of her disappointment. She would not have even said she was disappointed. The feeling was too monumental to name. Like the air we breathed, it loomed over us and came inside us all at once. And the effort she made to surmount this feeling was monumental too as she tried, within the confines she was given to make life perfect. Her china, her perfume, her waxed floor all beautiful, right. Though I loved my grandparents, by the time I was twelve years old I had already resolved never to be like either one of them. Their values were too narrow, their world too confined and small for me. At that early age I did not yet see that my rejection of them was a small form of self-hatred, nor did I understand how my grandparents' private failures reflected a public vacuity.

Who are we? Except in dreams of an abstract world, the self does not exist in isolation. This phenomenon is in every way a symbiotic creature. At the moment of my birth I learned to breathe. The air that filled my lungs became me. Months later, as my breath found a voice, the names I learned were for all that surrounded me. The sounds I formed were tailored to the capacities of a tongue, palate, ear that had evolved in tandem with the rest of life over billions of years. The words I used were handed down to me through centuries of history. The shape of my psyche, how I see, even what I think of as my needs, certainly my desires have come to me through the complex and refined processes of a particular culture. And it is even true that certain aspects of who I am that I value could not exist except for aspects of this culture I dislike or even detest. If the roles European culture has given to men and women were different, who would I be? Consider the fear of homosexuality. During all the years of suffering this fear has caused me not only anguished memory, frightened response, shame, but also insight; a deeper knowledge of my own psyche and of society has permeated the core of my thought and chiseled my character. The imperfections of the society to which I was born have provided the very *materia* of my soul.

The self is part of nature, but so is culture, and to know the self is to enter a social process. One does not know oneself except by being mirrored. Yet in the culture of my birth the reflection of being has been fractured into parts and parceled off to different identities. And the same identities which anchor existence in society also fragment experience along the lines of an old order alienated from nature.

This fragmentation creates a temporary reprieve from the fear of death and loss. But it also creates its own grievous sense of death and loss. When mortality is displaced onto others the roundness of life vanishes and with this what has also disappeared is that sense beyond measurable sense, pointing both to the unknown and to the known, giving a sharper intensity to what becomes, in the act of vision, more strongly present.

In dividing itself from mortality, the European psyche dulls its own experience of the world. If sexual desire, sensitivity to touch, taste, smell, love of color, movement, passionate emotion, all that which is the estate of those on earth, is consigned to others, it is also relinquished. What is lost is nothing less than the eros at the heart of existence.

The system designed to protect us from nature creates an unnatural frailty. Divided from life processes which cannot be extricated from death, from earth, the grounding of being, the self is confused. There is a crisis of identity. In America, a history of exile and relocation united with those European traditions which separate human existence from the earth have led to a particularly intense difficulty. As Ralph Ellison once wrote, "Since the beginning of the nation, white Americans have suffered from a deep inner uncertainty as to who they really are. One of the ways that has been used to simplify the answer has been to seize upon the presence of black Americans and use them as a marker, a symbol of limits, a metaphor for the 'outsider.' "

But in this field of perception, what is outside is also inside. All the qualities given to otherness are those that have been denied in a self that, severed from natural process, has become vague and pale. No wonder that, despite prejudice and hatred, the realm of the other has such a vivid presence to the Western mind. The West has fabricated a realm of being which symbolically preserves vitality. As Wole Soyinka writes of the European idea of Africans, ". . . they moved to construct a romantic edifice. . . ." In this sentimental portrait the African character was capable of intuition but not of analytical thought, was of the earth, and so, like the Western idea of nature, unthinking. This is an undermining praise, and yet it betrays the most intense ambivalence.

Is this also why women, placed lower on the social scale and in so many ways rejected, become the objects of an aggressive lust, and also a wholly ambivalent longing? "My wife with wood fire hair," André Breton writes, "With the heat lightning thoughts/ And the hourglass waist, / My wife with the waist of an otter in the tiger's jaws." In the Western imagination, woman's hair becomes a kind of fire through which images of mortality are burned into a reluctant mind, her waist an hourglass, alerting the beholder to the passage of time, and if she dies like the vulnerable otter, she is also the tiger who can bite into her lover's soul with the knowledge of his own death.

In the center of his poem, when Breton speaks of his wife's "mirror sex," evoking thus a frequently recurrent theme, woman as narcissist, a creature with a severely limited ability to see beyond herself, is he aware that by virtue of his identity a man enters a hall of mirrors? Looking at reflections of his own mind, the Western man confuses his own denied thoughts with what he sees. A longing for a part of himself is inextricably mixed with desire. Is this why distance arouses him? Wishing for yet also fearing a self he has relinquished, he comes to think that placing the woman he desires apart from himself is crucial to his passion. *Vive la différence.* In turn the passion he experiences in his body proves the rightness of the difference, as if it has been endowed by nature.

By his very desire, his identity takes on the compelling presence of nature. That he calls himself a man and that his wife *is* a woman seems to him to be identical with the facts of life. And yet, paradoxically, by the same move he has elevated himself above nature. Though we are all "unkinged," an old order still breathes just beneath the visible surface of what we call male. Masculinity is not merely meant to be a name for what exists physically. It is also meant to stand for a disembodied spiritual existence. Linked with immortality, the very mention of the masculine conjures up not only a mastery of nature but another world, immaterial and impervious to time. Even while the characteristics of masculinity—strength, courage, stoicism, toughness—borrow the power of bodily existence, masculinity asserts control over what is now defined as the weakness of the body, thus bending physical existence to submission at the feet of an idea.

If in the modern secular world there are no longer kings, an ascending order persists. Power stripped of any connection to the

cosmos has become, along with energy, the contemporary analogue of spirit. Now the old luster of divine meaning surrounds
masculine power. But though this ideal masculinity appears to be
universally available to the imagination, its social and political
privileges are reserved for an elite. When the revolutions of the
seventeenth and eighteenth centuries replaced royalty with the
rights of man, *man* was conceived as the ideal human being, the
standard by which every other existence should be measured, and
finally, as the *raison d'être* for creation itself. If in some usages *man*
was supposed to include woman, in the early documents which
established democratic rights, women were intended to be repre-
sented by the word "man" not as separate beings with their own
rights but as subsidiary beings, subsumed in male existence. Nor
was this *man* meant to be everyman. Even the masculine ideal has
a particular history. The idea of masculine being as the quintessence of power was never meant to describe all those who are
considered biologically male. The architects of democracy were
aristocrats and landed gentry. In early forms of democracy in
England and the United States those who did not own property
were disenfranchised. And in the early colonial period another
distinction arose. Whiteness, an idea constructed to set Europeans
apart from Native Americans, Africans, and Asians, became a
qualification for the rights of *man*. The significance goes beyond
ethnocentrism. The white European propertied man had placed
himself and his culture at the highest point on a scale of values
aiming toward transcendence.

What has evolved then is akin to the old order. Even without a
god there is still an above and below. And in this new plan no one
escapes the orientation. Even for those who are not white or
masculine, masculinity sets an ideal toward which to strive, the
direction of ascent. The form of deliverance for women or for all
those who are not white, or who are uneducated, working class, is
to learn to be more like a *man*. Just as Shaw's heroine, Eliza
Doolittle, once learned to speak correct English so she could pass

as a lady, women learn to be aggressive and competitive in business. As in a black ghetto where a boy who has spent his youth stealing cars speaks of the threat of incarceration as a kind of challenge, "a little Indiana Jones," a white, masculine mythos dominates the public imagination.

The ideal has foreshortened our social vision. If there is an arena of public discourse, an intellectual commons, this has been framed by the notion of *opportunity,* the illusion being that social equity can be established by training everyone to meet the standards of whiteness and masculinity, as if only by this elevation will everyone's existence become meaningful.

Of course the goal is impossible. Though the purveyors of technology have consistently promised and perhaps even hoped for the arrival of a more egalitarian world, the use of computers and other inventions eliminates many more jobs than it creates. What is left is a despair only slightly leavened by dreams of becoming a basketball hero or a movie star, as increasingly there is less and less room at the top.

Yet it is here in a terrain of implicit failure that too many men and women dwell, fed perhaps for a few years on dreams of ascent, soon to be trapped by what seems invisibly inevitable, blaming themselves or their families for a linear progression going nowhere, and ultimately the absence of meaning in their lives. For, what lies below in this geography of identity is not only the resource and raw material of the earth but human beings as functional objects. Only *man* exists for *his* own sake. It is out of the thread of utility that identity is woven for all those excluded from the ideal masculine world. In the conventional order, which is only just now changing, whoever is excluded from this world is defined at the core of being by usefulness.

The failure of imagination of the white European mind when confronted with the fully dimensional existence of those described as other is staggering. I am thinking of women in the culture of my childhood. And of Aunt Jemima and Uncle Ben. Little statues of black bootblacks. An epic novel of the Civil War with black slaves portrayed not as the central figures in a struggle over the abolition of slavery but as farm laborers and house servants, those who bring out platters of food, clean up after elegant parties, and help the heroine dress for her romantic encounters with the hero. Only recently have there been any realistic depictions of African-American women who have done domestic work for a living. But another tradition continues in which an African-American woman acting as a maid or an African-American man acting as a chauffeur becomes an icon of sustenance, nurturance, dependability, down-to-earth good sense, whose world revolves around the needs of a white hero or heroine. If in slavery black men, women, and children were openly measured, evaluated, sold, and treated like farm animals bred for specific tasks, since slavery a darker color of skin has blended in the white European mind with the maintenance of life.

All those whose work is of the body feel the divide. The life of the housewife is solitary and often lonely. But with every occupation bent on the basic tasks of survival one feels the sting of another kind of isolation. What one does has been separated from creativity and removed from any larger meaning. The more technologically sophisticated a society becomes, the more mechanistic become the accomplishments of the great majority, the farther away from an experience of significance this work becomes. To work is to suffer a silent humiliation in which the depths of existence are steadily erased.

But if the meaning of the other, female, dark, different, is reduced to functionality by this order, so has Western culture's experience of the world. In the Western habit of mind, the earth is no longer enchanted with its own significance. A forest exists for lumber. Trees for oxygen. A field for grazing. Rocks for minerals. Water for irrigation. Inch by inch the earth is weighed and measured for its uses and in the process the dimensions of the universe are narrowed. Consciousness has been diminished by this disenchantment. And of course the life of the body is also reduced in this truncated idea of use. Like the physical acts which bring sustenance, the needs of the body have become mechanical too; they are no longer numinous sources of knowledge.

An exclusively practical approach to existence permeated postwar American culture. Not only were infants fed according to scientifically devised schedules, and with formula instead of mother's milk, but the act of eating was charted for every age. A tricolored circle representing starches, vegetables, and proteins that was displayed over the chalkboard in my grammar school will be forever forged to my memory. As I grew older, frozen dinners became popular. They were supposed to lessen the labor of the housewife. They tasted like cardboard. Somehow it was metaphorically appropriate that these graying portions of food arranged on a divided metal plate be called TV dinners. One often ate them in front of a television set, the tube replacing firelight, canned laughter substituting for conversation between us.

Looking back, I see these meals as one more step along a path of mechanization that has led in this decade to serious debate over whether or not there is any difference between artificial and human consciousness. The fantasy has even been broached that in the future one might be able to download a mind onto a computer and achieve by one and the same stroke freedom from the needs of the body and immortality (or at least a life as long as silicon). A professor at MIT argues, "If you can make a machine that contains the contents of your mind, then the machine is you." The fantasy is that, with high-resolution, nuclear magnetic holography and ultrasonic radar, phased-array radio encephalography, engineers would be able to scan the brain to chart its chemical composition. This composition written into a computer program combined with computerized simulation of the senses would supposedly create a kind of life. "To hell with the rest of your physical body," the professor says, "it's not very interesting. Now the machine can last forever."

Now in my own mind I try to imagine what a truly disembodied consciousness would be. There would be the simulation of sight, taste, touch. But these would lose the complexity of movement, variation, depth and subtlety of color in changing light. And being separated from the curve of the life cycle—birth, death, love, continuity—life would lose its emotional dimension and sensual experience would finally become a mirror of what the Western mind has imagined it to be, shallow, no longer a source of wisdom.

And what would the downloaded mind do? In this technological apotheosis of utility, through which human needs have been virtually erased, the only activity I have been able to imagine is abstract thought: the image is terrible, so many minds locked in computers trying to solve equations garnered from research on high particle behavior or molecular genetic structure, all leading ultimately to a central philosophical question: What is the nature of existence and, perhaps more to the point in such a state, why do we exist?

In a civilization driven by fear of the full dimension of earthly experience, the question is difficult to answer. Exquisitely small particles of physical existence have been revealed. One can speak of neutrinos and quarks, decipher genetic codes, read the most intricate plans for the future in minute segments of cells, and yet common experience has been left unnamed and undeciphered. Whole worlds of being which are part of the human inheritance remain unexplored, unclaimed. Instead, the larger dimensionality of human experience has been stifled by narrowly proscribed ideas of identity.

Above all it is these categories of fear and hatred by which the experience of a whole culture is distorted. I am thinking of homophobia. The fear of homosexuality. Here again human experience has been reduced to functionality. One discovers this in religious prohibitions against a man and a man (or by

implication a woman and a woman) taking sexual pleasure together; the prejudice is revealing. The oldest biblical argument
against homosexuality is the same that is used against masturba-
tion and birth control. The seed is spilled. Semen has been
spent uselessly. Sexual union has taken place with no issue.
That is, with no purpose.

In a society in which the waste of precious resources essential
for survival, such as water or arable land, is wanton, and at the
same time overpopulation is a critical problem, the desire to save
sperm or sexual energy seems oddly anachronistic. Yet this obsession is not as far from the modern scientific sensibility as one
might guess. Like the drive for more and more sophisticated
technologies to simulate life, the prohibition against homosexuality springs from a fear of the full scope of sensual experience.

Homosexuality is not only a deviation, it undermines the grand
plan, a utilitarian salvation designed to rescue us from being. By
defining homosexuality as outside the boundaries of what is acceptable, all of sexual experience can be confined within the
dimensions of an idea of utility. This is the way that heterosexuality has been socially configured. A man and a woman do not
simply come together freely. Each has a consigned function. The
woman holds the egg; she is passive; she waits for insemination.
The man holds the sperm. He is active. He inseminates. Even
when conception is not desired and birth control is used, these
functional patterns are supposed to continue. The man is the
pursuer, penetrator, the aggressor, the powerful one. The woman
tempts, accepts, surrounds.

Despite the fact that in sexual practice these roles are often
reversed, repeatedly the attempt is made to describe this configuration as biologically determined. Even anatomy is not rigidly
determined along the lines of what we call male and female. And
certainly the possibilities of desire, of touch, taste, movement,
postures, including manners of entrance into the body, or where
the body is entered, and imagination, complexities of feeling,
memory, different kinds of intelligence, all the varieties of pas-

sion, tenderness, spill out way beyond this constricted and constricting notion of female and male behavior.

As with all experience, sexual experience is vast, not only in its possibilities but in the resonance of even the simplest sensation. Desire, longing, pleasure, passion, orgasm, move the body into states of being which defy all definitions, not only those of gender or sexuality but of the boundaried way European culture perceives existence. Moments of a seemingly infinite cavern-like interiority, sensations of enlargement or of dissolving, even decomposition, of engulfing or being swallowed, of merging with energy itself, change itself, breath, air, the lover's body, of becoming sound, light, as well as gravity, weight, stillness. Instant by instant any idea of who one has believed oneself to be is subject to challenge by the knowledge of this experience. And at the same time what is unknown in language, what has not been contained by a European tradition of logic, the felt presence of another universe, escapes from its bottle, which is the realm of the forgotten, into consciousness. Apart from any bond or relationship between lovers, in sexual experience an erotic connection to existence is kindled. This is spirit incarnate.

But this knowledge is prohibited. The experience of incarnation is disruptive to a familiar order of the cosmos. Not only sexual experience but every experience contains within it a dangerous knowledge, the direct revelation of the embeddedness of human existence in nature. This is why being must be ringed with fear. Rigid parameters of identity act as barricades against the possibility of the transformation in consciousness enfolded in the experience of being alive.

Is this why European culture has fashioned ideas of knowledge which serve as forms of resistance to self-knowledge? Just as a horse is broken in, so the mind has been broken into patterns of language, grammar, modes of perception, disciplines which themselves fragment existence. Not only has the capacity to know been consigned to the Manichean realm of masculinity, and the masculine mind disembodied, but knowledge itself, thought itself, has been torn apart into contorted shards of realization. Even the modalities masculine thought is divided into, such as analysis and intuition, metaphor or logic, rational or irrational, categories configured as mutually exclusive or opposed, are assembled according to the same hierarchy of being that elevates *man* above his own experience.

Nowhere is this so clear as in scientific investigations of the nature of reality. The fragmentation of knowledge which is part of the scientific method belongs to this fearful response, and it also deepens scientific ignorance. In laboratories substances, animals, plants, cells, or particles are torn from their environments and studied separately from the systems of which they were born and in which they thrive. This division mimics the entirely naive way in which a scientist is given to believe he can leave his feelings out of his calculations. Unconscious and under a cloak of coolness, for instance, science maintains an ignorance regarding the attitude of aggression which floods its processes. That one of the fathers of the scientific method, Francis Bacon, wrote of this procedure in the seventeenth century that nature should be put on the rack and tortured is not irrelevant to the environmental tortures scientific invention has wrought on nature today.

The branch of knowledge which Western culture claims as a mark of superiority over other cultures and designates as the final arbiter of truth has on principle severed itself from introspection. Even within the scientific world the left hand does not know what the right hand does. This winter I witnessed a group of reporters as they surrounded the physicist Dr. Edward Teller after a hearing held by Hazel O'Leary and the Department of Energy. The department had just released reports, long held secret, about experiments using radiation on human patients, most of whom were not told they were being irradiated, and who subsequently became severely ill or died as a result. Dr. Teller insisted to the reporters that the incidents were blown out of proportion, and that the danger to human

health from radiation had been exaggerated. Yet, though his accomplishments in physics are extraordinary, why should his
opinions about medicine be valued? A nuclear physicist knows
little of medicine or biology. In the way that we are accus-
tomed to thinking about and studying nature, it is as if human
bodies and atomic particles belonged to two separate worlds
entirely isolated from each other. And the creation of new disciplines such as molecular medicine or biological engineering
does little to bridge what is now an old gulf between these divided worlds. Mind apart from body. The human body apart
from nature. Physics and mathematics apart from biology. Each
of these divisions has by the very act of separation created distorted pictures of existence within each discipline. One cannot
simply patch the distorted pieces together. What is needed instead is a far deeper integration, and one that is not itself divided from another process, the movement and development of
emotions. And in turn, as part of this process, a new awareness of the social and ethical implications of scientific practice.

This disintegration does not belong exclusively to the scientific
mind. The same hierarchy of knowledge continues in a popular
culture which elevates science over poetry and regards physics as
superior to biology or ecology, which are more of this earth.
Ironically, the same European tradition, which fails to value experience for itself, rigorously defends the separation of scientific
questions from any other consideration, including ethical concerns, in the name of knowledge for its own sake.

Yet even scientific knowledge is not really valued as an end in
itself. Underneath the effort to chart the universe, describe species, understand the movements of subatomic particles, another
agenda persists. In European culture knowledge has been forged
into an instrument of power. In her brilliant essay "From Secrets
of Life to Secrets of Death," the scientist and science philosopher
Evelyn Fox Keller writes that "the urge to fathom the secrets of
nature" is accompanied by "the collateral hope that," through

this knowlege, "we will fathom the ultimate secrets (and hence gain control) of our own mortality."

Perhaps this explains the anxious atmosphere with which Western culture surrounds both procreation and the female body. The punitive distinction between a virgin and a whore which even today colors trials in which a woman accuses a man of rape, the idea of a "legitimate birth" (by which a birth is acknowledged only if the father consents to give his name to his offspring), the fear of menstruation, and an earlier prohibition against the "showing" of pregnancy in public, an unbridled rage against abortion, all testify to a profound discomfort with generation. The discomfort comes to rest on a woman's body, which is, as Keller writes, "perceived as holding the secret of life." One of the great secrets that women's bodies hold is the secret of how we come into being. So science tries to master the power of generation.

The atmosphere of hostility is only thinly disguised. The prevalence of Caesarean sections, as well as hysterectomies, unnecessary radical mastectomies, the virtual mechanization of birth, the persecution of midwives, come together with in vitro fertilization, molecular biology, or genetic engineering, as attempts to steal and control the capacity to create life. This purpose can be easily read in the words of Francis Crick and James Watson, the men who discovered DNA, when they describe their research as "a calculated assault on the secrets of life."

But something is lost in this assault. Writing at the turn of the century, Mary Shelley prophesied the present moment in her portrait of a doctor who tries to manufacture a human life from the remains of the dead. The novel's eponymous hero, Dr. Frankenstein, laments: "I had worked hard for nearly two years for the sole purpose of infusing life into an inanimate body. For this I had deprived myself of rest and health. I had desired it with an ardor that far exceeded moderation but now that I had finished, the beauty of the dream vanished, and breathless horror and disgust filled my heart."

Is it any accident that in this novel which has become a modern classic the character with whom we suffer most is the monster, a creature with almost human features, an almost human sensibility, yet locked out of life, half dead? Here in this tale, profound in the literature of alienation, lies a self-portrait of a culture where being itself has been diminished to a deadening idea of functionality.

Every act of perception has been affected. "I must walk with more free sense," Thoreau wrote in 1852, in his journal. "It is as bad to *study* stars and clouds as flowers and stones. I must let my sense wander as my thoughts, my eyes see without looking. Carlyle said that how to observe was to look, but I say that it is rather to see, and the more you look the less you will observe. . . . What I need is not to look at all, but a true sauntering of the eye." This other way of seeing, in which the eye does not divide but instead experiences the whole of existence with the whole of oneself, does not yield less insight. Rather the scope of vision is larger.

Examples can be found even in the practice of science. In her biography of the Nobel Prize-winning geneticist Barbara McClintock, Evelyn Fox Keller portrays a way McClintock had of working that was a departure from the usual scientific method. With an attitude of profound patience, McClintock developed a way of seeing, not only under a microscope but even with her own eyesight, which was close to meditation. This process involved hours of proximity, during which she discovered a receptive way of seeing. By observing corn in this manner she began to understand genetics in a dramatically different way. She found that genes could jump from place to place on the chromosome. Things are, she said, to Evelyn Fox Keller, "much more marvelous than the scientific method allows us to conceive."

A young scientist perhaps attracted to science because of a sense of wonder at life on earth, or what is shining in the night sky, finds that this sense of wonder is excluded from the scientific *Weltanschauung,* as it also is from the modern perspective that has been shaped by science. A utilitarian rhetoric has developed as part of modern science which banishes all emotion, particularly awe at existence itself. As the ecologist Edward Goldsmith writes, if Darwin once wrote of seeing a tropical forest in "all its sublime grandeur," this style, common to naturalists, is no longer acceptable in scientific papers.

What we are left with is a strangely efficient sensibility, like a vehicle capable of tremendous speed, yet traveling in a void. The most intense efforts are made to save time: faster and faster computers, the seductive idea of an data highway on which data races at high speeds to the far points of the earth. But time cannot be saved. Or increased. Only lived.

Yet the mind is not always reasonable. Paradoxically, perhaps what is also behind all these frantic attempts to streamline modern life is a longing to save time in another sense, to recapture the feeling of really living one's life. With the speed and stress that seem literally to lift one away from living, the meaning intrinsic to experience seems to vanish. Certainly this is the question at the tip of so many modern tongues: What is the meaning of it all?

What does it mean to be born? To come into being. To exist. In a social system bent to efficiency these questions are always being deferred. No wonder Western philosophy surrounds the question of being with cynicism about both consciousness and nature. The question is asked as if being were an abstract idea, generated, like Athena, from the head.

Yet being is generated from the body. Can the question of being even begin to be answered apart from the actual experience of birth? As riveted as Western philosophy has been upon the question of being, there are still no words to describe the knowledge that comes with this astonishing experience. This is partly because birth has within it a meeting with what in Judaism is known as the *Ein Sof,* the unutterable, that which cannot be spoken because even if fragments of this larger unknown presence can be sensed it is beyond the limits of human consciousness to contain. But this paucity of language has other causes. If in Victorian society birth was unmentionable, in modernity birth, along with all experience, has lost its intrinsic meaning. So language stops at the gate of the entrance into being. One can speak of intuition, or of dreams, of revelation, of clairvoyance, as well as of *Wissenschaft,* the knowledge of science, one can even speak of the unknown, but one cannot refer with the same certainty of recognition and respect to birth-knowledge as that which anyone who gives birth or witnesses a birth comes to know.

In my own life, I think of the birth of my daughter as one of the most extraordinary experiences I have had. Though birth is also among the most ordinary of experiences in the sense that it occurs often and all over the world, among diverse cultures, peoples, and species, still it is always astonishing. One can know from an early age that babies are born, even see the enlarged womb of a pregnant woman swelling her belly, even feel the movement of a small limb under the skin, or listen to the heart beat, and one can hold a newborn only hours after the birth, but none of this is quite the same as being present as the infant's head crowns at the edge of its mother's vagina and then begins to emerge between her thighs.

But in a language alienated from nature and disrespectful toward female experience of all kinds, how is it possible to describe this moment? One can speak of a softening in the room, or of what is, despite every sound in the room, a kind of silence which penetrates the air, or of that inaudible crack through which a nearly electric opening seems to appear in one's own consciousness, yet if a whole culture has conspired to deny the meaning of this event as part of a passage into being, these descriptions dissolve into sentimentality.

The experience of birth then is made smaller than it is. Even the mystifying idea of mother's intuition is reductive, not only because this kind of knowledge is regarded as innate and embedded in the body, and thus of a lesser order in a way that "higher" knowledge is not, but because this idea also trivializes the considerable learning and intelligence it takes to raise children. This mystification diminishes the revelatory quality of birth by enclosing generation in a kind of mute domestic realm which must remain elusive to the masculine mind. This is the back side of the scientific lust for the secrets in a woman's body. The wish is to possess knowledge without being affected by it, without being transformed.

The failure to receive the full dimensionality of *this* experience is especially unfortunate because birth and infancy constitute the beginning of all human experience. But the same tragedy repeats itself with death. Death which is the other door to existence has also been muted. As Walter Benjamin writes, modern society has made "it possible to avoid the sight of the dying." Yet, in this effort to escape the experience of mortality, an even greater lack is created. Because in this atmosphere of denial death loses its largeness, and an inexplicable sweetness has also vanished, that strange softening of the heart which accompanies the stunning motion that ends a life, breath curving with the curvature of earth, into nothing.

I remember when my grandmother died. I was not with the family in the hospital when she went into surgery. Nor did I see her body after death. The news came over the telephone. I was standing in an upstairs hallway looking through gray and opaque louvered windows. What came instead of weeping was a depression as gray and opaque. I left the house and wandered streets, feeling too vulnerable to be outside, yet too lost to settle anywhere.

My mother's death was very different. Over two decades later, along with many others in my community, I came to respect the significance of dying. During the last months of her life I brought my mother to a convalescent home near me. The home was run by friends with what in elder care is still unfortunately a unique approach. They believe every moment of every life is precious. My mother and I spent time together. She spoke openly about her approaching death, and what she felt in her body. Every time I said goodbye to her, I understood that I might never see her again. And I saw in her eyes that she was also thinking this. A profound and healing love passed between us. I reached her bed an hour after she died, and stayed there for a while. Her body was so thin it was as if she had melted away. My grief and sorrow were held in that room by an atmosphere of palpable tenderness.

During the postwar decades the idea that meaning is limited to earthly existence was widely adopted in intellectual circles almost as an expression of despair, fired by a kind of brave loneliness. According to a long lineage of European thought, in the absence of God, one finds oneself alone in a meaningless universe. Locked within individual existence, subjective experience becomes a form of isolation from which there can be no exit.

Yet the idea that existence contains its own *raison d'être* does not require isolation. The experience of birth and death include the presence of all existence. And the boundaries of being are permeable. The experience of one being enters and becomes the experience of another. Daily one takes the very substance of earth into one's cells and also into one's soul. These are the lines I remember from Whitman:

> *There was a child went forth every day,*
> *And the first object he look'd upon, that object he*
>   *became,*
> *And that object became part of him for the day or a*
>   *certain part of the day,*
> *Or for many years or stretching cycles of years.*

> *The early lilacs became part of this child,*
> *And grass and white and red morning-glories, and*
>   *white and red clover and the song*
>   *of the phoebe bird,*
> *And the third-month lambs and the sow's pink-faint*
>   *litter, and mare's foal and the cow's*
>   *calf . . .*

What is perhaps most miraculous about birth, especially to a Western sensibility trained in a strict idea of self as separate from others and nature, is that one life is born from another. In the cycles of nature, bodies feed bodies, and death feeds life. But this is also true of consciousness. Even in the most casual meeting, where no words are exchanged, by a glimpse, by desire, by admiration, shock, recognition, one mind is born from another. Language contains within it an infinite number of such births through which meanings have been constructed over thousands of years. Relationship is not tangential to consciousness. Consciousness as we know it, including a capacity for learning, focus, self-reflection, the ability to speak, think, to contemplate, cannot develop without the presence of others. Children who have been isolated from others find all these feats difficult if not insurmountable.

What is easy for a child, newly born, is to turn toward the mother's body. Groping with cheeks and mouth, the infant burrows over the mother's breast in search of her nipple. Finding this, her tiny lips must explore at the same time both the contours of the mother's nipple and their own movement, new, uncharted. With his first small acts the child finds nourishment, knowledge, and love all in the same efforts.

Only later does the child learn from culture to divide these things. Eating, he is no longer aware of taking life into his body. Even if she takes sensual pleasure in a meal, she has lost the memory of the mouth as an instrument of intelligence. He has forgone a deeper knowledge of his own existence as part of a continual process of transubstantiation, *bodies becoming bodies;* she loses the eros at the heart of becoming.

And yet the division is not really possible. All that is severed returns. Even when experience is unnamed and denied, what is denied shapes the mind. Placing the memory of sensuality, of an earth-bonded knowledge, at a distance, a man imagining himself as free of natural limitation projects the part of himself he wishes to forget onto the portrait he draws of a woman, someone he thinks of as closer to earth. Or a woman, defined by her culture as white, wishing herself free of earth, displaces the physicality of her own mind onto a woman or a man who is described as not white, and thus imagined as more deeply rooted in material life. But the story does not end here. This very act of separation and malignment begins to define consciousness with another kind of relatedness.

Nothing that is called masculine or white can exist without its corollary in these imagined feminine and nonwhite worlds. Nor does any part of this consciousness escape itself, its own misogyny, its own racism. The man who has learned to hate women is also hating the body from which he emerged into life, and the very process by which he came into being. All his thought about his own life, society, nature, the cosmos is woven with this hatred. And the same culture which produces racism is also produced by racism. Every part of that culture is laced and permeated with histories of fear and hatred. As Toni Morrison writes in *Playing in the Dark,* the abiding belief is that ". . . traditional, canonical, American literature is free of, uninformed and unshaped by the four hundred year old presence of, first, Africans and the African-Americans in the United States." But of course this strange and invented isolation is impossible. "It has occurred to me," Morrison writes, "that the very manner by which American literature distinguishes itself as a coherent entity exists because of this unsettled and unsettling population. . . . Through significant and underscored omissions, startling contradictions, heavily nuanced conflicts, through the way writers peopled their work with the signs and bodies of this presence—one can see that a real or fabricated Africanist presence was crucial to their Americanness. And it shows."

By the creation of fictional categories of otherness, the white, masculine mind makes itself profoundly ignorant of its own workings; in the act of diminishing the other, self-knowledge has been narrowed. And in turn this ignorance produces a troubled terrain of consciousness. Fragmented and disoriented, the landscape of this mind is permeated with anxiety. Edges of imagined selves fray with worry, as if identity, even being, were under assault. The question may be, Am I a *man?* But just behind another question lingers, barely audible. *Do I exist?* This is not simply detached epistemological inquiry. Doubt lies at the core of a consciousness which has banished its own experience. Ironically, in the effort to best mortality and place the inevitability of age, loss, and death into another world, the depth and meaning of daily life have been lost. In the wake of this loss, where existence is not colored with despondency, what remains is shallow.

And we are all affected. Although I am one of those who would be described as other, this mind is not foreign to me. From the earliest age I was educated in this manner of thinking and this way of seeing the world. The very medium of my own thought, the images, words, grammar, music I love and am familiar with, architecture, the shape of cities I have inhabited, ways that I live, have been born and bred in a European culture transplanted to America. And I have become all this. Slowly and painstakingly I have had to unlearn the more subtle forms of racism threaded into the fabric of these traditions I inherited. Just as I have accepted into myself and have had to unlearn ideas of woman or of sexuality that betray me and erase my own knowledge of myself. This, as Cornel West has written, is one of the cruelest effects of bigotry, that at some level those who are denigrated internalize this denigration. One becomes tied, even on the subtlest level, to inauthenticity by what is treasured and needed, by custom, family, education, even by the very cognitive forms through which one would reach for liberation.

What one is promised in return is meager. But in states of need, hardship, self-hatred, or worse, in witnessing the pain of loved children, family, it does not seem so. We are offered a share of a power over existence that almost daily grows more aggrandized in its plans, more heedless in its hunger for acquisition and control. If I long for freedom from the prejudices and deprivations of a social definition that has been imposed upon me, and if I am among a chosen few, I might be offered this freedom in exchange for another definition: to make myself over in the image of this power. That once I stood inside these boundaries, suffered this imprisonment, these prejudices, these deprivations, and had along with this the privilege of certain secrets, of knowing the backside of society, another relationship to the body, other sources of power, blood and birth at times foremost in my consciousness, and remembered a history of damages, suffering, injustices, including my own resistance to being categorized as woman, must now be forgotten. Now I must stand outside myself.

It is neither the death of God nor the idea of existence itself as the sole source of meaning that has created the feelings of isolation, loneliness, meaninglessness that are so much a part of the twentieth century. This abandonment has a much longer history. And the loss is more primary. The very knowledge at the heart of being, has been sacrificed. No one escapes this affliction. In a culture that has banished experience to a world of meaninglessness, the loss is general and touches everyone.

But what is also equally distributed among us all is another sense of power that is folded within being. And this power is not lonely. One day, taking a pause from this writing, I step out of my back door. I am tired, my thoughts unfocused. I stand dazed for a few seconds. Then I look toward a corner of the garden where the afternoon light has an extraordinary clarity. It is late October, the northern California colors are browning, and everywhere, scattered among the evergreens, are russets, yellows, burnished by this light. The air is newly cold. All this cuts into me with an intense force. For several moments I am transfixed. And I am not the same. I have been entered, ignited by this light, changed by this place.

4

Place

We know not where we are.

—Henry David Thoreau,
Walden

Forgetting occurs when all information of a particular kind
or mode about a situation is suppressed.

—Brian Rotman,
Ad Infinitum—The Ghost in Turing's Machine

Little fleece of my flesh
that I wove in my womb,
little shivering fleece,
sleep close to me!

—Gabriela Mistral,
"Close to Me"

The great mythos here in the country of my birth is movement. Ships filled with pilgrims, or protestants, or immigrants. The passages are almost abstract, as if all that lies over the waters is freedom. The release is from a corrupt world, from oppression, persecution. But of course there is another story, too, the underside of the ideal. The hellish middle passage, men, women, and children chained in the holds of ships, packed so tightly movement was all but impossible, drowning less often in the open sea than in the fluid of their own bodies. This passage was to slavery. And then there were the forced marches, the Trail of Tears of the Cherokee, the forced migration of Navajo, repeated all over the continent as one people after another were severed from their lands.

The dream was and still is forked. In one direction the movement is toward democracy. The underground railroad during the Civil War. The labor movement. The movement for civil rights. For women's liberation. The metaphor holds. More often than not, in this dream the pilgrim and the protester come to or from a place of meeting. Not only with each other but with existence, manifested intensely and freshly, newly revealed by a land less marked by familiar structures, a slate of assumptions wiped clean. The chance for a new start and the rhetoric of beginnings echo in the words of Thoreau, Whitman, Frederick Douglass, Margaret Fuller.

But this dream too takes another fork. The desire to be free of the necessities of place and the limitations of earthly life. Streets paved with gold. Robber barons. Vast wealth and lives of leisure built on the labor of slaves and indentured servants. The inventions of machines to replace every task. Gravity no longer a restraint; the American flag planted on the moon. Businessmen with cellular phones and powerbooks, no longer tied to the body, extending themselves electronically all over the world. Yearly migrations to better jobs, better economies; the search for cheaper labor, new markets. The freedom to grow endlessly. An infinity of power suspended in a space defined by no location, no settling ground, even if all the time the ground is here, and no one, except in these mad dreams, is apart.

Where does one leave off and the other begin? My hand curled around the pen. Paper and ink. Heavy gray clouds massing over the hills, and the wet air. Everywhere an exchange takes place.

One can make out differences, perceive outlines, boundaries, discover distinguishing marks. But the exchange continues at such a rate that the conclusion is clear. One cannot exist without the other. In the arc of existence, each being is wholly dependent on the matrix we all make.

One speaks of living *on* the earth but in truth life is held within the earth. An atmosphere woven from life circles the planet. Every movement, every breath, every response, the least thought is shaped to the curve of this mass. Even time and space bend to it. Like a child in a womb, all we know exists inside this outer body. And all is dependent on it.

But my mind was schooled differently. I remember being mystified in my childhood by the words "For dust thou art, and unto dust shalt thou return." So little else in my Christian cosmology pointed to that meaning. By every other lesson, I was taught to think of myself as somehow apart from soil and dust. Very little in my culture taught me that my existence depends on the existence of earth.

When in a dream of himself as a child Freud asked his mother where he came from, and she showed him bits of soil on the palm of her hand, he was terrified. The knowledge must have evoked fear, not only of death but of dependency. Because, if death is at a remove in time, dependency is always present.

Perhaps that is why a dialogue over dependency is built so solidly into the discourse of gender. In the Western tradition independence has been configured as masculine, dependence as feminine. Seeking liberation from traditional female roles, a woman is said to gain her independence. And as if her dependence prevented his liberation, a man calls his wife "a ball and chain."

But this pattern of thought conceals a reversal. Though men may complain about the dependence of women and children, what goes unmentioned is a man's dependence on female labor to meet the humble needs of his daily sustenance. That such a dependence embarrasses masculinity is clear even in the idealized trajectory of male development, which requires first that a man free himself from his mother's apron strings and then from his wife's. This is no simple story of autonomy. It has a subtext: the process requires mastery of women (which is to say of nature). Nor does the story allow for the ambiguity that shapes every relationship and always contains a mixture of give and take, complementarily and mutuality. To need is a form of trust and love.

But need is nothing but an enemy in this story. Yawning at night, hungering in the morning, a little cold in the afternoon.

Perhaps it is this too that inspires a fear of homosexuality. The image of a man's body curled into the arms of another man, letting his vulnerability be seen or even exist in the company of men, corrupting the masculine realm of independence with want. To recognize the necessity of earthly sustenance for male survival would strike an alarm. The whole scaffolding of male independence rests on the invisibility of a female foundation, a feminine world turned toward a masculine world ready to give what enables a man to produce the illusion of autonomy.

In this scheme, the private realm of domestic life becomes a place to hide dependency. The humiliation and vulnerability of nakedness and need can be hidden at home away from the public world. This is as true for society as it is for the individual psyche. In order to conceal the dependency of Western *man* on earthly process, private life must be carefully bifurcated from public life. For this life holds the secret of need.

Perhaps this is why a woman's body seems so threatening to the masculine psyche. Along with the home, this body has become the repository for an abandoned knowledge of dependency. One can read this fear in the traditional masculine hatred of women. Women know that men are dependent and with this knowledge they hold the power, either to reveal the secret or not. This revelation would bring with it a humiliation of cataclysmic proportions, one that holds within it the memory of a childhood fragility and the mother's power to erase one's own existence.

It is a fear that comes to play dramatically in the current angry debate over abortion. Intense arguements laid before both courts and public audiences attempt to prove that the fetus has separate rights as a human being. That even before the fetus can exist outside the womb independently, it is an independent being. So in the unconscious recesses of a psyche which imagines itself impervious to earthly frailty, to make abortion against the law would also banish any felt memory of union with a greater, enclosing, nourishing body.

But the union is all about us. It cannot even be separated from the progression of our thoughts. Here in this room I can hear water falling outside, see moisture on the ground in the garden, feel the dampness in the air and in a certain heaviness of mind that overtakes me in the rain. Yet this is not how I have been trained to see thought. I was taught to think of the mind as independent from place. Among all the fantasies of independence that are part of the Western mythos, the adventurer, the pioneer alone in the wilderness, the sailor on the open seas, the crusading knight, the heroic marine, perhaps the most enduring and profound in its influence has been the idea of a mind autonomous from any surrounding.

The concept that consciousness is separate from physical existence is deeply worn into the crevices of the European mind. This dividedness provides the metaphor through which an elevation over earthly process can be imagined. Only by considering itself independent of the earth can consciousness believe in its own transcendence.

Just as the natural process of human birth is reversed in Genesis to make woman born of man, so mental process has been reversed in the mythos of this civilization so that the physical universe is depicted as proceeding from abstractions. Plato's idea of earthly existence as a poor shadow of eternal ideas not only permeates the dominant traditions of Western philosophy but also reflects a fundamental posture toward existence, a hierarchy of values in which abstractions, theories, principles, ideas, mathematical equations, logic, and analysis are elevated above what is called concrete, corporeal, sensible, palpable, tangible, solid, physical, material, and contextual.

In the theology that preceded and yet still shapes modern scientific thought, the realm of the abstract was said to reflect the mind of God more accurately than a corrupt earthly life. The heresy of science was to observe the things of this earth. Science made a break from pure deductive logic by inserting experiment into the process by which truth is discovered. And to a certain degree, through experiment, what is palpable has been given value again. Yet, by an odd twist of mind, what is palpable has also been robbed of credence. Now what one perceives directly is no longer trusted without the intervention of the scientific method.

By what almost amounts to a kind of psychological sleight of hand, science has by one stroke seized authority over both concrete and abstract realms of knowledge. In this fabulous rendering of the scientific method, the scientist brings reality into his laboratory and returns with truth. This story gains strength through a subtle heritage which partakes of religion, philosophical assumptions, and the intrinsic authority of direct sensual experience. And so we do not notice that even scientific conjecture remains conjecture still. So inured have we become to the authority of science that when one "proven" scientific portrait of the world, such as Newtonian physics, is refuted by other portraits, such as relativity or quantum mechanics, we never question the scientific method itself, nor do we understand that all along scientific thought, like religious abstraction, is not the same as reality.

An experiment conducted in a laboratory is subject to many different kinds of influence and that is why experiments must be replicated in more than one laboratory to be taken seriously. But even what is taken as proof by the scientific community is not conclusive. A condition in one laboratory may be replicated in almost all laboratories because this condition is part of the ethos of a whole civilization. One of these conditions, a mostly unquestioned part of the scientific method, is the practice of studying any being in isolation from the environment in which it lives. But, as ecologists have shown, to study a creature outside of its surroundings is to study another animal altogether, one that does not exist in nature.

And as the philosopher and historian of science Paul Feyerabend has made clear in *Against Method,* no theory accounts for all of the facts in its domain. There are always seemingly stray aspects of reality that remain outside every theory's capacity to explain phenomena. There are even occurrences and test results that appear to contradict what becomes in the end an agreement about what is truth. Facts, whether from the laboratory or the field, do not make theory by themselves. They must be interpreted, and in science as in other fields this interpretation is not immune to diverse influences including political bias. And finally, as Feyerabend makes clear, even what is called a fact is constituted by scientific effort; it is *made.* Theory is implicit in the language of science, the method, the attitudes by which "facts" are discerned and shaped.

One of these prejudices is the enshrinement of numbers as the most reliable kind of data. Yet, as descriptions of the material universe, mathematical calculations must always be tried and proven by experiment. During the Manhattan Project, numerous mathematical calculations were done before the first experimental explosion of the atomic bomb. These calculations were partly based on smaller experiments such as the small chain reaction Enrico Fermi had created in the Chicago Metallurgy Laboratory, partly on conjecture, partly on mathematical theory. But, as the physicist Hans Bethe pointed out, no calculation can be relied upon to produce predictable consequences. Some early calculations, which were later "disproved," suggested that an atomic explosion could set off an endless chain reaction that would destroy the earth. In fact, the calculations which closely preceded the first experimental explosion of the bomb at Alamogordo were in error. The power of the blast was underestimated. The bomb destroyed the instrument designed to measure its force.

From hindsight, one might say that those earlier calculations which were dismissed had in them a grain of truth which was concealed by the limits scientific tradition places on knowledge. For the study of the bomb's effect was done by physicists, who were uneducated in botany, biology, and physiology. That infinitely small but also infinitely destructive nuclear explosions are still occurring in the bodies of those exposed years ago to ionizing radiation is a consequence which was not discernible in their calculations.

I am not immune to the great appeal of numbers. They have about them a kind of coolness which makes for relief from the chaos of need and desire, anguish or anger, the flood of words, not to speak of loud sounds, unpleasant sensations of any kind. When I think of numbers proceeding in orderly sequence, or balanced carefully into equations, my mind arranges itself into a kind of calm. I am reminded of Bach. Of quiet. Reason. This realm of the mind is as real as any place on the universe. But in the history of Western science, mathematics has taken on a specific metaphysical meaning. Identified by Kepler, among others, with the mind of God, the world of numbers not only claims to be real but to be more real than any other place.

The metaphysic continues but now transcendent truth is wrought from specimens of earth. If in the public mind, scientific knowledge rests on *hard* facts conjured from incontrovertible calculations and dense material evidence alike, this would appear to be a union of spirit and matter. But science is subtly arranged around an opposition between the two. Even if modern science no longer bifurcates matter and energy, by the scientific method, theory has been elevated above the realm of matter, as if scientific intelligence, like all intelligence, were not of the earth.

Yet, in the actual processes of thought, scientific or otherwise, no absolute division between material and theoretical or concrete and abstract actually exists. Thought not only moves continually back and forth on a continuum the West describes as abstract and concrete, but the human experience of knowledge can never at any instant be wholly one or the other. Even theory itself has a materiality rarely acknowledged in a culture still aiming toward transcendence. Ideas as well as poems, narratives of any kind as well as stories, sounds of words, even alphabets, certainly numbers, exist as physical entities, not only becoming flesh as they affect the thinker, the reader, or speaker, listener, acting as a kind of mortar for communities, families, peoples, but themselves emanating from, and participating in an ecology of mind that is as much of nature as are rocks and trees.

But in the West this commingling is veiled. If by means of duality Western culture has secured the illusion of transcendence, the culture is also blind to the order and pattern, the memory and intelligence, all the qualities of abstract thought, that exist *in* nature. By that hubris which in Western culture characterizes most thought about human intelligence, the ability to perceive pattern and order in nature has been elevated above nature while pattern and order are not perceived as qualities of a profound analytical intelligence in nature. Even the most abstract concepts of science, those which belong to mathematics, exist in nature. One has only to slice open an apple to find symmetry. Birth certainly contains a kind of division and multiplication at the same time, as do cell mitosis, DNA, the future lives within a seed pod, a copse of birch trees, splitting and reproducing even as they appear in repose.

Nor was sequence invented by the human mind but exists as a significant principle of order within all nature, most clearly perhaps with seasons, the progress of the earth circumnavigating the sun, or human growth and aging. Even the concept of the integer exists in nature, in beings and things which have a discernible integrity, a wholeness within themselves, such as one day, or, as the astronomer Caroline Herschel called them, ''the integer days." And computations made possible by the use of Arabic numerals, with their crucial use of position, can be observed in the meaningful arrangements of chromosomes which also change significance through where they are placed and in what sequence.

Gregory Bateson was famous for beginning his classes by throwing a crab on his desk and asking his students to describe the qualities of life, using the crab as an example. The symmetrical order is so clear. Near the end of his life Bateson argued that the capacity to symbolize, basic not only to all mathematics but also to what is called abstract thought, is also deeply embedded in natural process. In an interview taped for a Lindisfarne Fellows meeting, Bateson described metaphor as the "logic upon which the biological world" has been built, "the main characteristic organizing glue . . ." of what he calls elsewhere the mental world of organisms.

The manner of symbolic thinking he describes is not the symbolic representation of logos but the metaphor of poets. He compares two syllogisms, the famous example of "good" thinking:

Men die
Socrates is a man
Socrates will die

and the equally famous example of "bad" thinking:

Grass dies
Men die
Men are grass

Because the first example depends on the likeness of subjects rather than verbs it is a kind of logic not found in biology. For billions of years there has been no separation of subject and verb in living organisms. To extend the implications of his insight, one can see in the very insistence that the subject be separated from *this* verb a separation from the natural world and natural process.

A human death is made distinct from the death of grass. And the biological cycle of participation and transmutation at the heart of being, by which men and women are grass and grass is fed by and becomes animal life, is obscured.

But of course what is equally obscured and for the same reasons is the idea of thought as an attribute of the natural world. The possibility certainly exists that human beings have the capacity for and have invented forms of thought which are unique in the universe. But the assertion that what is considered the highest form of thought, namely abstract thought, is uniquely human has an emotional valence. This assertion takes the human thinker in the direction of a mythical world of ideas outside the biosphere. "For most mathematicians (and, one can add, most scientists)," Brian Rotman writes, "mathematics is a Platonic science, the study of timeless entities, *pure forms* that are somehow or other simply 'out there,' preexistent objects independent of human volition or of any conceivable human activity . . ." and, I might add, of any biological or earthly activity too.

If with arithmetic, algebra, geometry, calculus scientists are able to measure and begin to describe and in some ways even understand the abundant complex patterns in nature, this is an astonishing accomplishment. It is a mirror of human nature and of the dimensions of human intelligence, including the human desire to know. Yet in every aspect this accomplishment is also a mirror of the complexity and the vast intelligence which belong to natural existence. Human intelligence is woven from *this* complexity, the complexity of the universe.

But with the concealment of nature the full dimension of human intelligence is also sacrificed. Those forms of human knowledge associated with materiality suffer invisibility and marginalization. It is thus not only the natural world that is mechanized but one's own experience of the natural world. Sensual knowledge, seeing, tasting, smelling, feeling, hearing, crucial abilities through which the human species has survived for millennia in balance with other life forms, have been made subject to distrust, given a lower value, and hence, outside of a handful of artists and healers who are also marginalized, these capacities have been left under-developed in Western culture.

And what suffers equally in the estimation of modern science is what Pascal described as the reason of the heart. Human emotional knowledge, which has also evolved in community with natural existence, has been reduced to a problem that gets in the way of objectivity. By this method what is lost is the human experience of the beauty of a river, the trees along its side, the mountains rising behind it, rocks washed, polished by waves of water, silvery fish leaping within it, leaves falling on its surface, shining, illuminated by a setting sun, an experience central to what we would call any question of truth.

I can remember the intensity with which as a child I entered the Sierra Mountains, the deserts outside Los Angeles, the ocean just over the hills ringing the valley where I lived. Were I to put language to these experiences now I would describe them as meetings, transformational exchanges which touched me and through which I learned the nature of existence. I was taught. But I had no way to explain such lessons. The cosmology I had been given by my culture, its philosophies, would not embrace this knowledge. In the world view I have inherited, if nature seems to have meaning, this meaning is just an appearance, a sentimental overlay, one which only the naive, children, the uneducated, or those from lesser cultures, take at face value. If the child sees heaven in a wildflower, her innocent vision must later yield to a higher but severing wisdom which would have it that heaven exists on earth only in the eye of the human beholder.

What is sacrificed with the elevation of human consciousness above natural process is not only the idea of the intelligence of nature, but one's experience of being immersed in a larger whole. A deep and continuing relationship with all other forms of existence is an ancient aspect of human consciousness. One encounters it in children who delight in plants and animals. And this knowledge is kept alive in the myths and stories children learn about the natural world.

But the child becomes an adult. Culture schools her to imagine her own intelligence as unique and isolated in the universe. An older sense of participation in a world of meaning is traded for a mental world that, however dry and abstract, has the virtue of independence. To know is no longer erotic, no longer relational, but becomes instead a means of escape from enmeshment in material existence. By an incremental process of separation from the body, from emotions, from the direct experience of nature, nature becomes alien. Now independence from nature is supposed to provide safety from an increasingly menacing earthbound fate. Knowledge, which has become a form of power rather than intimacy, works a kind of magic in the psyche. Though, in this habit of mind, understanding and analysis bear with them the illusion of having captured the material world and bent it to submission, ironically the mind that imagines itself to be independent from the physical universe becomes more fearful. Because the fact of natural power is unavoidable. And in a withering cycle that is as inescapable as the fact of the human dependence on the biosphere, this fear grows more and more terrible if only because in the Western mind existence has become meaningless. To be swallowed by such a universe would be a preternaturally cold and lonely fate.

Yet the mind is already swallowed. Just as in any ecosystem the existence of each species or life form is dependent on the existence of the whole, so too human knowledge is dependent on the matrix in which it exists. As Hans Blumenberg writes of the Copernican revolution, the air we inhabit is just dense enough to allow us to draw breath and shield us from cosmic rays and yet thin enough to allow us to see the stars. Or, less sanguinely, one might imagine a nuclear winter in which the sky is darkened, polluted air stings the eyes, a lack of oxygen and the effects of radiation, not to speak of the trauma of events, affects the brain;

since the smell of ash expunges every other scent, food cannot be smelled to know if it has gone bad; because buildings, trees, shrubs, rocks no longer exist as markers of a familiar landscape, one cannot find one's way. Without the other and without other- ness, knowledge is limited to the point of extinction.

But any number of less dramatic examples might be drawn from the history of scientific discourse. Within the history of physics, two simple examples spring to mind. One is from the written work of Galileo. As Italo Calvino points out, whether he is describing a dialogue, the process of thought, or physical mo- tion, he is likely to use the image of a horse, racing, dragging sacks of grain, performing elaborate feats. The other example I use is more famous. That is Einstein's description of relativity, which at times he likens to the operations of an elevator and at other times a train. These concrete metaphors are not just illustra- tions. Human perspicacity is literally constituted by what can be perceived on earth and in the universe. Thought is impossible without such images.

The interdependency of human thought and the environment is a vast topic which has not been explored with anywhere near the same passion as the assertion of independence. But this mutuality goes back to the very origins of a human consciousness that evolved with the rest of nature. Answering Bishop Berkeley's famous epistemological question, If a tree falls in the forest and no one is present to hear it, does it make a sound? one might pose another question: If sound does not exist can there be such a thing as a human ear? For the ear and human knowledge evolved in community with other life forms and with the physical properties of an audible universe. Human knowledge, if nothing else, is a testament to the connectedness and interdependence of life. There can be no subject apart from an object. This understanding should transform our epistemologies by embedding not only being but the capacity to know in an earth imbued with intrinsic signifi- cance.

• • •

A return to what is a birthright of meaning is more than a philosophical journey. Something changes in the mood. An atmosphere of nihilism dissolves. Certainly I notice this shift when, turning away from the page or the computer screen, the living world is suddenly present.

When I rise and walk under the trees in my neighborhood, the russet color of their leaves burnishes my mind. Even turning in my chair, opening the window, feeling a cold wind against my face, my mind is joined, taken up, educated. This simple experience is one that most of us regard as an emotional necessity. A room, an enclosure, must have a window. Yet out of the mentality of this civilization we have made a windowless room.

What is at stake is sanity. There is a mad arrogance that flows from the diminishment of meaning in nature, one that approaches megalomania. A presumption of omniscience accompanies every dangerous attempt to control and dominate nature. Again and again disasters are created because human knowledge has been imagined as having no limits. A substance is given to young pregnant women because scientific tests indicate it can prevent miscarriage. Decades later this substance is shown to have no effect on miscarriage, but it causes cancer in the daughters born of this experiment. Fields are saturated with another chemical because this substance kills certain pests. But this substance finds its way into the bodies of birds and causes a silent spring. And then men, women, and children begin to grow ill and die too. But the lesson is never learned. With each new invention, a claim for safety is made that is founded on an idea of infallible knowledge.

In his beautiful accounts of peasant life in Alpine France, John Berger describes a very different attitude toward knowledge. The peasant farmer lives and works daily with an understanding of scarcity. This understanding, he writes, diverges from both the "bourgeois and Marxist ideals of equality" which "presume a world of plenty. . . . They demand equal rights before a cornucopia . . . to be constructed by science and the advancement of knowledge . . ." But the peasant ideal of equality is different. It "recognizes a world of scarcity, and its promise is for mutual fraternal aid in struggling against this scarcity and a just sharing of what the work produces."

The experience of scarcity delivers a dramatic lesson in dependency on the earth. Not only the dependency of the body but of the mind too. Closely "connected with the peasant's recognition, as a survivor, of scarcity is his recognition of man's relative ignorance," Berger writes. "He may admire knowledge and the fruits of knowledge but he never supposes that advance of knowledge reduces the extent of the unknown. . . . The unknown can only be eliminated within the limits of a laboratory experiment. Those limits seem to him to be naive."

It is these limits that are ignored when, in the case of possible pollution, from ionizing radiation, or one of hundreds of thousands of man-made chemicals released into the environment every day, no margin is made for the limits of human knowledge. If an effect cannot be measured by modern scientific and statistical means, it is presumed not to exist.

In an ironic footnote to both the history of mathematics, and also the history of a certain hubris, the symbol for zero, z, which came from the Hindu tradition, stands for the unknown. It was the adoption of this symbol and its use to occupy space that so radically advanced mathematical knowledge. Now, an older understanding of zero is crucial to human life, and that is the limitation before which we must learn to stand in respect as well as wonder.

Yet zero is also a circle. One is in fact encircled by the inutterable. And the edges of the unknown are closer than one would think. Behind every expression of belief in unlimited knowledge and power one can detect an earlier scene. In a half-forgotten, probably hazy, hardly focused memory an infant lies on his mother's lap. Everything he learns, he learns from her, from her body. He is learning even before he has words. Even if he fails to remember his early studies, his body will always remember them.

But as he grows to an adult and learns to equate power with independence, what his body remembers will threaten to humiliate him. Because what his body knows is not only that dependency is inextricable from his own existence, but that tracing the origins of his own knowledge back in time, to the body of his mother, and to the larger power of the cosmos he has met in her body, he arrives at the limits of his own understanding.

Is this why infancy is so often described in Western culture as telluric and primitive? The derision is ostensibly aimed at what the infant does not know. But in the guise of derogation, an old fear expresses itself. A fear of what the infant *does* know, including his knowledge of the limits of human knowledge.

Even now, that in the course of a day one holds within oneself not only the memory of infancy, but the same state of being, is wholly erased from consciousness. In the English language, except for pejorative descriptions, such as *regressed,* there are no words for this state of mind which is so much a part of human experience.

And if what is considered regressed is repressed, in the territory of mental exile to which this memory is banished, it mingles with other memories, all forbidden and frightening. The same social structure which creates a fictional divide between masculine and feminine, private and public, infant and adult experience, has also made of childhood a history of betrayal, trespasses, wounds. And it has produced a social amnesia about these events. Not only sexual abuse but emotional and physical abuses of many kinds are so common in childhood in Western society that such misery is more ordinary than a happy childhood. The memories of these traumas, whether conscious or not, contribute to the desire to forget the experience of infancy altogether.

Yet the erasure is not simple. Julia Kristeva explores the unacknowledged longing for the body of the mother as a source of melancholy. A closeness that has been forsaken even in memory. Within the very knowledge of dependency lies a sweetness. Here is an unparalleled intimacy and trust, the first knowledge of love, of belonging to a larger existence, merged with otherness. And this loss is also the loss of a matrix of meaning.

What results in the breech is a kind of paralysis. The psyche is cast into an arrested state, frozen between longing and fear, unable to carry the knowledge of infancy forward into adult consciousness. So that the state of being which is the birthright of the infant and has its own profundity, never ages, never matures, is never allowed to shape and illuminate an adult knowledge of who we are and what is the nature of the universe.

The dislocation is profound. In grief for himself, feeling at the core of himself an inner anomie, Western *man* has projected his inner state of mind onto the world. Because the world has no meaning for him he says it has no meaning at all. He invents a philosophy of nihilism. And in an atmosphere of denial and false sentiments, this philosophy has a ring of truth. Bearing the shock of honesty, cynicism at least approaches the emptiness that lies in the wake of the universe that has been abandoned.

By this chain of reactions, the fear of dependency creates an even deeper dependency. Were it allowed to become, to develop, the state of mind that the infant experiences with the mother would become part of an adult self. But the cost of adulthood in Western society, especially for men, is to lose the knowledge of infancy. Instead of developing this knowledge, the Western psyche replaces it with another kind of knowledge, not knowledge as intimacy but knowledge as power. And even here a disappointed, abandoned infant is concealed, one who in an adult body has become "infantile," and through power tries to extract limitless demands from others, society, the earth.

Paradoxically and yet predictably, primary among these demands is the wish for an earlier sense of knowledge, intimate, embedded, connected. By the same stroke with which it was severed from the self, this knowledge has been projected onto a woman's body. She possesses what he no longer has. And so once again he finds himself dependent on her for what he needs. But this time the need is exaggerated, even unmanageable, for what he imagines he desires really belongs to him, *is* him. He is not himself without it.

To regain a sense of himself, he may attempt to take possession of a woman's body, but erotic feeling can only intensify his sense of loss. Every effort only makes him feel more fragmented and without substance. If through the illusion of transcendence he achieves a certain sense of safety, this is only palliative. He may fantasize, along with Descartes, that his cognitive skills preceded not only his own infancy but birth itself, *Cogito ergo sum,* but his body knows that his thought followed. The existence of his own body. The existence of his mother. The existence of the earth. Unaware, his mind longs for its own lineage, wanders like an orphan seeking a substantial home.

In other, older cultures, perhaps at one time in the earlier history of most European and Mediterranean cultures, and even in the minds of the very young who are born into modern societies that have lost the sense of participation in a larger natural world, identity has been less an assertion of independence than an experience of interdependence. One is dependent for coming into existence not only on a mother and father but on an intricate web of life: one is born from the ground, the tree, the bird in the tree, the body of water feeding the roots, hence the rain, and the sun, and the air of course, the coolness of the mountain, indeed on all that one sees. Others in the family, each of whom contributes daily to make one's life what it is, neighbors, villagers, the farmers, the baker, the potters (for each thing used is made by someone one knows), are part of one's existence. In this matrix one defines oneself finally not by opposition to dependency but by a layered complexity that includes the process of exchange, of giving and getting, by which one's life comes into being and continues.

This is a rich identity. One that is not lonely, for it includes the great worlds to which we are all heir by birth, not as masters, but as participants, as members. And if perhaps we are small under the swirling clouds of the cosmos, as we cast our eyes over the night sky, or across the horizon when we awaken, knowing we are part of this vast, astonishing pattern, we are also large, as large at least as our own awe at what surrounds us and is at the same time who we are.

But along with the mourning one feels over a lost sense of connectedness, of immersion and placement, when this connection to the larger matrix of existence is sacrificed for the illusion of independence, one must also feel confusion. Who am I when I am separated from the ground of my being? It is here, at this psychological moment, that one can witness the birth of fierce nationalisms and fundamentalisms of all kinds.

In place of a widening circle, through which the self is both defined and extended, beginning with one's own body, the body of one's mother, father, family, community, tribe or village, the land on which one walks, where one's food is grown, where water can be found, where hills or mountains, a stream, an ocean, a forest nearby, provide markers, orientation, something else is substituted. A nation. A religion. A set of ideas which one comes to believe and to which one must *belong*. So a man calls himself American, or German, or Serbian, or French. And in time to be devoutly patriotic or religious is to embrace violence.

No one in modern society can be entirely immune to the anguish that must lie mute behind this state of mind. Severed from a world of meaning, one hangs on as if for dear life to an ideology. Belief is no longer an experience but a frail hope. One that must be fed continually by large and small evidence. And as this promise of fulfillment suffers the inevitable diminishment of groundless expectations, enlarging the boundaries of its purview would seem to be imperative. Only such aggressive growth makes the whole system seem alive. The doubt that must live daily underneath fanaticism can be projected on whoever resists conversion. Now there is a clear enemy to battle, to vanquish, to convince if even by force.

· · ·

But knowledge by itself can be a form of force. The experience is as close to rape as one can imagine: the psyche penetrated by ideas, a way of thinking, a way of perceiving that is not one's own. If women are in many ways socialized into submissiveness from the earliest age by rape and the threat of rape, whole peoples can be trained to intellectual passivity through invasive systems of knowledge. In the twentieth century particularly one has witnessed and is still witnessing many kinds of mental tyranny. I am thinking here not only of fundamentalist campaigns against homosexuality, or the fascist and anti-Semitic propaganda of the Third Reich, but of a modern culture that seems to spin itself out of almost nothing, extending into nameless space by wires and waves, producing dazzling images, and a resemblance to truth that is as monolithic as it is, by virtue of the very power of the medium, intoxicating.

That in the Western habit of mind knowledge is conceived as above life has led to a habit of dissociation which is also a dislocation. Wisdom has been separated from any particular place. In the modern sensibility knowledge is being severed from any earthly context as never before. Earlier in the century, Walter Benjamin had this to say about the mechanical reproduction of art: "Even the most perfect reproduction of a work of art is lacking in one element: its presence in time and space, its unique existence at the place where it happens to be." As he writes of patina, and more invisible marks, of a "sphere of authenticity" outside the capability of technical reproduction, he laments what he calls the liquidation of traditions which occurs as a result of the loss of context.

Within a wide range of cultural traditions—painting in Siena in the fifteenth century, the ninth-century bronze sculptures of the Yoruba on the Ivory Coast, the basket weaving of Pomo Indian women of California, Catalan music of western France and eastern Spain—one finds a wedding of place and art. That valleys of Tuscany appear as background in a portrait, or that Pomo baskets are woven from a grass that grows only in one area, is part of a process of rendering through which a mirror of a whole world, a specific moment in time and space is created. By these mirrors a story is told through which one can behold the coherence of self, society, and nature.

The contrast between these traditions and the new cyberspace is often difficult to discern. I am happy to walk across my room and slide a compact disc into a machine that will at one instant play back the reproduced sounds of a Beethoven quartet and at the next reproduce a choir of Buddhist monks singing traditional chants. My life is made richer; yet the relative lack in my own life of such a tradition is obscured by this seeming abundance. I do not know what it would be to be a Buddhist in a small village in which these chants have echoed for hundreds of years.

And what is also lost when knowledge is removed from place is a basic form of democracy. One which in the past has in many ways been able to elude tyrannous governments. This is the democracy of knowledge. A king or a dictator or the lord of the manor may pronounce that it will rain on Friday. But when I walk out of my house I can see for myself that it is not raining. Human knowledge and wisdom, the capacities to see, estimate, judge, make choices, decisions, have evolved over time together with all life in context, in particular places. Taken in this way, the capacity to know diminishes with distance.

But in the West the power to pronounce the truth grows with distance. As institutions of all kinds are increasingly centralized, authority is almost always elsewhere. And by this removal not only are citizens stripped of the most basic right, the right to perceive —but because those authorities who claim the exclusive right to determine truth are acting at a distance, they have become capable of the most monumental foolishness. Everyone can cite examples. American generals after World War II giving up a huge stretch of Eastern Europe to the Soviet Union because they were unfamiliar with the region. Soviet planners shipping tons of Georgian pine across thousands of miles and then shipping it back again for building projects in Georgia.

Once when I was teaching drama to a group of students whose families lived largely on small means and in run-down urban housing projects, I encountered a sociological "study" ordered by some funding agency. The study argued that this particular neighborhood of children had every middle-class advantage. One of the questions that the sample of children who were interviewed were asked was how many hours they spent a week mowing the grass in front of their homes. In this neighborhood I knew of only one plot of grass, and that was in the small city park where I taught. But the children had answered the question, imagining perhaps that they would like to mow a lawn sometime, or that they were supposed to have mowed lawns to pass the test, or just to jive the interviewer. That so many children had mowed lawns for several hours a week was cited in the study as proof of the neighborhood's middle-class status.

Increasingly, whether one is trained as a business executive, a teacher, an accountant, a doctor, or a lawyer, social power is derived from various kinds of such dissociated knowledge. One becomes dependent on this knowledge to survive, to rise in society, to earn enough money to feed oneself and one's children. Survival has been recast as primarily a social drama in which any collaboration with nature becomes nearly irrelevant. In this phantasmagoric atmosphere, to save the environment, the earth, and the complex processes by which we survive on earth is considered a luxury. For the knowledge of place that is being all but erased in the new technological consciousness is also a knowledge of the necessities and limitations of natural existence.

And yet even more is lost. The paradox is sad. The myth that ideas are independent from material existence promises to yield a ken of meaning beyond the petty and mundane considerations of daily life. Yet it is the habit of separating thought from place and the considerations of natural existence that makes daily life petty and mundane. And it is finally only within scarcity, in the smallest limitation, or through the most painful necessity of nature, that one begins to glimpse what lies beyond, a larger coherence to which we all belong. Dying or birthing, awareness opens and the heart is pierced with an unreasoned love that is also knowledge. The rounds of birth and death from which life emanates, the rising and setting of the sun, the course of seasons, every need of the body, all partake of the infinity of natural cycles and so can enlarge consciousness to infinite domains. They are there. Immense landscapes of the mind, just past that familiar pretense of power which is also a veil of ignorance.

5

Beyond

Every part of the earth is sacred to my people. Every shining pine needle, every sandy shore, every mist in the dark woods, every clearing and humming insect is holy in the memory and experience of my people.

—Duwamish chief

All that I could think of was to burn their houses and the towers in which they kept their idols.

—Hernán Cortés,
Third Letter to the Emperor

The New World. This is where I live, heir to a history I did not witness, though it has shaped my days. The events began as dreams. Sailing over the edge of the globe, the desire was for a faster way to the East, and hence to exotic treasures that trade might turn to wealth and power. Of course it was not a route to India or China the sailors discovered. Word spread quickly. New maps were etched, carried over water, unrolled before kings and queens who, in turn, drew their own designs on this expanded vision of the world.

What did they want? Land and the fruit of the land, gold, perhaps a fountain of youth, and something more. How would you name it, stature, glory? That move toward grandeur that often characterizes an inner sense of frailty. This was the end of the fifteenth century, the Renaissance. A time of dazzling achievement; the gates of knowledge had opened. But this was also a time of uncertainty and fear. The world, no longer accountable by the old explanations, loomed large and menacing. If the Christian God, though remote in the dimensions of His power, had provided, by His blessings and His rage, a feeling of intimacy with the very *raison d'être* of existence, now this feeling was fading.

One impulse was toward purity. Infidels, heretics, witches burned at the stake. Jews and Muslims were forced across borders. Yet the ultimate motion, like a pendulum, swings back and forth; the arc of expulsion must be answered by the push of expansion. The unintended effect of purity is loss. Diversity and variation make up the very texture of reality. Without them existence and certainly belief begin to seem lifeless. Somewhere in the shared mind of this frantic effort the thought must have persisted that the treasures to be found by each wave of explorers would not only line worldly vaults but fill the voids of spiritual regency as well.

The voyagers, however, do not go in search of meaning. At times naturalists are on board, making precisely beautiful drawings of the life forms they encounter. But otherwise, the captains, conquistadors, and knights, friars and priests go not to learn but to encompass and instruct. The feeling after all must have been heady. Like astronauts taking their first steps on the moon, the explorers are aware they are making history. So much so that it affects their dress, their composure, even the literary style through which they report their findings. So in his third letter to Charles V, the emperor of Spain, Hernán Cortés writes that ". . . we were fighting to preserve and spread the true faith, and bring to Your Majesty's service all those lands and provinces which had rebelled against him. . . ."

•   •   •

The word *rebellion* may sound odd here. The Spanish were invaders. In their efforts to conquer Mexico they had enlisted the aid of rebellious members of the Aztec Empire and neighboring people oppressed by and hostile to the Empire. And the soldiers of the Aztec Empire were not *rebelling,* but merely defending their own territory. Yet there is a consistent logic, no matter how perverse, to this vocabulary. It is the same logic that allows Cortés and his party to reassure those Aztecs whom they encounter that they wish them no "harm. . . ." This is less deceit than a fantastic conceit, the notion that the Spanish are superior to those strangers they encounter. Whatever they do to those who live in this New World the Spanish imagine as betterment.

Again and again as part of the same habitual greeting, the conquistadors tell representatives of the Aztec peoples that they will "come to know the knowledge of the true faith" and that they must acknowledge "our lords as the greatest princes of the world." But, of course, knowledge is also a form of power. At other times, according to the captain's letters, the Spanish pledge that the Indians will soon serve as vassals of the Spanish emperor.

Cortés's letters show no inner doubt, though he must have been dazzled by Tenochtitlán. Conquistadors compared this city to Venice or the enchanted cities of myths. Meeting Montezuma, who came to the edge of the great capital to greet him, the captain was given a necklace of shells festooned with shrimps fashioned from refined gold "almost a span in length." The refined craft of the jewelry, the precious metal itself, the architecture, the large and orderly markets, all these impressed him. He even remarked on the luxurious hospitality he was given. Taken into the city, he and his party were ushered into a "very large and beautiful house," in the palace of Axayacatl.

But he lost no time in this comfort. Almost immediately his soldiers placed Montezuma and his lords under guard. Soon after, the Spanish asked to attend the ritual dances for the feast of Huitzilopochtli. The most eminent of the Aztec nobility would be there, and there these nobles together with Montezuma and all the

Aztec leaders would perish at the hands of Spanish soldiers. Six years later, as part of his efforts to conquer the Aztec people and force them to Christianity, Cortés was to burn the palace which housed him and destroy the great city of Tenochtitlán.

"Our Lord was leading us to victory against our enemies . . ." Cortés writes in his third letter to the emperor. The Spanish conquerors enclosed their conquest and everything that was to follow in God's will. It was by such reasoning that Aztec people were bonded into slavery, that they were branded with hot irons, worked to exhaustion, that their lands were stolen, their goods plundered, their culture and their religion systematically destroyed by the Spaniards.

This was also the guiding logic of a chain of explorers and conquerors: Francisco Pizarro, Pedro Alvarado, Cabeza de Vaca, Francisco Vásquez de Coronado, Don Juan de Oñate, De Soto, as well as countless friars from the Franciscan order, and thousands of nameless young and single men, soldiers, or soldiers of fortune, seeking adventure, glory, wealth, who waged war on the peoples who lived throughout the Americas, in Peru, New Mexico, Florida, California, Oaxaca in an attempt to wrest control of their land and convert them to Christianity.

Nor was the approach Spain's alone. The argument of superiority accompanied sieges and massacres everywhere in this new place. The English, the French, the Italians, the Germans, the Dutch, even the Belgians made their own voyages, waged their own campaigns, enveloped their own lands. And it did not stop with the era of the great explorers. The conquests continued for over four centuries. Captain Cook, who landed on the shores of Hawaii near the end of the eighteenth century, declared that he had *discovered* the islands. And all through the nineteenth century the nations of Europe and the United States expanded themselves into other lands, claiming, if not discovery, possession of parts of America, Africa, Asia, Southeast Asia, all of India. Every effort had the same theme: those whose lands were taken were being *improved*.

• • •

I am so familiar with this history that only after a long passage of time spent thinking about these events have I begun to wonder at them. In encounter after encounter, civilizations, long separated by time and space, and entirely unknown to each other, meet. In a sense every meeting holds within it the possibility of astonishment. The difference one finds is also the means by which new worlds open. As strange and startling ideas about existence are revealed, beneath a familiar self another one appears and meaning reconfigures. The experience is often as frightening as it is wonderful. But what uncharted regions of the mind, what revolutionary possibilities, what chasms opened here! And how quickly *this* vast territory was closed. Though here and there, as a few explorers and colonists were intrigued, impressed, taught, moved, transformed by the unfamiliar cultures they had found, what predominated among these visitors was the drive to remake what was newly discovered after an image of Europe.

The closure of mind was in truth so quick, so final, so aggressive, imagining it now, I cannot help but think that the European psyche was in some way afraid of what it saw. Just five decades after Columbus landed, and less than twenty years after Cortés subjected the Aztec Empire to Spanish rule, Copernicus would publish *De revolutionibus orbium coelestium,* in which he showed that the sun and not the earth was the center of the universe. But the discovery of the Americas had already shaken the security of the sinecure by which the European mind had supposed itself the center of the universe.

Other manners of perception and ways of life had existed within or been known to exist outside Europe for centuries. But these differences had long been circumscribed by myth and ideology. Over time, the force of these differences could be gradually absorbed or explained away by layers of imagery and depiction, assertions of superiority woven into daily life. But the collective weight of variance which came all at once with the discovery of the Americas would have thrown the whole scheme off balance.

There were, of course, other reasons. That the fear of losing a familiar orientation to existence would have been so strong does not belie the potency of greed in the psychology of these ventures. Fear and greed belong together. In Western culture it is common for the psyche to answer disorientation and the terror of falling into meaninglessness with the accumulation of wealth and power. I know the impulse in myself. Yet the gain is only temporary. What the soul seeks cannot be met this way. The acquisition must always increase. And the life bent to this purpose becomes increasingly meaningless.

In sixteenth-century Spain a debate was formulated about the people newly encountered in the Americas. Were they human? The focus of the discussion was ethical. If these strangers were human, could they be baptized? And if they became Christian, was it right to make them into slaves? Yet just under the surface one can detect another direction of inquiry. What is it to be human? Here is the chasm which must have opened at the feet of Columbus, Raleigh, Cortés as they stepped on new land. At each meeting a self carefully constructed from centuries of culture seems to vanish. Stripped of crown, church, and all its social scaffolding, the self makes a terrifying descent. What lies below is the stuff of nightmares. Mortality, the great power of nature in and outside of the body, all that was obscured by European culture becomes once more visible, if only instantaneously, brought to consciousness by this meeting with a new continent.

It is strangely predictable then that the effort should be to force Indian cultures to mirror Europe. Though in so many ways, the meeting must already be like looking into a mirror. Yet one that reflects more than the beholder is willing to see. One wonders, for instance, how Cortés can fail to note certain similarities between Aztec culture and his own. He does liken the Aztec capital to Seville as well as Venice, finds the earthenware as fine as any in Spain, observes an order of governance not unlike that in Genoa or Pisa, but there are other similarities that escape him completely. Writing obediently and with a reverent tone to the emperor of Spain, he refers to Montezuma as a tyrant. And the Spanish Inquisition had been torturing and putting its victims to death in the name of Christianity for forty years when Cortés wrote to his emperor of the "very horrible and abominable custom" in Mexico of slaughtering boys and girls, men and women captured in ritual battle to the Aztec gods. Was the likeness too clear? Unfiltered by belief, the ghastliness would have been evident. But the Spanish did not recognize the contours of their own empire here. Rather the self-reflection possible in this moment was parried with more violence. In the siege of Tenochtitlán alone 240,000 were to perish.

One can see why this sanguine logic might require the thought that the massacred were not entirely human. Though the process of conversion was supposed to make the Indians more so, the prevailing mind held them to be lesser souls, even when made Christian. To rescue or to conquer; only in the most superficial reckoning of the colonizer's mind do these goals conflict.

Europe's true ambivalence takes place on another plane. An unfulfilled promise lies in the direction of discovery, not the hope of finding what is new, but the desire to reclaim what is old. It is a promise which is also a threat. I am thinking of a desire buried beneath layers of prohibition and silence. The unexamined wish etched between the lines of European arguments that the peoples newly encountered are less than human, more like children, uncivilized. A desire, perhaps, to regain a half-remembered state of mind, a past existence not so separated from earth.

Over time, for better or worse, throughout Europe the assumption grows that the original inhabitants of America are in a state of nature, unaffected and also undeveloped by culture. Even those who admire Indian cultures fail to recognize these as cultures or call them so. The erasure is often incomprehensible, as when, before the Protestant missionary Jean de Lery begins to describe what he has witnessed of the spiritual practices of the

Tupi of Brazil, he writes that they live "without any religion at all" or, he equivocates, ". . . almost none."

I am familiar with such eclipses of perception. They are almost always accompanied by exaggerated fantasies. Fantasy and perception mingle in most meetings. Perception lies at the core of intimacy. Seeing, touching, entering the body of the beloved, one is educated to another way of feeling, sensing, perceiving. Yet, fantasy has played a crucial role in the erotic literature of the West. Seeing the beloved, the imagination is opened, as sleeping images are awakened, experienced, explored.

But there is another kind of fantasy through which a meeting can be experienced, one that arises independently, apart from perception or even in opposition to it. Encountering a woman, a man refuses to acknowledge who she is. In place of her presence he substitutes an idea of who she is. The idea is usually the repetition of a convention, whether archetype or stereotype. She is, for example, a virgin or a whore. That he does not see his lover is clear. But what is less obvious is the degree to which his image of himself is also occluded. The ideas of both the virgin and the whore belong to him, represent states of feeling in his own psyche, symbols of a conflict that, unexamined, remain unchanged, tormenting him within.

But the state of nature in which the European describes the Indian to be depends as much on the Western idea that nature exists apart from spirit as it does on the desire to regain a nature that has been lost. And this tinges the wish with terror. The nature that has been sacrificed is depicted as dangerous, tempting the soul to satanic regions or to unreason, madness. Over time, aspects of the self that have been relinquished become monstrous in the imagination. These are what the Buddhists call hungry ghosts. Certainly they must accompany any psyche shaped around power and denial.

• • •

From my own childhood I can remember two recurrent images of what was described as a more primitive life. One was of groups of dancers, feathered, skirted in grass, or in bright colors, sometimes breasts revealed, moving in synchronized rhythm to drums, chanting words and phrases that were never translated but remained instead on the borders of consciousness as somehow menacing, a speech that gathered like a thunderstorm, and without cause or warning might break apart the fabric of a reasonable life.

The other image showed an alarmed white man, decked in khaki clothes, the regalia of an explorer, submerged shoulder deep in an iron pot set to boil over an open fire. His image was inevitably joined by figures of natives eagerly waiting to consume him. The implication was that the natives were hungry. That cannibalism was a religious ritual, not practiced to abate starvation, was hardly understood by Western culture.

The thought of eating human flesh, even under the most severe conditions, is abhorrent in the West. As I child I spent my summers at a Girl Scout camp in the Sierra Mountains near Donner Pass. The story of what transpired there at the turn of the century was an early part of my mythic world. Pioneers stranded in an early and terrible blizzard survived because they ate the members of their party who had already succumbed to cold and hunger and had died. Those who spoke of this lowered their voices to a hush, as a debate unraveled in the mind. Was this worse than death?

Even the hearing of such a tale causes the Western soul to shudder. Writing of the passage home from Brazil, Jean de Lery describes a harrowing experience of hunger which drove the European voyagers to glance "at each other sideways, harboring evil thoughts regarding that barbarous act." Depicting the state of mind arising from this hunger, he writes that when "the bodies are weakened, and nature is failing, the senses are alienated and the wits dispersed;" and all this, he says, "makes one ferocious, and engenders a wrath that can truly be called a kind of madness."

Here is the image of cannibalism which the West projects on

strangers. Though De Lery speaks of his nature failing, the common explanation for this moment is that it is a reversion to a state of nature. That is how the Donner party was configured in the popular imagination of my childhood. And certainly the horror of such a deprivation is a fate that can befall any group. Yet if one rewinds the narrative to begin at an earlier point, at the inception of the exploration and conquest of America, or the movement of pioneers west, the genesis of this "state of nature" seems not to be so much a reversion as development, an expansion of what is called civilization, driven to desperate circumstances by the cycles of an inexhaustible hunger for power.

Later in his life and back in France, De Lery will witness the St. Bartholomew's Day Massacre, part of the religious wars of the late sixteenth century. He will see Frenchmen roasting and eating the hearts of other Frenchmen. This sight will lead him to contemplate more richly the similarities as well as the differences between his own culture and the foreign one he visited. But his meditations will not significantly alter the West's idea of its own absolute and moral superiority. Nor will it stop the Western mind from projecting an unclaimed image of a wild voraciousness on what it calls primitive peoples.

Aiming to swallow the continents of America, Asia, and Africa, Europe set upon *civilizing* these places. Notwithstanding the argument that the American peoples had no civilizations, everywhere different religions, philosophies, cosmologies, ways of life were encountered, prodigious efforts were made to obliterate them. One might ask why such a massive campaign was conducted to destroy cultures that were, according to Western logic, not supposed to exist at all. But to the tyrannous habit of mind, which is also the same habit of mind which opposes itself to nature, whatever contradicts belief is experienced as assault rather than correction.

The process was harsh. In what was to become the state of New Mexico, the family structures of Acoma pueblo Indians were deliberately destroyed. Pueblo children were torn away from their families. Forbidden to speak their own language. Severely beaten for doing so. Admonished by their Franciscan colonizers to accept these monks as their spiritual fathers, the children were taught that the friars were in every way superior to their own mothers and fathers.

Not only were cultures which held the land they lived on as sacred damaged by so many forced exiles, and bases of livelihood and religion such as herds of buffalo holy to the Plains Indians deliberately ruined, but across the Americas religious ceremonies sacred to the Sioux, the Navajo, the Cherokee, the Iroquois were outlawed and held punishable by imprisonment. Even in 1913, Indians in North Dakota had to beg the Bureau of Indian Affairs for the right to teach their songs to their own children.

Certainly anyone who has traveled to a foreign place knows the great disorientation one feels when one cannot use one's own language. Even when one speaks the foreigner's language fluently, so much is lost. Not just the ability to express one's thoughts more subtly, but the time to dwell in them. Speech is always associated with memory. I think, for instance, of the word "street." It is a word I like. So many meanings rush to mind. The phrase "mean streets" which only an urban American can really grasp. Words in a song: "on the street where you live." The rhyme with sheet, the half rhyme with stream. From the sound of the word, the unique shape of American cities arises, the image of houses with lawns, a sense of the citizen, democratic, untitled. And hearing the word spoken, I remember a welter of addresses, all the streets, avenues, terraces, and drives where I've lived, my own child's handwriting, in pencil, on a piece of cardboard in an old red wallet I keep, 1310 Keniston Avenue, the house my parents brought me to just after I was born.

Whole worlds exist in language which are lost as language is lost. Each language is a repository of unique wisdom. Vocabulary and grammar contain and bear forth singular ways of experiencing existence. The Wintu, for instance, do not use a possessive adjective to describe their own bodies. Instead of saying, "My head aches," they say, "I headache." Nor is ownership asserted over a family member, a house, a piece of clothing. One does not say, "Her dress was red," in this language but rather, "She was dress red." By this grammar, instead of a collection of "isolable individuals" the world becomes a continuous whole. And what a revelation to read that in many Californian Indian languages verbs are elongated with suffixes which indicate the direction of the movement. In Karuk, for example, one adds a suffix such as *varak*, meaning hither from upriver, or *furuk*, meaning into an enclosed space, to a verb describing motion. By this usage the dependence of human action on a circumstance, a particular terrain, the earth, is made more evident.

The beauty of a consciousness, accruing layers like rings on a redwood tree over centuries, preserved and passed from generation to generation, woven into every daily effort, reflecting births and deaths, meals taken together, the artful labor and life breath of families, villages, tribes, nations. Was it perhaps ignorance that made European culture so destructive? But there must have been at least the shadow of a memory. When John Smith met Powhatan or John Elliot began to preach to the Massachusetts tribes, was there not the slightest trace of recognition, even if buried quickly?

Yes, the cultures Europeans encountered were strange to them, inexplicable in ways unsettling and weird. Yet here at the heart of disturbance in this meeting lay another mirror that must have reflected some inkling of grief. The memory perhaps of earlier loss of culture, an earlier forced conversion. It is there in the root of the word "weird," which can be traced to the Anglo-Saxon word "wyrd." Once, before the Roman invasion of Britain and the forced conversion of Britons to Christianity, this word referred to the "sacred and unexplained force of existence." According to this vision of life, the universe was a matrix of fibers where each being, each act, affected everything else. A vision not unlike so many of the cosmologies *discovered* in America.

The signs of dislocation are still here. Including a continuing identification of authority and prestige with distant power. By the third century, most of Europe was colonized, exploited, ruled by envoys from the Roman Empire. Even today vestiges of that earlier event are with us. The identification of authority and prestige with Roman culture. If once by the hand of the conqueror, everywhere in Europe the power to determine truth and to govern were associated with Rome, Latin the language of religion, learning, and authority, Roman the symbols of military might, governance, and prestige, the pattern continues into modernity. There is the Latin nomenclature of law, science, and medicine. Or the famous image at the very birth of the modern age, in that illustrious painting by David of Napoleon's coronation as emperor, in which Bonaparte wears Roman robes. Even today men who assist the British monarchs during the coronation ceremonies wear coats fashioned after those of the men who ruled the Roman Empire. And in the United States, *E Pluribus Unum* is the official phrase supposed to bind us together.

The association of excellence and superiority with Roman culture, and inferiority with the pre-Roman cultures of Europe, persisted in the conventional histories of Europe I learned in school. By this reckoning, Europe suffered a dark age because the classical texts from Rome and Greece had been lost in the sacking of Rome and by the burning of the library at Alexandria. As tragic as this loss was, the sense imparted by this version of history was that all human creativity, ingenuity, and wisdom was contained in these scrolls and perished with them. Thus, the story went, the monks who preserved knowledge were forced to focus endlessly on what few texts remained, copying and annotating them. They engaged in introverted scholastic debates, enshrining this activity in a language and

realm removed from ordinary life and common people, because they had lost a more enlightened approach to knowledge
when the texts of the empire that had conquered Europe perished.

According to the same history, it was also this loss that caused
what has been portrayed as the loutish and dissolute behavior of
peasants, working people and common folk, from which the
monks were said to barricade themselves in monasteries. That
monks most often came from the common people and partici-
pated in the life of the village is not part of this rendering. Nor is
there any reckoning in this version of events with what it means to
be conquered, to have authority put at a remove and into another
language, to suffer the imposition of a foreign cosmology, another
religion, another way of life at the hands of one's conquerors,
those who in the recent past have killed one's ancestors.

I am familiar with this kind of selective history. Because a brand of
alcoholism runs through the Irish side of my family, I have paid a
closer than usual attention to descriptions of this problem among
the Irish. Rarely is this behavior, and the desperation it springs
from, traced to that long history by which the Irish have been
colonized. Like accounts of alcoholism among American Indians,
the drunkenness of the Irish is both exaggerated and isolated from
an earlier history in which dignity, the means of sustenance, and a
whole culture was destroyed.

If in being Romanized Europeans did not, like many pre-Co-
lumbian Indians, lose their land, they did lose their footing. The
place where they lived lost its significance in consciousness; it was
no longer sacred, no longer the site of reference for memory and
imagination. The site of meaning had been removed to ''antiquity,'' the ancient history not of various European cultures but of
one culture alone. By this process, parchment copies of Latin and
eventually Greek words, embroidered at the borders with em-
blems of earthly fecundity, gilded images of flora and fauna, became the ground of meaning. It is no wonder, then, that scholasti-

cism was bent away from the direct observation of nature. Such an approach requires presence. Though the Dark Ages were not as dark as has been supposed, and though all the while a more vibrant religion came into being through the meeting of Catholicism with peasant traditions, yielding, among other gifts, an intense worship of the Virgin Mary, still one might trace the introverted and oddly abstract aspect of a great deal of monkish scholasticism as much if not more to an attachment to classical texts as to the loss of them. A greater loss, the ground of meaning, had been traded for these texts.

From this perspective, I detect a breath of grief in the most quixotic, inexplicable acts of a later time. Those ill-fated attempts to recover holy lands. Waged as if the survival of the spirit depended on this recovery. If these efforts failed—neither the Holy Land nor the experience of land as holy had been regained—it would perhaps remain for a New World to promise that recovery, a century later.

The New World I was born to did dream of itself as released from a prison of European tyranny and intolerance. Yet if in America the thirteen colonies gained independence from Britain, this was not to be an independence from European culture. Despite a pride in America as a place that gave refuge to immigrants, the dominant American ideal remained European. Even in the middle years of the twentieth century, in the time when I grew up, the study of American culture, American art, literature, and ideas, was a new and radical departure from the old canon. Looking to the beginnings of literature, the first stories and first voices, one turned in the direction of Beowulf and Homer. And the idea of what *was* American culture was oddly constrained and monolithic. Ancient stories and poems, weavings, paintings, pottery by American Indians, African poetry, storytelling and imagery brought to America by slaves, Yiddish culture that gradually became part of American culture, the great and varied Asian influence that so affected California, and had influenced Thoreau and Emerson in their ideas of transcendentalism, and Hispanic cultures so vividly present in the Western states were not included in the American self-image.

At the same time everything British had a gloss of superiority. England was the lodestar in a sea of history by which one oriented oneself. Though we disapproved of kings and queens, the royal couple continued to hold an almost mystical attraction for us. Among the treasures my mother saved from her childhood was a small round dish, suitable for candy, that had emblazoned on it an image of King George VI and Queen Elizabeth. A wreath of laurel leaves surrounds them, and above is written the word "Coronation," accompanied by the date made significant by this event: May 12, 1937.

One might say this reverence was in part due to my particular family history. Yet the truth was far more complex. Though I always thought of myself as somehow from an English background, over time a more complicated picture became evident, including ancestors who were French, German, and probably Jewish (though the family denied the latter), and others not from England but from the British Isles, Wales, Scotland, and Ireland.

My father was born in Canada and my mother in California. But as I was growing up, neither of those histories seemed much to belong to me. In the place where I lived, at the outer rim of the westward expansion of European culture, we seemed to rest lightly on the ground, as if in some spiritual sense we still existed elsewhere. Nearly all of the buildings were new, built in cheap imitation of modern architecture; they seemed to hover over the ground rather than rest there. Housing developments proliferated. Landmarks were rare. In this atmosphere I longed for age with nearly the same passion as a sailor longs for land.

Beset by our small miseries, on many occasions when my father, my sister, and I were reunited after the family divorce, we would set out in his car looking for monuments to visit. Among our favorite destinations was the mission at San Juan Capistrano. In some way we never articulated to ourselves, we were in search of a sense of history we could see and touch. Those stucco walls were made so much farther back in time than the new buildings, new sidewalks, new grass where recently we had lived together. We would go to the mission when the swallows returned, as they did every year to nest in eaves and porticoes. I remember one year the three of us stood as swallows flew in and out while the setting sun illuminated patches of sky and turned the Spanish buildings pink. This is one of the first moments I recall when all my own worries dissolved in a larger landscape of time.

I had no knowledge yet of all the suffering that had transpired there. Indian children taken from their families here too, forced to use English, forbidden to speak their own languages, forced away from their own religion. When Fray Geronimo Boscana, who spent much of his life at this mission, wrote an account of the Juaneño religion, he described this faith as "horrible" and "ridic-ulous," and declared that the "Indians of California may be com-pared to a species of monkey."

The period sings with sad ironies. The beauty of the missions, the terror of what transpired there in the name of St. Francis of Assisi and the God he worshiped. No doubt these friars were well acquainted with St. Francis's vow of poverty and had, in joining such an order, made this vow themselves. In the gospel according to Matthew, Christ asked his followers to "be not solicitous of what you eat or what you shall wear." He suggested that God would provide. Did the friars believe this was the reason the God of Christianity made the Indians? To serve the friars? Here these men and women were enslaved, beaten, and worked to death by the monks.

Though I knew little about the atrocities committed, what transpired was not entirely unfelt. If in some way Los Angeles seemed as yet unsettled, and if the culture of my childhood felt shallow, even vacant in some way I could not explain, certainly the loss of this history helped to keep us on the surface of our-selves.

I had recovered some knowledge of our family's place in this

chronology. At the age of six, after my parents' divorce, my
mother's parents, with whom I was to live for several years, took
me on a journey across the country to the farmland where they
were born. As most people did in those days, we traveled by
automobile and hence I saw things. The red formations and desert
rocks of Arizona, the high crags and forests of the Rockies, the
green pasturelands of Kentucky. Despite all the wonders, there
were long stretches of repetitive highways, and I was frequently
bored. We would stop at intervals, for lunch, or orange juice, or a
milk shake, at gas stations, adorned, I remember now, not with
crosses or plaster saints, but with cigar store Indians, or small
black grooms proffering the reins of invisible horses, icons of an
older order that had paved the way for the modern age.

The farmland we visited was in southern Illinois and I loved it.
Milk warm from a cow, a white and black spotted pony I was
allowed to ride bareback, wheat taller than I was, berry bushes by
the stream. Knowing this was where they were born gave me an
understanding of my grandparents I could have had in no other
way. Years later, another part of the picture came to me when I
went to lecture at a university just a hundred miles south, near the
Mississippi. A graduate student took me out for the day. She
showed me a series of mounds made by Indians. The risings
reminded me of similar mounds I had seen in England, at Glaston-
bury, supposed to have been made by Britons before the Roman
invasion. The particular civilization that had existed here was very
old and had disappeared by the time European settlers came. The
mounds probably held the bones of ancestors and were sacred
places. She showed me the river and told me that all this area had
once been marshland, crisscrossed by waterways the Indians had
traveled by canoe. No more. Now much of the marshland has
been filled. And at the banks of the river more than one factory
spews out smoke, silently emptying chemicals into the water. Her
mother was Indian and her father German. As she helped me
imagine what it might have been like, centuries ago, Indian villages and settlements living in a close way with the river all

around, I could feel veins of water lace a delicate design through the body of the land. For some reason now, as I write this, my eyes still fill with tears.

There is a loss here too I have strained against all my life. My family history, a history of farmers from the East, or from Ireland, France, Germany, pushing west, settling on land that had a history which was all but erased. The region had been famous for the beautiful paintings of the piasa bird. But they were destroyed by mining operations in 1847. The land my great-grandparents farmed was once the homeland of Algonquin tribes, perhaps Tamaroa or Cahokia, or Kaskakia people. Unwilling exiles had transpired here, people forced from their land, and there were murders, untimely deaths. I imagine that the land held this suffering, mingling with the crops, the daily life. Even as the heat of the day migrated into a night filled with fireflies, dreams of these forgotten ancestors must have arisen along with the grief of those so displaced.

And something else was here too. Another chapter. My great-grandmother's side of the family, the Branches, related to my great-great-uncle, the writer James Branch Cabell, who had come to Illinois by way of Virginia. This part of the family had been in the United States since before the Revolutionary War, and could be traced back to a General Green. But this illustrious history probably had another side. There must have been slaveowners among us.

In an inarticulate way this history came to touch me after all, bringing me along with so many of my generation into movements for social change. Struggling to be free of the sad and constraining fate of my family, the ideas of freedom and democracy appealed to me even as a young child, learning American history. But the best education I had in democracy, one that raised the deepest questions regarding power and process, came to me from the civil rights movement. What it meant to be disenfranchised, the multitude of subtle and insidious forms disenfranchisement can take, the social and political effects of stereotypes, and the terrible psychological toll such ideas take when they are internalized, the cumulative economic loss which occurs as the result of years of prejudice, a poverty that engenders despair, and depression in every sense, eroding the soul in its own way, the manners by which those in power hide the fact of their power, even while wielding it to ensure they lose none of it, the theft of history, dignity, unacknowledged cultural debts and influences, language undermined and undermining.

Though those of us who were part of the civil rights movement did not achieve equality, even in our own small societies, we had begun to redress something in ourselves. An ignorance. Those who were white had much to gain too. Probing the meanings of the civil rights movement, the historian Vincent Harding writes of white Americans who lived "daily lives in absolute denial of their prayers, speaking with forked tongues to their children." We were learnng to speak more honestly and see more deeply.

A few years later, educated by the civil rights movement, I would begin to articulate feelings I had had since childhood, first as a girl, then as a young woman, about the pattern of discrimination that had shaped my life according to gender. This influence echoed an earlier history. The nineteenth-century struggle for women's rights and then suffrage had commenced as part of the movement for the abolition of slavery. I began to understand that racism and sexism were intimately connected. I could see that the racist idea of the other and the misogynist idea of a woman echo one another. And over time I could also see that both prejudices mirror a conflict in a mind alienated from nature.

It would take me longer to see that the origins of these patterns of mind shared a common history. A history whose outlines are obscured by the very habit of mind it created and which created history in turn. Only in writing a very particular history, the history of war and the development of nuclear weapons, could I delineate the threads, the degradation of nature, the development of masculinity, traditional ideas of gender that could not be understood apart from a history of European empires and their armies, the same empires that led to colonization, slavery, and what today we know as racism.

Socratic dialogue. The eloquence of Pericles. The towering tragedies of Sophocles. The epic battle of Troy. The figure of a Greek warrior, exquisitely turned, his thin, muscular legs rust red against the graceful curve of an ancient vase. Western ideas of masculinity claim a lineage going back to antiquity, and the length of this lineage is used to justify patterns of violence and domination. In the West manliness is gilded with these glories. Yet by another light, what one considers manhood is not ageless, but an aspect and a consequence of a particular history of slavery and empires.

Wherever empires require large standing armies, not only to establish colonies but afterward to maintain them, military training and service become the defining marks of masculinity. In the Greek empire of Alexander the Great a boy was culturally indistinguishable from a girl until he began his military training. In his youngest years he was raised in his mother's quarters, along with his sisters, according to the ways of women. During this period of his life his dress was the same as a girl's dress, his behavior tender and sensual as that of a woman. Then at the age of eight or nine he would be taken suddenly and roughly into the men's quarters, where he would not be allowed to grieve for his mother or his old way of life, but instead was introduced to sensual deprivation, habituated to hardness, and prepared by competition and physical prowess for the life of a soldier.

The change was not all loss. In place of his earlier pleasures the young soldier received something else. If masculinization dissociated a young man from an emotional and sensual life, creating in the breach a strange feeling of dismemberment and undoubtedly also boredom, war offered him a way to regain the vividness of life. The intensity of battle, the mud and blood of combat, a heightened sense of danger, the intimacy men feel with one another when threatened by death, even the selflessness and sense of belonging to a larger world, to a country beyond the self, came to replace that immersion in sensate life which is a birthright.

And in the realm of an exclusively symbolic life which, more and more over centuries, has become a refuge for a masculinity forged out of the fear of death and the daily friction of smaller brutalities, the battlefield yields the promise of a paradise returned. The land itself, that territory won by combat, becomes a kind of Eden in the warrior's mind, a symbol for a lost empire of experience, possession of this ultimate prize configured as honeyed balm, the wellspring of life, exotic and golden. The passion is barely concealed in these famous lines by Kipling:

> Lived a woman wonderful
> (May the Lord amend her!)
> Neither simple, kind nor true,
> But her pagan beauty drew
> Christian gentlemen a few
> Hotly to attend her.

> Christian gentlemen a few
> From Berwick unto Dover
> For she was South Africa
> And she was South Africa
> She was Our South Africa
> Africa all over!

So a metaphor of pleasure and excitement is created from cycles of privation, death, and warfare. To a masculinity created out of the necessities of empire, the colonized nation becomes an illicit lover in whom the excised life of body, heart, and mind can be, if not retrieved, captured.

The metaphor was made flesh. The Greek and Roman empires regarded the bodies of women as part of the spoils of war. Girls and women of vanquished nations were regularly taken into sexual slavery. Homer's long account of the Trojan War begins with a fight between Achilles and Agamemnon over possession of a girl stolen from her father for the sexual pleasure of Greek heroes. And rape and prostitution are so much a part of modern warfare that, earlier in the century, the soldier going off to combat would be initiated twice into manhood, once in bed and once on the battlefield.

But the ultimate symbolic goal for the martial life is glory. This is what the young man is promised in exchange for risking his life. Just as Plato proclaims earthly life to be only a faint shadow of a more ideal existence, according to the symbolism of warfare, victory or death on the battlefield earns the soldier an airy immortality, an infinite residence in an afterlife which is imagined as loftier and more preferable than any life on earth. To die fighting is the apotheosis of the masculine ideal. The entire Greek ethos turned on this premise.

Which came first, one wonders, the battlefields of empire or the ideas of gender that circumscribe existence by severing dualities? The question cannot be answered. The movements of history are not linear. Cause is folded into consequence the moment it occurs. Between a body of ideas and social life a continual resonance transpires, one echoing, enclosing, determining, shaping and shaped by the other, not only in rapid sequence but also simultaneously. That a division between mortal life and eternity seems somehow believable must be in no small part because such a dividedness mirrors a psyche taught by the necessities of war to dissociate from earthly experience. And yet such a lesson is possible only within a view of the cosmos that elevates spirit above the matrix of earthly life. An intricate dance of causation and effect, idea and practice accompanies the movements of empires expanding their boundaries, until eventually expansion becomes a way of life, affecting every social form, providing its own *raison d'être*.

The reasoning born of empires continues to press into our lives, shaping us along the lines of an old story. A continuous line can be read through time which connects Alexander the Great and Caesar with the crusades of Frederick II, emperor of the Holy Roman Empire (styling himself as "ever Caesar Augustus of the Romans Fortunate, Victor and Conqueror of Italy, Sicily, Jerusalem and Arles"), to Frederick the Great of Prussia, who proved his manhood and his worthiness as a leader by expanding the borders of his kingdom into Silesia and then Poland. By the end of the nineteenth century European nations had established empires throughout the world.

Even today, in democratic countries, young men are made into soldiers in the same way. Though because of the nature of modern weaponry warfare is no longer fought in drill formations, following a series of repetitive movements designed by Frederick the Great, soldiers are drilled constantly. The purpose of these tedious exercises is to habituate men to respond to the orders of a commander instead of the impulses of their own bodies. Deprived of sleep, food, overworked, isolated from women, family, friends, humiliated and ridiculed, soldiers learn to disregard their own sensual knowledge and to dissociate from what they feel.

As I write I am aware that the image of a squadron of young men, dressed in high uniform, with a spit-and-polish shine to shoes and weapons, is oddly anachronistic, even romantic. Though the impression remains that to become a President of the United States one must prove oneself through military experience, military valor is not quite the *sine qua non* of accomplishment that once it was. War is more impersonal. Missiles fired from thousands of miles away, bombs dropped according to mathematical coordinates flashing in coded colors on a computer screen, the technologies of modern warfare have perfected dissociation and ironically, in so doing, have nearly eliminated battlefields as the test of masculine mettle.

The erotic glow of sword and shield has shifted now to the

nearly miraculous operations of tools. Tools themselves take on the heroic capabilities that once belonged to warriors. Wily missiles that cut a path over and around a landscape of buildings to find their targets. Satellites suspended in space that, like generals with a longer view, photograph terrains, positions, armament factories. Brave and invincible tanks. Stealthy airplanes that cannot be detected by any radar. In the perfection of machines, cleansed of the vulnerabilities of the human body, the immortal hero, unattached, without weakness or need, has been made to exist on earth.

Yet even machines have histories. That so much scientific invention has occurred during a time of war reveals an underside to efficiency. In the West, the origins of technologies are inseparable from empires and their philosophies. To the masculine psyche, on or off the battlefield, tools of all kinds, electronic, nuclear, chemical, biological, are imbued with the excitement of combat. The design, manufacture, and use of tools are all configured as a kind of conquest.

The ethos of the warrior does not stop at the boundaries of the battlefield. Just as warfare has shaped the masculine appeal of technology, the military psyche shapes the entire social body. The sensual privations the soldier learns to embrace, the foreshortening of emotional response that is called courage in warfare, the aggression necessary to survive, these are all characteristics of civic masculinity, qualities required for business, politics, law, even medicine.

In this light, the development of Western economies and economic theories can scarcely be understood except as a form of participation, even if only imaginary, in warfare. On the simplest psychological level, the deprivations of a masculinity shaped to the purposes of warfare lead in turn to a kind of greed and a hunger for power which is a species of expansion. And because, through the separation of matter and spirit, ordinary life has lost its significance, this greed is accompanied by a longing for significance that is expressed as ambition. Meaning, no longer the province of a shadowy afterlife, belongs to a less elusive realm, an elite class, to which, in a democracy, anyone can aspire. Rather than a bridge connecting the self to all that exists, significance has become a possession over which warring interests and parties compete.

Yet the psychology of civic masculinity can include those who are not biologically male. The realm of social meanings into which women too are educated has been shaped to the contours of a warrior's psychology. One cannot participate in society at all, let alone succeed in public life, without this education. And though in traditional roles women are allowed a wider range of sensual and emotional experience than men, the confinement of female life, and the separation of all that is called feminine from meaning, creates in turn another kind of void and its own longings. And because inside traditional roles a woman locates the meaning of her own life in her husband's fate, even the most feminine woman has been militarized.

Ultimately no one can escape the psychology of the warrior because the psychology is inscribed into the economic order. And the circle of causation folds back on itself. Economic order also causes warfare, the ways of the warrior causing a drive toward expansion, and war created by that drive. What precedes both is a manner of living, an idea of survival formed toward the conquest of nature. In such economies, because the limitations of nature exist only as barrier and not as source of wisdom, no meeting with nature ever takes place. Human society becomes embattled with existence.

One can read a certain ignorance in the history of the Roman Empire. In Rome an economy that regarded nature as an inexhaustible resource eventually produced the exhaustion of land and forests, which in turn produced a need for expansion. Yet if by expansion land was acquired for the growing of grain, those granaries and forests were depleted by the hunger of armies marshaled to gain and govern new lands. The result of conquest was a kind of *samsara,* an endless wheel of suffering.

• • •

For the modern age, the dream has been to rescue humanity from the limitations of nature through machines. Capitalism and communism had this wish in common. But although in the Marxist vision the means of production would be owned by everyone equally, what has actually occurred in both systems is a separation between the great majority of people and a direct control over any means of survival. What have been created instead are vast structures of concentrated social power. Structures inapproachable for most people. Not only communist bureaucracies but corporations which are increasingly centralized as they are becoming less and less accessible to any democratic process.

In such a world, everyone must be afraid. That fear of starvation, cold, or privation which is existential to the human condition grows in direct proportion to the distance placed between oneself and the means to survive. If I have access to land or to a common forest, yields may be low, but I can always grow or gather. I will have firewood, water, something to eat. If I have a craft or skill, in difficult times, I can work harder. There is always something I can do to keep myself, my family, and my community alive. Such is hardly the case for the growing numbers of unemployed in the modern, industrialized world.

But the terror which comes from this preternaturally powerless state is not limited to the poor. One witnesses this fear not only in violence on the street but in the most lofty corridors. No amount of wealth or social power can quiet the ghost of nature whose necessities society denies at its peril. Even though the rich attempt to barricade themselves from feelings of vulnerability, those who are powerful must feel uneasy, as if the long-neglected foundation of their safety were about to crumble. Is this why one encounters among them such an unreasoned fear of those who are weaker, the deprived, the homeless, women and children who rely on the pittance of relief we call welfare?

• • •

The wheel of suffering sweeps up every human experience in its course. If at the heart of expanding economies what is missing is a meeting with nature, the capacity to meet at all is also damaged. I am also thinking of the failure of intimacy between men and women. An eros shaped to the model of conquest; masculine sexuality configured as a means of strength, seizure, and possession; feminine sexuality drawn after the image of a passive, mindless earth. In this conception eros has been transformed into an index of power. But by this transaction the authentic power of sexual experience is lost.

And even beyond the roles dictated by ideas of gender, in modern society the absence of a respectful relationship with a living, growing, intelligent environment leaves the psyche that develops in this atmosphere increasingly ignorant and unskilled, unable to relate on any except the most shallow level. As if the body were trained only to walk on a ground constructed from the imagination, ideal, responding to every need smoothly, the effect of disregarding the exigencies of nature is ultimately disabling. For it is by limitation, difference, surprise, unpredictability, even friction and certainly difficulty that the soul is honed. By defining nature as without spirit, the modern habit of mind becomes spiritless.

Though it was heretical in the decade of the fifties, when I was growing up, to question the idea that the American economy should be without natural limitation or any restraint, it seemed then that European democratic nations had made a break with the tradition of empire. In this period, one after another of the nations which were held as colonies of Britain, France, Spain, Portugal, and the United States gained independence. What I was taught and what I believed was that a great change in the Western imagination had occurred. In place of the aggrandizements of empire, what was valued now were self-determination and human rights.

But the age of empire has not ended; instead empire has merely shed its more archaic forms. Only the leitmotif of expansion has changed. Where once one spoke of Christianity and saving souls, now the reigning idea is progress. In place of missionaries raising crosses or explorers planting flags on foreign lands, a fleet of economic advisers, loan officers from the World Bank, investors, agronomists, and salesmen offer material deliverance, a "better way of life" through the inevitable machines and technologies invented in the industrialized West. Yet though the symbols of this advancement appear to be more beneficial than missions and Bible schools, what seems to be only a gift of electronic equipment, or scientific knowledge aimed at a better standard of living, continues a history of imposition. As the template of one culture—its manner of thought, its way of life—extends throughout the world, diverse and complex cultures, including their stories, architectures, ways of living on and with the earth, and unique processes of understanding, are disappearing.

Nor have the manly virtues of the warrior vanished. Now it is the technician and the scientist pursuing *new frontiers* in the service of a conquest of nature who are trained to another kind of dissociation, a studied detachment. The atmosphere is strangely abstract. With the revelation of the interior world of the atom, physicists may have dismantled the idea of "objectivity," but Western science still wears the mantle of an absolute truth. The judgments of various experts come as if from ephemeral regions of knowledge existing outside the cave of daily experience and above any culture. Bestowed with authority by scientific findings, legions of bankers, speculators, administrators, diplomats, corporations, development agencies speak an oddly elevated language, disembodied, dislocated, neutered. The style creates the illusion that the modern approach bears no vestige of any flesh and blood existence, belongs to no invested point of view, has no history.

And as much as this language of momentous decision making appears to come from nowhere, it also seems to go nowhere. Only the vaguest tracery of an indication, euphemistic and obfuscating as bureaucratic reference often is, tells us how such decisions actually affect the lives of those who will unwittingly fall in their path. Though the argument has so often been that technology is innocent in this grand scheme, it is stunning how the technology which delivers these plans for the future, as well as being offered as a prize for participation in it, mirrors and accelerates a state of disassociation. Here again as meeting is avoided, sensibility is diminished. Just like the soldier sitting in front of a video screen who aims electronically at fluorescent colored coordinates to complete his bombing raid, masterminds of finance are able to make vast changes in the lives of people largely unknown and even obscure to them while they sit thousands of miles away, isolated, shielded, staring into an unblinking light which can display "information" from around the world at the light stroke of a finger.

Writing of the same phenomenon in an earlier time, the critic Walter Benjamin tells us, "The invention of the match around the middle of the nineteenth century brought forth a number of inventions which have one thing in common: one abrupt movement of the hand triggers a process of many steps." He describes the mechanical proclivity of the twentieth century, including the telephone and the camera, as illustrations of what the poet Paul Valéry has called "the smooth functioning of the social mechanism," an efficiency that blunts the "feeling of being dependent on others, which used to be kept alive by need."

The push-button devices of modern technology move in a perverse kind of harmony with societies which repeat the same patterns automatically, without self-reflection, doubt, or question about what we do, how or where we are going. Filled with mechanical, electronic, and chemical marvels, the West creates a kind of magic show through which life seems to be lived effortlessly and with no limits. Countless glossy, appealing, inventive images render the illusory possibility of an ageless life, independent of gravity and weather alike.

But what is not visible in this picture of comfort and productivity is the utter dependence which the industrialized West has on those nations it calls "underdeveloped." When natural limits to land, forests, minerals, plants, water, labor, or even markets appear in the West, the continuous display of splendrous abundance is achieved only by reaching beyond the West to take and use what is there.

Yet today one does not call it plunder. Instead, surrounded by a more secular nimbus of charity, the modern expansion of European power is known as aid. Economists, agronomists, and other experts present scientific arguments for elaborate projects of betterment. One after another new programs, first industrialization, then the Green Revolution, now the Information Highway promise the poor outside the West that they will benefit.

The chosen standard for success is inevitably Western. Taken from the West itself, as well as from those idealized self-portraits of the West which television imports throughout the world, a half-conscious collage of objects, modes of living, images and expectations, everything from the inevitable blue jeans, to Coca-Cola, to refrigerators whose lights go on when the doors are opened, to microwave ovens, to sidewalks, business suits, computers, portable telephones, automobiles, frozen food, and light-skinned bodies, to acquisition itself, has come to stand in many minds as a universal symbol for happiness.

But something sad transpires in this process. Though more often than not the circumstances which have led to poverty, disease, and starvation in developing countries have been caused by colonialism and Western ideas of development, the most common belief in the West is that these conditions have always been the lot of life for men and women in pre-industrial societies. In this atmosphere acts of industrial development seem as if they were natural imperatives. Not only has improvement been made synonymous with European world views and a Western style of life, but the West has been defined as more advanced and thus superior, the third world somehow slower to achieve happiness, and always behind in efforts at advancement. In a word, inferior. As Gustavo Esteva, who once served in the Mexican Ministry of Planning, writes, the word "development," ". . . for two thirds of the people of the earth . . . is a reminder of what they are not. It is a reminder of an undesirable, undignified condition. To escape from it they need to be enslaved to others' experiences and dreams."

But the effect is more than humiliating. What also occurs is an even more devastating event which the Indian social philosopher and agronomist Vandana Shiva has called "intellectual colonization." Contrary to the air of beneficence which developers so often adopt, like earlier missions to convert other cultures to a Western way of life, the process is violent. What is destroyed is culture, history, an inherited way of seeing the world, of making judgments. "The first level of violence unleashed on local systems of knowledge," Shiva writes, "is not to see them as knowledge." In the lens of the colonizer, local culture virtually disappears. Or, when it becomes visible, "it is made to disappear by denying it the status of a systemic knowledge and assigning it the adjectives 'primitive' and 'unscientific.' "

Unknowingly I was a witness to the unfolding of this violence, though I did not understand what I was seeing. The posture in mid-century America was benevolent; everywhere lives were going to be improved, even in rural America, if only the uneducated could be convinced of the wisdom of betterment. One thought of ideas that lay outside the ken of Western scientific rationality as backward. I remember watching a film on television one afternoon about the efforts of the Tennessee Valley Authority to build a dam and bring hydroelectric energy to the region. The promise was that electricity, jobs, and prosperity would follow. The hero argued with recalcitrant farmers and folk of the valley who did not want this change. I knew nothing of the Appalachian culture and way of life that was perishing, even while I sat watching that flickering screen which had been introduced so recently into my life. My sympathies were with the hero, not the others, characters less delineated in my mind, whose superstition defined them.

It was common then to speak of the problems of poverty throughout the world as the consequences of this kind of recalcitrance to change. One spoke disparagingly, for instance, of the sacred cows of India, as if religious ignorance were causing the starvation of millions. I adopted this attitude along with another current of my thought. I had rejected my own religion for its narrow prejudices and hypocrisies. As a younger child I loved the teachings of Jesus, the songs in church, the feeling of a larger presence, and the communion with this presence that Christianity gave me. But anti-Semitism and rigid attitudes toward sexuality alienated me. By the time I was fourteen, I began to call myself an agnostic and then an atheist.

In a certain sense, I replaced the feeling of communion I once had through religion with a vision of social justice on earth. In this I was typical of my generation. Yet though I believed passionately in equality, I was unaware of a certain arrogance that I had inherited along with my education. I assumed that Western ideas of progress were good for everyone. For my generation, "sacred cow" was a metaphor for literal beliefs impervious to scientific reason. But there was a wisdom in the Indian idea of the sacred cow that eluded us. I hardly understood at all the actual problems of starvation in India or other parts of the world. I grew up in a meat-eating culture. Hamburgers, hot dogs, beef stew, corned beef hash. Almost every Sunday night we had roast beef which my grandmother had bought from the butcher section of the grocery store in our neighborhood. To be poor was to have to eat beans. Aside from the writings of Sinclair Lewis, I was hardly interested in how that beef got to the butcher, where the cows pastured, what they were fed, or how the way food is produced shapes economies, affecting, among other things, social justice.

Everything in my social environment had taught me to believe that whatever one wanted, whether it was to eat steak every night, or own a convertible Mercedes, or have a television in every room, was limited only by money. If the orange crops just outside Los Angeles failed one year because of early frost, we still had oranges. They were trucked in from Florida or Mexico. I had learned about certain cycles of nature in school, the conversion of carbon dioxide into oxygen by leaves on a tree, the need for leaves and manure to constantly build the soil. But I remained in some way uncomprehending about a crucial aspect of my existence: how it is the food I ate came to be on the table.

I had no understanding that commercial ranching, to quote Frances Moore Lappe and Joseph Collins, "squanders precious grain," which could feed so many more than could the cattle raised in this way. And that Western culture had a great deal to learn from the idea of the sacred cow completely eluded me. As Sir Alfred Howard, one of the earliest and most influential founders of the movement for sustainable agriculture, has written, the agricultural practices of Asia have "passed the supreme test—they are almost as permanent as those of the primeval forest, of the prairie or of the ocean." Lands that would have been depleted in a few decades if farmed according to Western scientific methods have remained arable for centuries in the alluvial soils of the Gangetic plains in India because they were cultivated in a manner inextricably woven with ancient beliefs in *Kamadhenu* and *Kalpataru,* the sacred cow and the sacred tree.

Vandana Shiva, who has worked for years in rural India, tells us that these two holy beings "are the inviolable links of the inviolable food chain in Indian agriculture." For the worship of cows and trees turns out to be profoundly practical. It is trees and cows that provide the humus and organic matter which replenish the soil. And if respected and allowed to live unhindered, they will also replenish themselves, perpetually. That Indian peasants live in and with a vision of the cosmos that has held the earth as sacred has also engendered wise techniques of farming that keep the soil alive, such as the practices of shallow plowing, rotational cropping, and the use of a mixture of crops. Only now is the value of such methods becoming better understood in the West.

• • •

But the understanding must run deeper. Again and again Western experts fail to recognize the wisdom of older ways of life which are based on a respect for the wisdom of nature. In the West the curious idea of human existence as isolated from and above natural process has shaped our idea of economy. This idea has put us on a disastrous course, but nevertheless it is this idea which for the last two centuries we have been imposing on the rest of the world.

That at times the interventions of the West into local economies has been well meaning does not allay the gravity of their consequences. In the Sahel, for example, where French taxation policies and the incursions of commercial farmers on grazing land led to the gradual impoverishment of nomad pastoral peoples, the United States Agency for International Development, known over the world as A.I.D., responded by drilling deep-water wells to provide drinking water for the nomads' herds of cattle. But, as is so often the case with thought couched in a paradigm that fragments the cosmos, the thinking behind this strategy was perilously fragmentary. For centuries within this region, the natural cycle of rainfall which alternated between dry and wet periods had maintained a balance between cattle, their drinking water, and the grass they grazed which grew on marginal, unarable lands. After the new wells were drilled herds increased, the fragile lands were overgrazed, and then cattle began to die in unprecedented numbers. This was one of the Western ideas which led to terrible famine in the Sahel. Images of women, men, and children starving, bone thin, dying, shocked us in the West. But we had only the narrowest knowledge of the causes of this suffering.

In the European habit of mind, one which conceives of both capitalism and communism as outside the concrete conditions of earthly survival, perhaps the most abstract idea is the concept of the free market. This marketplace is, of course, not real. It does not exist in any location; there are no oranges carried by mule or truck to a square, a stall, an open building.

Barter, of course, is outmoded. One never trades a sack of apples for a dozen eggs. The currency is always money, an abstract symbol, not only for real substances and materials, such as food or wood or stone, but also for labor, such as cultivation of the soil, carpentry, factory work, computer programming, and also as the valuation for economic transactions themselves, interest and the various fees and costs of commodity trading. But, in this abstract market, whatever money has come to stand for has vanished almost completely from view, except as a subsidiary circumstance which must be considered from time to time only as adjunct to the real goal, which is the acquisition of more money. In this atmosphere, money becomes more real than physical existence, and the illusion grows that survival has far less to do with watershed systems and soil and air than it does with the climate of this abstract marketplace. This is especially so in the ether of electronic communication. It is as if through commodification and capital the world might be transformed into pure number. And of course, in the realm of mathematics, which is not bounded by the earthly dimensions of time and space and the cycles of living things, the idea of limitless increase can seem not only possible but even necessary.

If nature limits economic life by the yields of soil, the slow growth of trees, the availability of water, fish, the needs of animals, the concept of free market and its corollary free trade recognize no such barriers to constant growth. Though the mythos of economic freedom conjures Darwinian images of what is described as the naturalness of competition and even greed, the mandates of the free market run in an almost diametrically opposed direction to the necessities of natural existence. Starting with the illusion of an endless supply of goods limited only by want or need, the imperative of the market is to continually create new desires and dependencies.

Economists and investors who have designed Western policies toward nations they call underdeveloped are not unaware that the effects of this course are often disastrous in the lives of the poor. The historian Jean Berthoud, who has been studying and writing about markets for decades, unearths this passage by J. L. Sadie, published in 1960 in the *Economic Journal:*

> Economic development of an underdeveloped people by themselves is not compatible with the maintenance of their traditional customs and mores. . . . What is needed is a revolution in the totality of social, cultural and religious institutions and habits, and thus in their psychological attitude, their philosophy and way of life. What is therefore required amounts in reality to social disorganization. Unhappiness and discontent in the sense of wanting more than is obtainable at any moment is to be generated.

If this causes misery in the lives of others, this misery is justified as a means to a greater end. "The suffering and dislocation that may be caused in the process may be objectionable," Sadie writes, "but it appears to be the price that has to be paid for economic development; the condition of economic progress."

Yet as wearily realistic as this last sentence sounds, it is still astonishingly vague. What is this "economic progress" that justifies so much pain? In plan after plan the vision of this future is left curiously abstract. One might well argue that this is purposeful. The progress which will occur in fact rarely comes to benefit those who have been dislocated and made to suffer. Nor will this new social and economic order benefit their children. They have instead been sacrificed to increase the wealth of a small segment within their own nation, and to aggrandize the wealth and power of Western developers.

But something else is expressed here. I am thinking of the word "agora," ancient Greek for both meeting place and marketplace. An economy is more than just an exchange of goods and services. The ordering of economic activity is also an ordering of significance. Meaning arises from meeting, from the congregation of a people and the nexus that they make through need and desire. (The etymology of the word "allegory" reflects this understanding of the genesis of an intellectual common ground. As *ger,* standing for meeting, comes together with *alle,* which denotes other, a system of shared symbolic significance, allegory, is created.)

What is at stake in any economic order is the shape of consciousness itself. Though greed and the desire to exploit others are certainly ample motives, another psychology is also present in the imposition of an economic order and this is the desire to possess and control meaning itself. For this reason, one can read the same colonial attitudes in the history of communist economies. One encounters in communism the same hubris, the same arrogant certitude, the same willingness to cause pain and suffering to others in the interest of a progress that is also strangely abstract, even when those who are making economic and social plans for others are committed in principle to the collective good. But, like the abstract idea of a free market, this concept of collectivity is more ideological than real and strangely severed from the communal aspect of existence which is part of nature. In the former Soviet Union and China ancient ways of living in communion with land, trees, and animals, as part of cultures that shared common resources, have been sacrificed to the designs of planners who marked indigenous cultures for eradication.

The Sami way of life, for instance, was disrupted in the Soviet Union by the collectivization of reindeer herds. And this economic reordering was accompanied by efforts to enforce assimilation which intensified greatly in the 1960s, during which the government made the Sami language and shamanism illegal, confiscated sacred objects, forced children into boarding schools and thousands of indigenous people into centralized farms and factories. In the name of communism a deeply communal way of life was nearly destroyed. An ethos that existed within Sami culture for millennia called for no privileged ownership of the means of production, shared streams, forests, land, work. Vladimir Afanoskie describes the traditional life his family lived before 1917: "My Grandfather and uncle fished on the open sea. My mother fished for salmon in the rivers. Every fall people moved their reindeer to a winter range, returning in the summer when the grass was high." With this way of life, the Sami people did not need employers or jobs or factories or government aid.

But once the reindeer were taken, Sami society began to unravel. In this culture, reindeer were not simply resource or raw material or a means of survival. Sami religion centered around the reindeer and the work, migration, and way of life that caring for reindeer required. These animals were at the center of a sacred communion between the Samis and the earth, an earth which they conceive of as intrinsically spiritual. "When they took the reindeer away," Afonoskie said, "it was as if they took the life right out of us." Now the Samis struggle to survive according to a way of life lived in towns and factories that is alien to them. Poverty, alcoholism, suicide, a higher rate of tuberculosis and mortality in general are among the costs of a loss the dimensions of which can never be calculated.

Whether Marxist or capitalist, Cold War nuclear technology, fascist eugenics or Western genetic engineering, the continuing movement in the twentieth century to unify the world and nature according to one scientific idea has all the characteristics of a Greek tragedy. As system after system fails to produce the abundance and freedom from suffering it promises, what becomes more and more clear is that the desire to spread one way of life over the globe is not entirely rational. This is perhaps most evident in the madness of certain technologies. One thinks, for example, of monocultures, the reckless diminishment of the great variety of seeds and species to just one or two kinds that decreases nature's capacity for survival under a variety of conditions. Or of the production of nuclear power, which in every aspect is so dangerous to human health. Of the human genome project, which, setting as its goal the mapping of all human genetics, has actually patented the genes of native peoples. Or one thinks of the various projects in genetic engineering which promise miraculous results and yet include no reckoning of all that in nature still seems miraculous because it is beyond our reckoning, past the limits of our knowledge.

And yet that is the point. At the core of what is an irrational appeal of modern scientific ideology is the promise of limitless knowledge. Not the wide-eyed and wondering wish children have to understand everything. But another kind of wish. As Vandana Shiva writes, "The prefix 'scientific' for the modern systems and 'unscientific' for the traditional knowledge systems has . . . less to do with knowledge and more to do with power." Underneath the obvious lust for social and political control that this *use* of knowledge evinces dwells an unexamined wish, the dreamlike desire for the power to define reality.

And what is the interior landscape of this dream? Here there is no easy posture of receiving. No casual meeting. No subtlety or free play. No sultry slow descent to an erotic knowledge by which, just as one takes in knowledge, one is entered by the known, capsized, transformed. Rather the motion is all swift, driven, edged by anxiety, aimed like a weapon is aimed, aggressive, conquering. Because dominating every effort to know in this terrain is an unmistakable atmosphere of terror.

The moment is hardly ever revealed. Not the contemplation of death, though death too is feared, but of life, of existence itself. Rilke writes, "Beauty is nothing but the beginning of terror." But this terror has a history. If once we were at home on the earth, we have grown used to imagining ourselves otherwise.

Is this why fear is elemental to the experience of knowledge? Not only what we learn but the state of learning itself challenges every idea of sovereignty over creation that we have. Because to know is an erotic act, one is made vulnerable to what has been before unknown; all knowledge enters the self as the force of change. Yet the Western self, ordered as it is around dominion, does not want to submit. Like eros itself, which has been divided by categories of victory and submission, knowledge as an erotic act has been shaped to conquer, determine, and even annihilate that which is known. The strategy is predictable. Just as the West, through pornography and the larger system of gender, shapes sexuality (which is in turn a form of knowledge) to the contours of power, so knowledge has been made to be not only an agency of power but a form of power.

Given the underlying psychological mood of this approach to knowledge, one should not be surprised that for so long the West has been bent upon shaping the rest of the world into an extension of itself. The existence of other systems of knowledge always poses an implicit challenge to the assumptions of one's own culture. Yet the challenge is especially threatening if the process of knowledge itself has been made into an act of domination.

But dominion does not come easily. Not only knowledge but the experience of knowing must be diminished and reduced. For to know is to encounter a power within oneself that is also greater than the self. In the process of knowing, one is met by a larger, more powerful presence, a world beyond the carefully constructed boundaries that culture gives to being. Through knowledge one is immersed in otherness, a difference which is all the more troubling because it is not entirely distinct from one's own being but exists on a continuum with it.

The signs are so common, one scarcely reads them. Yet in so many ways the issues of knowledge and sexual congress have been treated as one and the same. That it has been crucial in the traditions of the West to mold sexual knowledge into a pattern of dominion is clear. Yet that this pattern is woven together with the epistemologies of empire has been less obvious. I am thinking of the term *missionary position* and all the resonances of that phrase. The Western concept of knowledge as a form of dominion is threaded with a fear of women. After the convergence of Christianity and the Roman Empire, women became the most potent symbols of a sexual knowledge that could corrupt the purity of spiritual knowledge. In the iconography of Christianity a woman's body was the vessel for the earthly desires Christian theologians would excise from consciousness.

This is why women were eventually banned from the priest-hood. But the struggle was waged internally as well as externally. Just as the Western psyche longs for the exotic with a passionate desire, the portrait we are given of the pious monk is of a man tortured by his own longing. So as early as A.D. 500 Benedict of Nursia, sheltered in the desert from every worldly pleasure, but still thinking with desire of a woman, rolled himself in a clump of thorns and briars, "till his body was all one wound, but also till he had extinguished forever the eternal fire which inflamed him. . . ."

What is telling here is the contradictory idea that one can extinguish an *eternal* flame *forever*. But this momentary lapse in logic expresses a state of mind which may, on another level of consciousness, understand that within a living being the desire for an earthly life and the knowledge of the body will never be silent. And in the same lapse, beneath the arrogant claim, one senses a desperation, the knowledge that the struggle to separate oneself from earthly existence will be endlessly futile.

The same struggle continues, in more secular times. One reads, for example, that in the seventeenth century the Royal Society of Scientists founded by Robert Boyle preached celibacy to its members for the sake of purity of thought. But always an ambivalence expresses itself. This is audible in the words of Rob-ert Hooke, student of Boyle and secretary of the society, who said that for him the study of mechanics "was his first and last mis-tress." And at the dawn of the nuclear age one can hear the same conflict in these words written by the chemist Bertram Boltwood:

I am beginning to believe that Thorium may be the mother of that most abominable family of rare-earth elements, and if I can lay the crime at her door I shall make efforts to have her apprehended as an immoral person guilty of lascivious carriage.

This tension which arises in the effort to understand nature expresses a profound conflict in consciousness. The real culprit here is self-knowledge, both desire and the unavoidable apprehension of desire. But the conflict is inevitably projected outward, toward other beings called closer to nature, as well as nature itself. It is no accident that so strong a resemblance exists between what is an essentially pornographic portrait of women in Western theology and the idea of indigenous peoples as backward, bestial, uncultured, more carnal, living in a state of sin. In the nineteenth century Christian missionaries, men and women alike, turned toward wayward women and native people around the world with the same desire, to save their souls.

No wonder, then, that Western developers so often overlook or purposefully undermine the power of women in societies they are marshaling toward scientific progress. One pattern in particular repeats itself. Whether it be in the eighteenth century in New England, or in the nineteenth and twentieth centuries in India and Africa, colonists and developers have ignored social structures that placed women in control of farming and the planned use of local resources. Vandana Shiva, citing Murdock's *Ethnographic Atlas,* notes that, in half of one hundred and forty-two "advanced horticultural societies, farming was the exclusive domain of women, and it was shared on an equal footing with men in another twenty-seven per cent." The knowledge women have of agriculture is considerable. For centuries women in these older cultures have integrated their own survival, that of their families and communities with an ecological understanding. As B. Hyma and Perez Nyamwange write, the prevalence of this division of labor has made ". . . women's traditional tasks, experiences, knowledge and concerns about local problems . . . essential in solving

emerging environmental problems such as deforestation, soil ero-
sion and the scarcity of food, fodder, fuel, wood and water.''

But throughout the world this way of ordering society is being
destroyed, as first colonists and then developers impose their own
ideas of gender on native peoples. Carolyn Merchant writes of the
efforts of colonists to "civilize" Indians in New England. This was
a process which "meant converting their female-dominated shift-
ing horticultural production into male-dominated settled farming.'' That "despite the power of women in production, the
colonial fathers dealt only with Indian men'' is a pattern which is
being repeated disastrously in Africa today, where land which
once belonged to women to farm is being deeded to men who are
also offered monetary inducements to grow cash crops. In the
societies where the West has intervened in this way, these policies
have led to malnutrition and starvation as well as the increase of
alcoholism and despair which are always part of the devastation of
a way of life.

What remains hidden in this picture is how, in the name of
progress, the West has reproduced an image of its own devastation. Poverty, alcoholism, a widespread feeling of nihilism, social
disintegration, desperation, these are all common in the West. Yet
this is the way of ambivalence. That one feels lost in the world and
has begun to believe existence has no meaning creates an almost
unquenchable thirst for something one cannot quite name. Always
it exists someplace else, or belongs to someone else, and must be
gotten, wrested, won. It is gold or the fountain of youth or spices
or just a vitality observed in other cultures but which one cannot
locate in oneself. So, by almost the same motion with which the
West tries to replicate itself all over the world, the industrialized
habit of mind projects the image of that which has been lost, this
unnamed and irretrievable quality, onto those the West would
improve. Ghosts of forgotten selves, peoples whose cultures have
been described as backward and impossible to preserve in the
modern world, become, in this mind's eye, noble savages, living
in a state of nature, uncivilized, naive, childlike, primitive. So

traditional cultures, appealing to the imagination that dooms them, begin to dwell in the Western mind as dreams and fantasies.

The fantasies do have a reality. They describe a region of the mind, a capacity with which one is born. It is perhaps this which the word "development" reveals about industrialized psychology. Originally borrowed from evolutionary thinking, this word also refers to the natural growth and learning of a child. It is as a child that one has a different experience of what it is to know the world. Eros not yet restricted to a game of dominance. Flowers, animals, hummingbirds, and dragonflies that still speak. A wave crashing on the shore, leaves falling one by one in a forest, the sun rising up over the crest of a hill, all this is magic and portentous with meaning. One knows oneself as a being born of the body of a woman, sustained by the body of earth. One exists in a matrix that is both nurturance and meaning, and it is by this matrix that one is defined at the core, by myriad connections with everything around one that is named and held.

But in order to enter the world of those one loves, the social matrix, one has to unlearn this early knowledge and to suffer the subsequent loss of a largeness uniting everything on the face of the earth, a largeness to which one once belonged. Even if here and there daily one senses the presence of this larger life, what one must do to survive pits the mind against it, for in a society bent to power one must participate in building in an illusion of power.

The cost is inestimable. Yet the pain and hunger of the loss of connectedness have fueled the building of empires. It is impossible to say now what is cause and what is effect. What one finds under layers of history and the denial of history is a self-perpetuating cycle. An idea of masculinity, which has been shaped over time to purposes of empire, becomes in itself a cause of war and violence. Required to fulfill an ideal of manhood, political leaders act from the smallest of motives. But the diminishment is general. For the drive to dominion creates an unnatural deprivation in the soul. What has been relinquished is a sense of the natural coherence of life, the textured complexity of implicate meanings which braid together every moment of existence. No longer held by the matrix of existence, the troubled soul of a civilization seeks power, and just as a way of life that is out of balance with nature creates the need for greater and greater resources, so too a civilization disconnected from the weave of nature tries to unify the world, in a vain attempt at totality, under one flag or according to one ideology.

And if the erotic relationship which binds all existence has been erased by a masculine ethos, violence, particularly the violence of warfare, comes to replace this eros in the life and the imagination of empire. Engaged in battle, the soldier once again feels part of something larger. Serving others, even sacrificing his life, he experiences for a brief period that connectedness which is his daily birthright. Even on the home front, war effort fulfills the same need to feel part of a larger whole, to work as one cooperatively. The desire can be as passionate as any other. At the apex of the British Empire, by contrast to ideals of individualism and a social Darwinism that preached the survival of the fittest, service to the empire was regarded, as Joanna Trollope writes, with "absolute devotion."

Now though I am well past the romance of nations and warfare I still feel this desire. Marked with all the disaffections of my time, trusting only the loosest structures, unable to define myself by any order of belief, still I find in myself the wish to serve, a longing to place my life in the amplitude of a larger meaning.

Other ways of life exist. Settled at the periphery of vision, images of vastly different orientations migrate at times into focus through tales of travelers, chance meetings, journeys, photographs, history books. For unspoken reasons these glimpses of otherness draw the soul. One feels an authority in the weave of a rug, its patterns symbolic of a life passage, or in the dark smooth surface of a pot, shaped as if this shard of earth could hold all existence, in a group of dancers through whom the most intense of energies seems to pour, or in stories that chart the cosmos with delight. The temptation is to try to steal the power. But the power cannot be stolen.

Yet meetings with other cultures can inspire awareness. For a civilization driven to possess or conquer, the attitude is unfamiliar. But a quieter act is called for now. An act of perception. Other approaches to knowledge exist, other forms of social order, other cosmologies from which the West can learn. This is no textbook lesson. The examples are alive, changing, variable, no more perfect than they are primitive, not without problems, injustices, or inequities of their own. Nor is the influence of the West on other cultures always destructive. Yet all over the world there have continued for centuries cultures that do not pit forest, water, air, land against human existence, or one human fate against another. And what has been steadfastly underestimated in the West is how much those cultures we call undeveloped have to teach. The lessons are critical to our survival. As the Iroquois Basic Call to Consciousness states, "The traditional native people hold the key to the reversal of the processes in Western Civilization, which hold the promise of unimaginable future suffering and destruction."

Despite the expansion of Western culture all over the planet, this culture faces a crisis. Yet, since one of the attributes of our civilization has been the capacity to innovate, question, and change directions, the calamitous course we have pursued can be reconsidered now, and altered.

As Helena Norberg Hodge writes, ". . . I used to assume that the direction of progress was somehow inevitable, not to be questioned." I too was brought up to believe that technological progress must keep on as it always has, that European civilization cannot go backward. And yet, in truth, what is backward and what is forward?

Hodge writes of her life in another culture, a Tibetan village: "In Ladakh I have had the privilege to experience another, saner way of life and to see my own culture from the outside." Living in another way, she became aware of the assumptions which her own culture had imbued in her. "I . . . assumed human beings were essentially selfish, struggling to compete and survive, and that cooperative societies were nothing more than utopian dreams." What she encountered in Ladakh was another psychology that, together with a different epistemology, regards neither the earth nor other human beings as separate. In a traditional Tibetan village there is no strict boundary between self-interest and the needs and concerns of others. As Hodge writes, ". . . one person's gain is not another person's loss. . . . A high yield for one farmer does not entail a low yield for another. Mutual aid, rather than competition, shapes the economy."

In Ladakh compassion is less an ideal than a way of life. Embraced by the traditional customs and institutions of this culture, much work is structured communally. There are many practical reasons for collective labor. But this way of working also reflects and supports an understanding that life is communal at heart. Being together, talking, singing, visiting are all crucial to the entire culture; the countless tasks necessary for survival are circumscribed by a larger meaning in this collective presence. So in the practice that the Tibetans call *bes,* the harvest of each farm is done by all the villagers, and even by neighboring villagers. With the practice of *rares,* by turns, one or two people in the village will shepherd all the animals belonging to those who live in the village. And in the observance of *paspun* groups of families help each other out at the times of births, marriages, and deaths. It is not in contrast to everyday life but from the fabric of it that a Buddhist ethos of compassion for all sentient beings arises.

Because daily efforts to survive are shared in small and palpable ways in this economy, another experience of self comes into being. The lattice of connectedness that is constantly felt does not obscure the uniqueness of each soul so much as create a feeling of safety within which that uniqueness can come into being. The great awakenings and soul changes one seeks in a solitary way in the West have been intrinsic to a shared life in these villages. And though certainly vices, moments of greed and jealousy arise, the shape of this way of life supports the growth of spirit and flesh as one.

Here is a world beyond worldliness the Western mind has sought with little solace. The search has failed so often that in common usage one speaks now of an *ideal* world as a world impossible to realize on earth. Hope fades with age into bitterness or resolution. And there is cause for grief. Despite the most extensive global expansions and the appearance of an almost mythical abundance, industrialized society has constructed a meagre and impoverished experience of the universe.

Ths history of this construction is not without pause. There have been and still are countless subversions, forms of resistance, counter-motions, parallel and simultaneous histories, influences that are either concealed or unrecognized. Within Europe and the New World, fragments from pagan, peasant, African, American Indian cultures survive. Though the cosmologies which weave these images, artifacts, rituals, stories, recipes, architectures, songs into transformative meanings have been obscured, traces of another coherence persist, even at times taking a place at the heart of public discourse. Shards of other histories can be found everywhere. And if, as Jerry Mander writes in his critically important book *In the Absence of the Sacred,* the "Great Binding Law of the Iroquois Confederacy" was quite probably a "primary model and inspiration for the U.S. Articles of Confederation and for the Constitution," what is also true is that along with democratic institutions, a dream of a deeper consensus continues. Just as Jefferson, Adams, and Franklin witnessed an Iroquois society in some ways more egalitarian than American democracy is today, the American mythos contains within it a memory of societies arranged along another line of orientation, societies that bend with and not against what has been called wilderness.

But the dream is also memory of a more intimate kind. The wish for communion exists in the body. It is not for strategic reasons alone that gathering together has been at the heart of every movement for social change from the abolition movement to the union movement to the movements for women's, gay, and civil rights. These meetings were in themselves the realizations of a desire that is at the core of human imaginings, the desire to locate ourselves in community, to make of survival a shared effort, to experience a palpable reverence in our connections with each other and the earth that sustains us.

If the common belief in late twentieth-century modern society is that human nature is small, narrow, and selfish, this belief is symptomatic of a habit of mind that engenders despair. Yet the possibility for something else exists not just in other cultures but within European history, a capacity in the nature of human consciousness. It was under the oppressive sway of an empire that the words were uttered, "The kingdom is at hand." Everywhere another impulse surfaces. One longs not only to help, to be of use, but to participate, to be defined by the largest arcs of meaning that connect flesh and river, sky and word, revery and the least act of survival. What lies beyond is here, present in every moment of daily life and each meeting, resonant and calling up response.

6

The Eros of Everyday Life

. . . the individual self is . . . a fleeting meeting-
ground of intricately woven relations, its nature is pro-
foundly participatory, but is, for that, no less endowed with
distinctiveness, particularity.

—JOANNA MACY,
The Dharma of Natural Systems

To us, each object is imbued with invisible fibers of light
that reach out into the universe. . . .

—ALEX JACOBS, IROQUOIS ARTIST

In the late spring of the year my mother died she came to live closer to me so that I could take care of her. She had one room and her own bathroom in a convalescent home that I could reach by driving up through the tree-covered hills in back of my house or by a hot freeway that skirted the bay for a few miles and then turned inland. My sister and I knew she had only a few months to live, but still we arranged to move a small number of her possessions up north, so that she could have them with her. The presence of these things made her feel more of a piece, as if the familiar fabric and enamel and wood of these objects formed some kind of bridge between past and present.

I would visit her in the afternoons, doing some errands for her on the way, checking to see that all her needs at the home were met, handling the paperwork that seemed to multiply itself continuously, and completing small tasks for her. On the afternoon that the moving truck arrived, I went out earlier than usual so I could help her arrange her belongings. The drawers of one chest were so covered with grime that, not wanting to release this dust into the room, I took them outdoors to clean them. But just as I set to work a strong wind whipped over the hill in back. As I held the wooden drawer up in the air, layers of dust inside, built up over several years, dispersed, and bits of the sweet-smelling hay that covered the hills were blown into it.

I was surprised and moved. I felt as if the surrounding air were helping us, mother and daughter, through this passage. I had had a difficult childhood. Troubled in her own mind, my mother had been by turns neglectful, abusive, and kind. I had forgiven her many years ago. But, like a dust that accumulates over time, remembered sorrow has many layers. Recently, during my own illness, moments of an old anger welled up in me again, and though I did not express these feelings, a silence grew up between us.

But the frailty of her body approaching death was like a strong wind. We were present to each other as never before. I liked caring for her. And she was grateful for what I did. My own experience with illness made me understand her fears, and she let me comfort her. I began to feel that the direction of caring, who was giving, who was receiving, was far less important than the intimacy of the gesture. I was losing her and gaining her in the same moments. And yet we both had love.

Bound by little domesticities into closeness with my mother, we were being held in an ancient pattern through which rain, gravity, sunlight move particles of earth, energy, spores, leaves, or water moves from one place to another, composing and decomposing life. It was this that struck me when the wind came up that day.

The idea of a world creating itself through small chores. The universe as a place of constant cooking and cleaning, merging and separation. Plant life taking nourishment from earth, fusing with the bodies of animals. Air entering bodies, changing, reentering the atmosphere. Genes fusing, replicating, differentiating. At one moment, particles suspended in fields of energy and at another matter and energy existing as waves. Everything dissolving into the whole and then separating, resolving into being.

In these months, I became acutely aware, as I never had before that I had come from my mother's body. For a period of time I had even been part of her body. Then by the brief but transformational passage known as birth I emerged from this commingled state into being. I remember the first time I looked into my daughter's eyes. She had just been born and a nurse laid her on top of me. Her eyes were as dark and intense as they are now. I realized I was meeting a new life.

Perhaps this is why one travels from union to diaspora and back again. That we are all one is true. And yet the differences among us are so crucial, determining fate, experience, perception, consciousness. Discerning, discernible being is at the heart of knowledge. Without difference and separation, there would be no meeting.

Several years ago, when a group of friends gathered for dinner, we began to tell each the stories of our first sexual encounters. The psychologist Rollo May recalled himself as a gravely serious young man, shy and completely inexperienced in such matters. An older woman, sophisticated and "European," as he told us, invited him to her room. He was stiff and uncertain of himself, she the pursuer. At the door she moved to embrace him, holding him close to her and then moving away, close and apart, close and apart until an irresistible force field existed between them. This was, he said, among the most erotic movements he had known.

Time, if one pays attention, is filled with such meetings. Not only between lovers, or parent and child, but also friends, com-

munity, and the common air. Waking, my hand meets the cotton
sheets on my bed, my mouth meets the water I drink as I arise, my
eyes meet the morning light, shadows of clouds, the pine tree
newly planted in our backyard, my ears meet the sounds of a car
two blocks east. Everything I encounter permeates me, washes in
and out, leaving a tracery, placing me in that beautiful paradox of
being by which I am both a solitary creature and everyone, everything.

Isn't this what shapes our days? The paradox accounts for gravity, which is a kind of eros. The great mass of the earth curving
space and time around it, the greater mass of the sun drawing the
earth in an even circular motion, balanced between fusion and a
solitary direction.

There is an eros present at every meeting, and this is also sacred.
One only has to listen inwardly to the histories and resonances of
the word we use for religious experience. In Sanskrit the word
satsang which translates into English as "meeting" means "godly
gathering." In the English language the word "common" is
linked through the word "communicate" to "communion." And
earlier meanings of "common" point to levels of meaning that
have been obscured in our idea of the sacred. Gary Snyder gives us
the etymology for "common" as *"ko,* 'together,' with (Greek)
moin, 'held in common.' " And he also traces the word back to
the Indo-European root *mei,* meaning " 'to move, to go, to
change.' " This ". . . had an archaic special meaning of 'exchange of goods and services within a society as regulated by
custom or law,' " he writes, as in "the principle of gift economies: 'the gift must always move.' . . ." And the gift does
move.

To exist in a state of communion is to be aware of the nature of
existence. This is where ecology and social justice come together,
with the knowledge that life is held in common. Whether we
know it not, we exist because we exchange, because we move the

gift. And the knowledge of this is as crucial to the condition of the soul as its practice is to the body.

I have been taught by many religions: Christianity, Buddhism, Judaism. Many other religions have also influenced me: Sufism, Taoism, Hopi and Navajo traditions, traditions of the Yoruba and the Kongo brought to the Americas by those who were enslaved, the Hinduism practiced by Mahatma Gandhi. If once I was schooled according to a hierarchy that placed a meeting with God above every other meeting, I have found another meaning within all these traditions, that what is called God exists in every meeting. In meetings of minds, or of bodies, between humankind and animals, plants, earth.

When the divide between the sacred and the profane falls, everyday life is graced and all that is holy is heavy with vitality. Communion is not only an isolated ritual; it is also a manner of living. One can say that all of life is illusion because it vanishes over time, and that to desire or take pleasure is vain. I climb a tree, reach for a plum, and eat it, but in moments the plum is gone and I have nothing. The sad conclusion of this way of seeing is that the search for the sacred must go on someplace else. In texts and words which grow more pale the farther away they are placed from life.

But one can also say that in placing that plum in my mouth I have experienced joy. The fruit of many months of sunlight and earth and water has entered me, becomes me, not only in my stomach, my blood, my cells, but because of what I have learned. The plum has been my lover. And I have known the plum. Letting the plum into the mind of my body, I will always have that taste of sweetness in my memory.

But I cannot know this sweetness, the full dimension of it, unless I am aware of the holiness of this meeting. If I think that the plum tree exists only to feed me, I have lost the meaning that is mixed with every pleasure. The tree exists for the sake of its own being. And it is also part of a commons, its fruit the inheritance of bird and animal and soil alike. I must know this to receive the full value of communion.

Because within every meeting other meetings occur. They take place in the mirror of consciousness. To exist is to reflect and consider. One meets oneself, one sees a trajectory, a certain possible path into what is yet unknown, recalling histories, detecting patterns, weaving the fabric of existence out of every moment. And for each of us, as for every community, village, tribe, nation, the story we tell ourselves is crucial to who we are, who we are becoming.

As we tell this story we shape our minds and the minds of our children to the contours of a shared territory of mind. In this way we create an intellectual commons, a landscape as central to our survival and the quality of our lives as any other. How and what do we choose to see? What do we value, celebrate, anticipate, mark? By what measure do we express our love for the living?

When I was a child I was taught to memorize a map of divisions. By this geography I learned to think of myself as apart from the earth. And by the same plan the names that society gave me divided me from others. Consigned to the background by one idea, elevated to a privileged fate by another, by none of these names could I recognize myself. And all this that fractured my own experience into constrained ideas of spirit or body, intellect or sexuality had also shattered the shared consciousness which I inherited. The atmosphere was permeated with all that could not be said, stories that were not told, hatreds spoken among us that obscured the larger life that belonged to us all. And the separation of sacred from profane, numinous from quotidian, holiness from the life of the polis, narrowed my vision of all existence.

Yet the communion *is* here. Even as I touch my hand to my face I can feel it. That radiant love that is an undeniable part of the body. What June Jordan calls an "intelligent love." Seeking to see, to know, to take in all that is, as it is. To meet all that exists.

It is by such a sacrament that wounds will heal us. Any healing will require us to witness all our histories where they converge, the history of empires and emancipations, of slave ships as well as underground railroads; it requires us to listen back into the muted cries of the beaten, burned, forgotten and also to hear the ring of speech among us, meeting the miracle of that.

And if we weep in the apprehension, let us take the capacity to weep and marvel as proof of a wisdom in the stuff of our existence, at one with the ancient redwood forests on the western-most coast of America, as it is with the watery cells of our own bodies, or the star, just now, bursting into a distant brightness. Our sorrow and joy belong to *this* history, have evolved from the cooling planet of Earth, the fern spore settling eons ago and growing in the new mud, the slow appearance of a human form. The tears and laughter with which we meet this moment are as much a part of intelligence as any reason and can move us deeper to the core of things.

By the light of our desire to meet and communicate, language can be taken as proof of our commonalty and of a commons in the mind. Nor is the life of the mind irrelevant in this critical, trag-edy-bearing time. By what and how we think, we coerce, confine, distort, and damage or sustain, encourage, create, coax ourselves and otherness into a fuller realization of being.

And no one acts alone. No one thinks alone. I was aided in my effort to meet my mother in her death by countless other meet-ings, great marches protesting social injustice (which were above all protests against indifference to suffering), the community that surrounds me and cared for me in illness, countless stories of help, succor, and care told by others, even those no longer living, written and remembered. Even to write these words today some-thing unspoken between me and an intimate friend had to be said. The threads of connection run everywhere and to unexpected places.

And so the change, too, must be made together. It is not a single vision but a common one that calls for alteration. To change how we see involves some loss, certainly the death of habitual metaphors for order. And the changes needed are great as well as small. It is not only philosophy as it is written in books, but philosophies written into our lives, in institutions, social systems, economies, and governments which need to be reconsidered. For it is by and through these living structures that communities think and perceive. If we would change a habit of mind that has become destructive we must revise the social architecture of our thought.

Yet this is the only hope for the familiar world we cherish. Not only Bach's Magnificat, Sappho's lyric, the stories of Coyote, the smooth surface of marble columns, the shape of piazzas, the sound of John Coltrane, or a golden sculpture of the Buddha reclining, the fate of everyone, everything we love, but the fate of that subtle weave that holds it all, giving each of us eyes, ears, heart, mind, and breath, rests on the question. Can we rise to ourselves and see what is in the nature of the soul to see—that we exist on this common ground together?

Notes

8 "cultural decay and moral . . ." Cornel West, *Race Matters* (Boston, 1993), p. 58.

10 "History . . ." John Edgar Wideman, *Fatheralong. A Meditation on Fathers and Sons, Race and Society* (New York, 1994), p. 101.

18 "There's a time . . ." Mario Savio, cited by Kenneth Cloke in *A Brief History of Civil Liberties Protest Movements in Berkeley—From TASC to SLATE to FSM (1957–1965)* (Santa Monica, 1994), p. 127.

20 Regarding abstract art, see Cornelia Schultz, "Searching for Meaning in Abstraction." An unpublished paper, delivered at the University of California at Davis, 1993. See also April Kingsley. *The Turning Point, The Abstract Expressionists and the Transformation of American Art* (New York, 1992).

22 "Ginsberg read *Howl* . . ." Michael McClure, "Writing One's Body," *Lighting the Corners, On Art, Nature, and the Visionary* (Albuquerque, 1993), p. 3.

23 "Experience, adventure . . ." Joyce Johnson. *Minor Characters* (New York, 1994), p. xiv.

24 "Woman?" Simone de Beauvoir, *The Second Sex* (New York, 1957), p. 3.

25 "Beginnings are . . ." Rachel Carson, *The Sea Around Us* (New York, 1958), p. 3.

28 "Undulated valley . . ." Mary Wollstonecraft, *Letters Written During a Short Residence in Sweden, Norway and Denmark* (Lincoln, Nebraska, 1976), pp. 118 passim.

37 "it raged . . ." Vaclav Havel, "Politics and Conscience," *Living in Truth,* ed. Jan Vladislav (London, 1990), p. 140.

38 "Your mob . . ." Thomas Carlyle, *The French Revolution* (London, 1973), p. 201.

39 "humanity's philosophy of life . . ." Theodore Barber, *The Human Nature of Birds* (New York, 1994).

48 "It is glorious . . ." Henry David Thoreau, *Walden and Other Writings* (New York, 1992), p. 292.

49 "alive to all the nuances . . ." See Cornelia Schultz, op. cit.

52 "Since the beginning . . ." Ralph Ellison, "What America Would Be Like Without Blacks," cited by Cornel West, op. cit., p. 1.

52 ". . . they moved to construct . . ." Wole Soyinka. *Myth Literature and the African World* (Cambridge, 1976), p. 129.

52 "My wife . . ." André Breton, "L'Union libre," *Selected Poems* (London, 1969), p. 31.

57 "If you can make . . ." Gerald Jay Sussman as cited by Jeremy Rifkin, *Biosphere Politics, a New Consciousness for a New Century* (New York, 1991), p. 246.

59 "Even anatomy . . ." For a more thorough discussion of these issues, see the work of Judith Butler, *Gender Trouble, Feminism and the Subversion of Identity* (New York, 1990).

61 Regarding Francis Bacon's imagery, see Carolyn Merchant, *The Death of Nature, Women, Ecology and the Scientific Revolution* (San Francisco, 1980), p. 169 passim, and Susan Griffin, *Woman and Nature, The Roaring Inside Her* (New York, 1978), pp. 15–17.

62 "the urge . . ." Evelyn Fox Keller, *Secrets of Life, Secrets of Death, Essays on Language, Gender and Science* (New York, 1992), p. 39.

63 "a calculated assault . . ." Watson and Crick as cited by Evelyn Fox Keller, *Ibid,* p. 45.

63 "I had worked . . ." Mary Shelley. *Frankenstein,* ed. and annotated by Leonard Woolf (New York, 1993), p. 86.

64 "I must walk . . ." Henry David Thoreau, *Journals,* as published in *The Heart of Thoreau's Journals,* ed. Odell Shepard (New York, 1961), p. 99.

64 "much more marvelous . . ." see Evelyn Fox Keller, *A Feeling for the Organism: The Life and Work of Barbara McClintock* (New York, 1983).

65 See Edward Goldsmith, *The Way, An Ecological World-View* (Boston, 1993).

67 "it possible to avoid . . ." Walter Benjamin, "The Storyteller," *Illuminations, Essays and Reflections,* ed. Hannah Arendt, p. 93.

67 See Barry Barkan, "The Regenerative Community: The Live Oak Living Center and the Quest for Autonomy, Self Esteem and Connection in Elder Care," in *Enhancing Autonomy in Long Term Care; Concepts and Strategies;* ed. Lucia Gamroth, Joyce Semradek, and Elizabeth Tornquist (New York, 1995).

68 "There was a child . . ." Walt Whitman, *Leaves of Grass* (New York, 1958), p. 290.

70 "traditional, canonical . . ." Toni Morrison, *Playing in the Dark* (Cambridge, Massachusetts, 1992), pp. 4–6.

79 "no theory . . ." Paul Feyerabend, *Against Method* (London, 1980), pp. 47 passim.

82 "logic upon which . . ." Gregory Bateson, "Men Are Grass, Metaphor and the World of Mental Process," in *Gaia, A Way of Knowing, Political Implications of the New Biology,* ed. William Irwin Thompson (Great Barrington, Massachusetts, 1987), pp. 46, 44.

83 "mathematics is a Platonic science . . ." *Ad Infinitum—The Ghost in Turing's Machine, Taking God Out of Mathematics and Putting the Body Back In* (Stanford, 1993), p. 4.

83 "Sensual knowledge . . ." For a more thorough discussion of the co-evolution of human sensuality and intelligence with all life, see Ty Cashman, "Philosophy of Natural Systems," a work in progress.

85 "Copernican revolution . . ." Hans Blumenberg, *The Genesis of the Copernican World,* trans. Robert M. Wallace (Cambridge, Massachusetts, 1987), p. 3.

86 See Italo Calvino, *Six memos for the Next Millennium* (New York, 1993), pp. 42 passim.

87 "bourgeois and Marxist . . ." John Berger, *Pig Earth* (New York, 1979), p. 202.

93 "Even the most . . ." Walter Benjamin, "The Work of Art in the Age of Mechanical Reproduction," op. cit., p. 220.

98 "we were fighting to preserve . . ." Hernando Cortés. *Five Letters of Cortés to the Emperor,* trans. J. Bayard Morris (New York, 1991), p. 166.

99 "harm . . ." *Ibid.,* p. 4.

99 "come to know . . ." *Ibid.,* p. 4.

99 "our lords . . ." *Ibid.,* p. 11.

100 "Our Lord was leading us . . ." *Ibid.,* p. 165.

102 See Ramon A. Gutierrez, *When Jesus Came the Corn Mothers Went Away: Marriage, Sexuality and Power in New Mexico, 1550–1846* (Stanford, 1991).

104 "without any religion . . ." Jean de Lery, *History of a Voyage to the Land of Brazil,* trans. Janet Whatley (Berkeley, 1990), p. 136.

105 "at each other . . ." *Ibid.,* p. 212.

106 "He will see Frenchmen . . ." *Ibid.* See Janet Whatley, Introduction, p. xvii.

106 "the family structures of Acoma pueblo . . ." See Gutierrez, op. cit.

108 "The Wintu . . ." See Leanne Hinton, *Flutes of Fire, Essays on California Indian Languages* (Berkeley, 1994) p. 62.

108 "the word 'weird' " . . . I am indebted for this etymology to Brian Bates, a scholar of European shamanic traditions.

113 "horrible . . ." Boscana, as cited in James J. Rawls, *Indians of California: The Changing Image* (Oklahoma, 1984), p. 26.

116 "daily lives . . ." Vincent Harding, *Hope and History, Why We Must Share the Story of the Movement* (Maryknoll, New York, 1991).

118 "Lived a woman . . ." Rudyard Kipling, "South Africa, 1903," *Complete Verse* (New York, 1989), p. 207.

120 "ever Caesar Augustus . . ." Frederick II cited himself so in his compilation of law, *The Constitutions of Melfi*, cited in Jill Meredith, "Court Art of Frederick II," ed. David Castriola, *Artistic Strategy and the Rhetoric of Power, Political Uses of Art from Antiquity to the Present* (Carbondale, Illinois, 1986), p. 42.

126 "the invention . . ." Walter Benjamin, "On Some Motifs in Baudelaire," op. cit., p. 174.

128 "for two thirds of the people . . ." Gustavo Esteva, "Development," ed. Wolfgang Sachs, *The Development Dictionary* (London, 1992), p. 10.

128 "The first level of violence . . ." Vandana Shiva, *Monocultures of the Mind, Perspectives on Biodiversity and Biotechnology* (London, 1993), p. 10.

130 "Squanders precious grain . . ." Frances Moore Lappe and Joseph Collins, *Food First, Beyond the Myth of Scarcity* (New York, 1978), p. 47.

130 "passed the supreme test . . ." Sir Alfred Howard, An Agricultural Testament, as cited by Vandana Shiva, *Staying Alive, Women, Ecology and Development* (London, 1988), p. 105.

130 "the inviolable links . . ." Vandana Shiva, *Ibid.*, p. 106.

133 "Economic development . . ." J. L. Sadie as cited by Jean Berthoud, "Market," *Development Dictionary*, p. 72.

135 "My Grandfather . . ." Vladimir Afanoskie as quoted in Art Davidson, *Endangered Peoples* (San Francisco, 1993), p. 107.

136 "The prefix . . ." Vandana Shiva, *Monocultures*, p. 10.

138 "till his body . . ." David F. Noble, *A World Without Women, the Christian Clerical Culture of Western Science* (New York, 1992), p. 83.

138 "I am beginning . . ." Bertram B. Boltwood, cited by Brian Easlea, *Fathering the Unthinkable, Masculinity, Scientists and the Nuclear Arms Race* (London, 1983), p. 61.

139 "advanced horticultural . . ." Vandana Shiva, *Staying Alive*, p. 105.

139 "women's traditional . . ." B. Hyma and Perez Nyamwange, "Women's Role and Participation in Farm and Community Tree-Growing Activities in Kiambu District Kenya," ed. Janet H. Momsen and Vivian Kinnard, *Different Places, Different Voices, Gender and Development in Africa, Asia and Latin America* (London, 1993), p. 30.

140 "meant converting . . ." Carolyn Merchant, *Ecological Revolutions, Nature, Gender and Science in New England* (Chapel Hill, 1989), p. 92.

142 "absolute devotion . . ." Joanna Trollope, *Britannia's Daughters, Women of the British Empire* (London, 1994), p. 117.

143 "The traditional native people . . ." Cited in Jerry Mander, *In the Absence of the Sacred, the Failure of Technology and the Survival of the Indian Nations* (San Francisco, 1991), p. 193.

143 "I used to . . ." Helena Norberg Hodge, *Ancient Futures, Learning from Ladakh* (San Francisco, 1991), p. 1.

144 "I . . . assumed . . ." *Ibid.*, p. 2.

144 "one person's gain . . ." *Ibid.*, p. 51.

145 "a primary model . . ." Jerry Mander, op. cit., p. 226.

II

ESSAYS, 1980 – 1990

Red Shoes

The imprisonment which was at one and the same time understood as the imprisonment of the female mind has a larger boundary, and that is the shape of thought itself within Western civilization.

It is an early memory. Red shoes. Leather straps crisscrossing. The kind any child covets. That color I wanted with the hot desire of a child.

On one level, one thinks simply of the conditions of imprisonment which affected, for instance, the intellectual life of George Sand. How it was necessary for her to dress like a man in order to attend the theater with her friends. She wanted to be in the section just beneath the stage, and women were not allowed in that section. This transgression was a necessary one if she was going to, as she did, enter the realm of public discourse within her mind.

When was it I first heard the title of the film, The Red Shoes? *My older sister had seen it. Did she speak of it with my mother? I must have overheard it. I was often excluded from such conversations. I was too young. And my mother preferred my sister.*

The female world, bounded as it is, contains, as does any world, rich layers of meaning. It is not simply that a woman must stay within this world but that signification itself is kept away from it.

Whatever lies within the confines of the feminine province is defined *sui generis* as either trivial or obscene (as in housework, or lovemaking) and as such not fit for public discourse.

I was, I suppose, shopping with my grandmother in the department store with the X-ray machine that made a green picture of the bones in my feet. I have the vague feeling my grandmother finds red impractical.

In this light it is no wonder that the novel became a literary form so widely practiced by women, a genre in some of its popular manifestations, and in some phases of its development, dominated by women. The novel is allowed to describe what we think of as the private sphere of life, which is also the sphere of life given over to women. And is it any wonder that so many ''classic'' novels written by men have a heroine at the center of the story? *Anna Karenina. Madame Bovary.*

In my mind, as I remember my grandmother, I can feel the shape of her larger body next to mine. Her elbows are wrinkled in a way that fascinated me. The flesh on her forearms hangs in beautiful white lobes, not so different than the lobes of her breasts.

Why is it the novel can enter the private sphere in a way, for instance, that the essay cannot? One answer presents itself immediately. The novel is fiction. It is not true. It exists in an epistemological category unto itself. Yes, it is lifelike, it evokes or even, as is said metaphorically, creates realities; still the reality of fiction is not to be confused with *reality.*

I cannot remember whether or not my grandmother let me have those shoes. Despite her somberness in my presence, a mouth habitually turned down, and her air of dutiful weariness at having to raise a child at her advanced age, she has another side. I am twenty-one years old when she pulls a black silk robe out of a closet where she has kept it for years and gives it to me.

• • •

In the public imagination the feminine world has the same flavor as a fictional world. It is present but not entirely real. Men enter the home in the evening, as darkness descends. They may eat there, play with the children, make love, confess certain feelings hidden during the day to their wives, sleep, dream, but all that fades away into near obscurity with the dawn when they must emerge again into the world of work.

Perhaps she did buy me those red shoes. I can see them now in my closet which was also her second closet, the closet of the black silk robe, the place where she kept her rarer treasures, her two fur coats, worn only on the more special occasions . . . and, am I embellishing here, her sweater with the rhinestones on it, or were they pearls? Whenever I wore those red shoes, which was as often as I could, they gave me a secret sustenance, the liberatory feeling of a rebellion conspired between my grandmother and me.

Secrets within the private life are like obscurities within an obscurity. Private life is *private,* walled off, unseen, unscrutinized. To write a history of the private life is a recent departure, an ingenuous idea, and has an erotic edge, not only because of the sexuality which is part of private life, but because in doing so one penetrates a contained world. The secret alcoholism or indiscretion or sexual abuse within a family history is, being an obscurity inside an essentially obscure world, seemingly less real than the rest of private life, and has even more the flavor of fiction. At the same time the novel, being fiction, is congruous with this world. It is formed to the contours of the way we hold the private life in our minds.

When I put the red shoes on it was not only on special occasions. I wore them even on ordinary days. They followed me into a child's world, one that no adult ever saw. If I took them off to play in the sand or the mud, they witnessed me from the sidelines and kept my secrets.

• • •

In fiction the whole life of the body, of sensuality, is opened to view. The form of the novel or the short story and even more of the poem allows the reader to enter imagined experience as if within a body. Pain, pleasure, color, taste, sound, smells are evoked. The literary devices of fiction are meant to admit this material world.

I wore them walking the twelve blocks I regularly walked to school. The shoes became so much a part of me that I forgot I was wearing them. I let my mind wander. I looked into the windows of the houses along the way and imagined the lives of the inhabitants.

In depicting the sensuality of the world and our bodily experience of it, fiction is also portraying the mind itself, which always thinks in a sensual context. Without the body, it is impossible to conceive of thought existing. Yet the central trope of our intellectual heritage is of a transcendent, disembodied mind. As the essay moved further away from meditation and reflection, further from what we call "confessions" and closer to science, with its claim of objectivity, it began more and more to resemble this celestially detached brain. At a fairly recent point in the history of the essay it became a radical act to use the pronoun "I."

Perhaps she did not buy me the red shoes. But even if that were true, the fact is she might have.

The idea of an entirely autonomous mind has a subtext, and that is the desire for unlimited freedom from natural limitations.

In the lay and ken of her soul, this was a possibility. As I imagine that she gave me the shoes, which perhaps she did, am I bringing part of her soul into being?

And yet limitations are a necessary predisposition for any existence, including the existence of something we suppose to be abstract and cerebral, like the essay. And when the essay is built on the purposeful "forgetting" of the body, these limitations paradoxically grow greater. The form of the essay circumscribes imagination. At its edges many other imagined possibilities are hovering.

Was this the reason for her attachment to the peach-colored bedspreads? They covered the single beds where she and my grandfather slept. They had a luxuriant feel, suggesting an erotic dimension that otherwise was absent in her house.

To speak of housework, or childbirth, or sexuality, or rape in the form of the essay represents, in each instance, a crumbling of the fortifications erected by a masculine world against the feminine world. But still, in each instance, the sensual reality of these phenomena are stripped away so that they may enter public discourse. And when these subjects are made into sciences, they gain a certain legitimacy. Though it is often marginal, as in Home Economics.

Or perhaps not entirely absent, but never more open, never so frank, as in those bedspreads. They were luminously sexual, the sort of bedcover Mae West might have had. Of course we never spoke of this quality. It could never be spoken, only suggested.

One might think that, because fiction brings one into a fully sensual world, the subject matter would be more rigidly policed. But this is not the case. The idea that fiction is untrue allows it a greater radius. I am thinking of Virginia Woolf's *Orlando*. At the time of its publication, it was her most popular novel. What she suggested about the malleability of gender was far more palatable in this form than in her essays, which treated the subject, by comparison, more conservatively.

. . .

The bedspreads were symbolic of many aspirations. She cosseted a desire to be socially elevated. In her mind we were finer than all our neighbors, though I, with the working-class language of my father, and my childish ignorance of manners, constantly endangered our superiority.

Just as the reader is protected by the supposition that fiction is not true, so too the author of fiction is shielded by this idea. Stories can be told that otherwise could not. But what is even more interesting is that, because fiction evokes particular social and natural worlds in their entirety, many possible stories exist inside the narrative world implicitly, without being explicitly described. They exist as possibilities or even likelihoods. A door to a barn is described. The narrator does not open that door. But it exists. And therefore the reader can imagine what is behind the door. The shape of circumstances in both *Jane Eyre* and *Wuthering Heights* suggest sexual abuse. One knows a racist political history has preceded *Their Eyes Were Watching God*.[1] Neither writer nor reader needs to have delineated these events. The experience is part of the reality that is conjured.

I was fascinated by my grandparents' bedroom. The family story was that they slept in a double bed until one day my grandmother woke to find my grandfather's hands around her neck. He was having a dream. I am certain the significance of the dream was never discussed. Only thereafter they slept in single beds. I can't remember when I heard that story. Now it is as if I've always known it.

But unless one knows the history of racism or the configurations of sexual abuse, one does not see them in the narrative. They are felt perhaps, sensed, but not delineated, unnamed.

In this bedroom, they lived as if in separate worlds. I liked to watch my grandmother at her dressing table, trying on her earrings, her perfumes; I

---

[1] An extraordinary novel by the African-American writer Zora Neale Hurston.

felt privileged to catch a glimpse of her fleshy body, her long pendulous
breasts emerging from her corset. I preferred to look at my grandfather's
desk when he was absent. What I loved best was his collection of fountain
pens.

Reading a book about the documentation of torture in Brazil, I
come across this distinction made by Thomas Nagel: ". . . the
difference between knowledge and acknowledgment." He defines
"acknowledgment" as "what happens to knowledge . . . when
it becomes officially sanctioned, when it is made part of the public
cognitive scene." The essay is a forum for the "public cognitive
scene."

One evening when my grandparents went out and I was alone in the house
I was pulled as if by a magnet to my grandfather's desk. I wanted to write
with his fountain pen, which he never let me use in his presence. But the
ink was heavy in it. Many times I had seen him shake it down to the nib,
and so I did this, but not with the same experienced gesture. The ink sailed
across the room in a sure trajectory toward my grandmother's satin bed-
spreads. Both covers were evenly spattered.

The integration of knowledge into public consciousness is more
than a simple act of education. Perception itself in human consciousness is a social act. It is not only that knowledge and language are socially derived, but the moment of perception itself is
prismatic. A single viewer will react differently when part of an
audience. Certain responses are amplified. A small gesture made
on the stage, whose meaning otherwise might be ignored or even
forgotten, brings the whole theater to laughter. In the assembly of
others, perception becomes a demarcated event. And, as it is said
in the same book about torture in Brazil, the process of trans-
forming knowledge into public acknowledgment is also "sacra-
mental."

. . .

I tried to wash the spots out but only made them worse. I can feel the terror of discovery now. It is hot under my skin. I would have preferred the discovery to be private, between my grandmother and me. I was rarely physically punished. But she beat me this once, with a belt. My father and grandfather were in the next room, and I was angry at them, not because they failed to intervene but because they were witnesses at all.

Sitting in the public gardens that are close to my house, I hear a white-haired woman exclaim to her friend, "The color is so intense!" Their bent bodies are as if curled together around a rosebush. The gardens are tiered and shaped like an amphitheater and so her voice travels easily. It is an extraordinary moment. All at once I am pulled into her passion and the brightness of the roses, and I begin to think how closely twinned in human consciousness are experience and the expression of experience. Something happens, indefinable yet palpable, as all of us in the garden are pulled simultaneously toward the sound of this old woman's voice and the color of the rose.

What was it I did not want them to know? That I had committed a crime and been found out? Or that I had become abject, shamed by the pain itself of my punishment? I had been in such abject states before, when, through the neglect of my mother, I was cold, frightened, perhaps hungry. Afterward I would feel a profound embarrassment. Writing of his experience of torture, Jean Amery recalls that "one never ceases to be amazed that all those things one may . . . call his soul, or his mind, or his consciousness, or his identity are destroyed when there is that cracking and splintering in the shoulder joints." It is this that is humiliating and, as Amery writes, "The shame of destruction cannot be erased."

After a time I leave my bench and walk up the tiers of the amphitheater. I hope to catch a glimpse of these two women. In my imagination I have already given the speaker a rich mystical life. But they are gone.

•   •   •

*Such a memory is perhaps more easily recalled when it is only an abstrac-
tion of itself. One says, "I was tortured," or "I had a difficult childhood," without entering the experience in any concrete way, and thus also
without reliving the feeling of destruction. But sensuality and abstraction
are mutually dependent. In the mind, the capacities are inseparable.*

I had wanted to see the old woman's face. There was something in
the tone of her voice which led me to believe she had crossed that
barrier which we so often erect against what is seen. Did she fall
into the color of the rose?

*Fiction, as opposed to the essay, is often viewed as an escape from reality.
The storyteller can make up a world and has no moral reason to stay loyal
to this one. Shame and suffering can be left at the boundaries of this
imagined world.*

I imagined the color of the rose to be red. As I entered the garden
I saw a rose whose deep burgundy color drew me. This red is
replete with associations. Some of them wonderful. Some terrible.

*But any really good story includes both pain and pleasure, sorrow and joy,
in infinite complexities. And any imagined world, if it is to be believed,
will soon be replete with its own requirements, consequences, and limitations, just like this world.*

Falling into that color, was she not also falling into herself, as I fall
into myself now, my own memories of red, and my own redness?
For me this is still a color heavy with menses and childbirth, with
violence and loss. But in her voice I hear something different. All
that, yes, but an added dimension, a kind of lightness, an aspect of
this color that comes to one perhaps only in old age.

*The freedom that fiction affords is a freedom not from concrete limitations
but from the limitations on the mind imposed by ideas. This is a secret*

liberation, the same liberation given by direct experience. For the limits of physical reality are not the same, nor as distinct in experience as the limitations described in abstraction. As John Berger writes in his long work on the peasants of Alpine France, those who live on the land "never suppose that the advance of knowledge reduces the extent of the unknown."

It is easy for me to imagine beginning to perceive another dimension of color in old age. Imagining this, I am pulled toward a future I have never until now predicted.

The extent of the unknown borders all language. One's relationship with it is erotic. One has a passion to know. But one can never entirely know what is other. Telling a story, no matter how much you know, you are very soon pulled into unexplored territory. Even the familiar is filled with unexpected blank spaces. The usual Sunday drive is all of a sudden a wild ride into terra incognita. You are glad to be going, but there is a vague feeling of discomfort. Where are you?

This is not a dimension of color acknowledged in our culture. Still, it exists within the culture. It has been painted. I am thinking of the work of Helen Frankenthaler. Color as she paints it takes a different place in the mind. Or rather one might say the mind takes place in the color. One is infused with it, the same way one is taken in by water, swallowed.

I am thinking of a Sunday drive with my grandparents. We went to the country place of friends. They had an orchard filled with peach trees. I have remembered it all of my life. The vividness of the peaches I pulled from the trees. The sharply sweet taste in my mouth, nothing like store-bought fruit.

Is this experience of color had by some in old age, and others who are artists, a return to an earlier state of mind, the beginner's mind of infancy? To a perception untutored, not yet muted by the mediating presence of language?

Now as I remember that peach, it is a taste indistinguishable from the shapes of trees, the tall grass surrounding them, the summer heat, the breeze blowing, the sight of my grandmother in a white blouse standing on the ladder. And was there a kitten, or am I confusing the memory of my great-grandmother's garden, and her kitten, with this one?

There are of course two experiences of the red color of that rose. One is acknowledged. It is the social red, the historical red, the red, as Merleau Ponty writes, "that is a punctuation in the field of red things." The other red is unacknowledged, it exists in an exiled region of consciousness. But can they be separated, these two reds? And what of the tension one feels between experience and the forms experience assumes in the imagination? One feels it while writing. The words are not quite right. They betray. Lie a little. Fail to make a perfect fit. Take off in another direction entirely on their own.

Of course I am embellishing. I doubt that my grandmother wore white. It is the color one is supposed to wear if one is a woman in a pastoral setting.

In recent critical discourse, the awareness that in the mind experience is replaced by a construction of experience has led to a despair of the possibility of describing reality. But in the sway of this despair, how do you point out a lie? How do you answer the contention that torture in Brazil never took place?

That day in the country I breathed in a certain state of mind. One that I never had before with such force. Later, when I encountered the same mood in certain paintings, certain myths, I mixed not only my memory but also my hope with these images.

. . .

I love that moment in writing when I know that language falls short. There is something more there. A larger body. Even by the failure of words I begin to detect its dimensions. As I work the prose, shift the verbs, look for new adjectives, a different rhythm, syntax, something new begins to come to the surface.

Looking back, I see a maze of associations I must have had with the color red. I know my mother also loved the color red. That she would have bought me those shoes unhesitatingly. That she wore bright red lipstick. That she used red henna on her dark brown hair. But I cannot remember if I thought of her that day I chose red shoes.

The manner of telling lies in public life is seldom direct any longer. Far more pervasive is the habit of ignoring an event of great significance. No official need argue that torture never existed. The torture is just never mentioned. No one goes to trial. No torturer is ever named. A general, vague reference is made to troubling events of the past which must be changed. The actuality of the torture begins to fade from public consciousness.

She had faded away from my life. I could not remember her at all as my mother, but only as a woman I would visit, and whom I liked. Liked her in a way unaccountable even to myself.

Among those who were tortured or those who lost a loved one to torture there are two reactions. Some wish to evade the memory at all costs. Even though the memory is always there in some form, the pain of recall is too excruciating. Others live to tell the truth, or hear it told, and never tire of the telling. Of course, this is also too simple. For most of us, who have not been tortured, but experienced lesser pains and fears, the two impulses, to remember and tell, or to deny and forget, are side by side, and mixed together.

· · ·

She was not easy to remember. It was not only neglect but abuse I suffered from her, a nastiness when she drank that came from her, as if from a demon, and which she herself would forget the next day.

I underline this passage in a recent issue of the *Paris Review,* in which Nathalie Sarraute is being interviewed. ". . . it seemed impossible to me," she said, "to write in the traditional forms. They seemed to have no access to what we experienced."

It seems possible to me then that even as a child I would be drawn to the color red, and yet also welcome my grandmother's common interdiction. It is certainly not a practical color. It won't get you anywhere.

Form can be transgressed for transgression's sake, but it can also be transgressed in an attempt to lean in a certain direction. It is a tropism toward the light and heat of another knowledge. And is this knowledge a memory?

Even so I cannot forget my desire to wear red. Even if my grandmother failed to buy me those shoes, years later as an adult woman I make up another story. I investigate the possibility that she did buy them. This is not an escape from my desire. It is instead an instigator of grief. I learn more fully what it is I have lost.

What we would wish to remember and what we might wish to forget are so intricately woven. Would we perhaps like to forget the life of the body, of the inner self, the private world, the world of children and childhood, of sucking and orgasm and death? This world which is a privacy within a privacy, protected by the double walls of house and skin, the conventional forms of expression and silence.

It is not the inner place of red I am seeking but the right to wear it outwardly. To wear it brazenly. Like a sequined dress. Or a scarlet letter.

• • •

There is then a hypnotic movement of the mind. We are used to it. We move back and forth from fiction to essay. From private to public. The arc of the pendulum has put us to sleep. But when the two poles meet, and the swaying stops, someone in us awakens.

It is one thing to love the color red and quite another to wear it openly. For my mother, wearing red was an act of defiance, a flag of another kind. Despite everything, she has won some territory for me, her daughter. I am like the daughter of Madame Bovary. The daughter of the fallen woman.

Bringing the public world of the essay and the inner world of fiction together, is something sacrificed? The high ground? Perspective? Distance? Or is it instead a posture of detachment that is renounced, a position of superiority? The position of one who is not immersed, who is unaffected, untouched? (This is, of course, the ultimate "fiction.")

And she, my mother, was the daughter of a respectable woman. But that is not the whole story. My grandmother had her own rebellion. She was a club woman. In the organization that was defined as auxiliary to my grandfather's club, she was made president. The proceedings of the club were secret. It was a secret realm of power, a fictional world, closed off from that other world described as real life.

But there is always the other side of the coin. Behind the "superior" stance of the essay a quality of fragility is concealed. Theory pales when faced with the complex world of experience. Almost as soon as any idea reaches the page, another argument comes to mind. And while it is true that in the realm of ideas one can diminish the reality of everything outside these ideas, this is at best a temporary diminishment and one that always rebounds upon the self. For ultimately this diminishment requires a lessening of one's own knowledge, one's perceptual experience and, even, existence.

• • •

It was to these clubs that my grandmother wore her best finery. Treasures sequestered from her closet, the closet of the fur coats and the black silk robe, which was also my closet.

On the other hand, the realm of experience longs for more than knowledge. What goes on in the private body, in the inner quarters of the mind, cannot fully be redeemed, or even understood, without public acknowledgment. I am thinking of the tears of the victim who has finally heard her assailant convicted. In this case, paradoxically, it is not an imprisonment which takes place so much as a liberation from the imprisonment of an enforced privacy.

On the nights when the family could attend dinners or occasions given by my grandmother's club we were given little party favors and corsages. These had been made by the women in their secret sessions together. They contained bits of plastic fruit, sprays of pine, sparkles, all tied together with a bit of ribbon, most often red.

Is it possible to write in a form that is both immersed and distant, farseeing and swallowed? I am thinking now that this is what women have been attempting in the last decades. Not simply to enter the world of masculine discourse but to transform it with another kind of knowledge.

My grandmother has been dead for nearly two decades, and now my mother, who is old herself, has become respectable. Yet it is an astonishing moment for me, now, to recall these two women, and myself as a child, my red shoes, my mother's rebellion, my grandmother's secret wardrobe, the inner meanings of these, and the threads of meaning that reach out like tendrils in the larger landscape of mind.

If I rise from my desk, leave my pen and paper behind, walk to the door, the play of life before me and inside is suddenly dazzling in its intensity. Is it because I am thinking about consciousness that suddenly my experience sharpens? And when I return to write will I be able to reshape the form so that more of this world falls on the page? One can spend a whole life writing, I think to myself, and still hardly begin.

Where No One Dwells

At seven years old am I too young for literary images or just lacking a common mythos that might make my existence on the planet less lonely?

When I think of the highway that runs up the middle of the state from south to north, the feeling is harsh. Something has been stripped away, shorn, and the land like a lamb left shivering.

At least twice a year since my parents' divorce I travel this highway with my grandparents or my father. I live in the South with my mother's mother and father. My sister lives in the North with our great-aunt, our maternal grandmother's sister. That is why we travel this road. Up the San Joaquin Valley, hot and dry, then moist farther north, in the summers brown fields, cotton in the fall, near Thanksgiving. To bring us together again.

The landscape tells a history I know little of—farmland, few houses. Occasional Orange Julius by the side of the highway. Then that solitary farmhouse stark against leveled fields. The flatness of the land rolling as if endlessly. Then an uneventful town, squat new buildings, miniature Los Angeles, wide intersections suggesting continual passage.

. . .

Year after year the farmhouses will look more neglected. Relics replaced by the monolithic plains of agribusiness, where no one dwells.

All my life I will have a map of the state of California in my mind forged by these journeys as regular as the seasons. The topography of this state where I was born feels as if part of my body. As I write the Pacific Ocean swells out from the left side of my body. To my right I can feel the presence of the Sierra Nevada range.

It is in these mountains that my sister and I spend a month every summer. Our family knows little of our life there. It is a life apart, and that is the virtue. That pain and trouble passed through so many generations has been left behind. Sitting on a flatbed truck moving toward the mountains, I wait for the sight of red soil, the smell of pine that will wash me clean of the family mood.

At home in the late afternoon, I sit watching Westerns on the gray television screen. Images of cowboys on horses unattached to anyone, even the land. Hollywood Indians, with feathered head-dresses and war whoops, but no villages to return to, Davy Crockett in his beaver hat, Kit Carson, all his belongings on him, free as the wind.

I have not yet read Thoreau, thought of that solitary life at Walden Pond. But a place has already been made in my imagination for that place to exist.

I do not like the maps in school we are encouraged to paint. Murals of the United States with tiny pictures of apples, wheat bales, gold mines indicated by pickaxes, all the "resources."

One of my old schoolbooks, however, captures my imagination. It is the story of an Indian child. It shows villages. The child learns the skills of the elders. How to live in the forest. This is the only image I can recall of a life *in* nature lived in community.

What does that mean, "in nature"? I cannot say now. But in my child's mind it is a clear demarcation: the difference between Los Angeles in the 1950s, the orchard in the San Fernando Valley, that farmhouse and field, disappeared by the time I am eleven years old, and the landscape of Indian life shown in my schoolbook.

Where did it come from, this loneliness one breathes in the atmosphere of my family? And it is there beyond the threshold too. On the streets where neighbors scarcely know each other. Inside the bigger buildings where they do. It is an American tradition. Everyone moving. From the East to the West, home-steaders, living apart on their land, because the laws of home-steading require it. Yet the image is right. My grandparents have moved from their small farming town in Illinois to California.

Was it the odor of constriction one finds in the South and the Middle West, narrow-mindedness, prudery? The urge to move out in ever widening circles is powerful. H.D., Ezra Pound, Hem-ingway, Kay Boyle, leave for Paris, Spain, Italy. Paul and Jane Bowles off to Tangiers. And later, James Baldwin. All my life my mother and I share a longing for Paris. I send her back postcards of this city she will never see.

But the move out began in Europe. French, German, Irish, Scotch, Welsh origins in my own history. I am thinking of that earlier journey. The imagination of Eden. Safe harbor from the tyrannies of Europe. Freedom.

And perhaps also a culture grown weary of itself, reaching in a certain sense a dead end. The metaphors gone stale.

•   •   •

America as wildland, nature uncorrupted by society. At the heart of American literature, *The Deerslayer* choosing solitude and the woods over society.

A sense of freshness in the language. Walt Whitman declaring "a greater age to celebrate, greater ideas to embody, than anything ever in Greece or Rome . . ." In America, he writes, the mythic names should commemorate "things belonging to America and dating thence. . . ." The task, he says, to destroy the old and erect a "new earth" in its place.

But the new from a different perspective is also the old. I picture Europe extending out over space, searching for a site of renewal, Ponce de Leon's spring of eternal youth. The encounter in time is paradoxical. Journeying halfway around the globe, explorers meet the past, what the forest looked like before destruction. And older cultures. Lineages stretching back thousands of years, a more ancient way of life.

Of the proper names Whitman suggests should be used in the new American language, one is *Niagara,* word from the language of the Iroquois nation.

All the Indian words for plants, trees, animals, mountains, valleys. Then later Spanish words, words I grew up hearing in California. And then the Latin words, identifying species, the words by which we locate reality in European civilization.

Latin the language of church and science. Which before was the language of the state. *E Pluribus Unum.* Language of the Roman Empire. The Conquerors.

Did the explorer glean even a hint of a forgotten self from his first encounter with these peoples he called "savage"?

· · ·

Evidence throughout Europe of pre-Roman cultures conceiving human existence as part of rather than apart from nature.

Once separated from nature one must act upon nature, affect, possess this other.

A grammar inherited from Latin requiring a subject and a verb. An action. And preferably an object acted upon for the sentence to be whole.

Exploration of the New World coinciding with the witch burnings. In the century of Columbus's voyages, the official church position shifts. The acts of witches, once called illusion and fantasy, are declared by the *Canoni Episcopi* to be real.

Cotton Mather. Child prodigy. Enters Harvard at age twelve. Becomes minister of North Church in Boston at age twenty-five. Continuing his father Increase's argument against godless rationalism, he believes that to show the existence of God one must prove the existence of a Devil and witchcraft.

God as one end of a polarity. Dependent in some strange way on His opposite.

At the other end of this polarity, the Devil, who meets with old women in the forest.

The geography of *The Scarlet Letter*. The dark woods of Massachusetts. Place of adultery. Witches. The town square, center of the community, place of judgment.

•   •   •

All the secrets in the novel provide the structure, even the *raison d'être* of the work. Paradoxically, the secret is the mode of revelation to the reader.[1]

Art as the means of protest, but also as the mediator between the secret (life in the woods) and society.

The old theme of the return, the journey back home, to one's roots, or to a more natural self, whether found in the city or the country.

At the age of six I accompany my grandparents on a trip to the region where they were raised. I stay overnight on the family farm just outside Champaign-Urbana in the southern part of the state. Rich pastures. It is as if the land has curled up to embrace me. Everything is erotic. The intense yellow of the fields. The heavy heat and deep shadow under trees buzzing with insects. Fireflies at night. Dark sudden rain clouds. Early morning milk warm from the cow. Berries bleeding into my hands and then into my mouth as I pick them. Rough hair and sweat of the pony I ride bareback.

But this memory has no anchoring place. It floats without attachment in my mind. There are only two stories about this land I can recall my grandmother telling me. One I heard during our visit. She took me into the yard to a gravestone. These were her twin brother and sister, she said, who died very young. The other I heard more than once. About how she had taken a pledge at church never to drink. And kept the pledge even when she was ill with a fever and the doctor suggested whiskey.

Of course later, in Los Angeles, she put the pledge aside. Her life more sophisticated, which was what she wanted. But the atmo-

---

[1] Chloe Levy, "Outing the Novel: the Open Secret of Subversive Intent in Faulkner and Hawthorne." An unpublished paper.

sphere of that pledge remained in the corners of our lives. I could not be romantic about our rural past.

The story told over and over in many forms, the hero or heroine who must escape society in an attempt to save her, his soul. Madame Bovary. Huck Finn.

European culture imagining the mind as separate from nature.

Yet the contours of the mind resemble nature. (Thoughts flowing like water.) Knowledge and memory inextricably bound up with matter.

As I cut my grapefruit this morning I remember how my great-aunt taught me to section the fruit. Even forty years later I can see her sitting across the table. How we learn.

The mind with its own ecology inseparable from the body. *Remembrance of Things Past:* not just the taste of madeleine. But the turning of the body in bed.

The dependence of even the most abstract reasoning on nature. I cannot imagine mathematics without fingers. Digits.

Yet there is this too. Art as a counterpoint, a standard against which unruly nature is measured, controlled. My great-aunt believed herself all her life to be plain. The aesthetic of that time of her youth (*fin de siècle*) in which her beauty was not recognized. Her soft features, the lovely subtle color of her hair.

The imagination of the New World as an act of rebellion from an aesthetic so layered and ornate that experience itself was lost through that lens.

•　•　•

The American kinship with Buddhism. Emerson and the transcendentalist circle meeting Zen. The journey back becoming then a return to the fundamental, the direct, existence itself (the red wheelbarrow).

The Oversoul. But what about the Insoul?

Dickinson's poetry. Simplicity *in* the *form*. An attitude stripped of assumptions. Beginner's mind.

> *The largest Fire ever known*
> *Occurs each Afternoon . . .*

Her capital letters a half mockery of puritan sermonizing. So close to that usage, that sound. And yet, like a slant-rhyme, so different. The difference being one of direction. For Truth, do you look toward Heaven or Earth?

The underside of the City on the Hill. Rage against sensuality, the body. Perhaps this control is comforting companionship when confronted with what we call wilderness.

The wilderness of course being in the mind.

My memory of being an artist's model. One student was looking with great intensity and drawing with an almost abandoned ferocity. During the break I go to see his work. It is a scribble. Not abstract. Nothing. Just a monotony of nearly angry pencil marks. Somehow I conflate this memory with another event that happened in this same period. The woman who lived next door, and had had a series of violent lovers, was found murdered a month after I moved, and the principal suspect was an art student.

America a country of extremes. European culture at the apex of scientific development. A technological Camelot. President Bush flying down to Rio to reiterate his refusal to sign the accord which would protect animal species and plant life. The imagination of human beings as outside the circle. Therefore American industry need not be limited.

And at the other end of the pole, Robinson Jeffers. Harshly condemning humankind. The cragginess of his mood resembling the steep Californian coastline. That strange notion of freedom in America. Not the freedom of *The Federalist* papers, or the Constitution. A social contract hammered out from years of trials, agreement, practice. But another kind of freedom, beyond time and space. Rejecting any limit. Any necessity. Jesse James. Outlaw.

The hero in *An American Tragedy* who murders his pregnant lover because he does not want to be tied down. He wants to rise.

Hawthorne hinting at another way of thinking of one's existence, as he writes of Pearl, the "illegitimate" daughter of Hester Prynne:

> God, as a direct consequence of the sin which man thus punished, had given her a lovely child . . . to connect her parents forever with the race and descent of mortals. . . .

The feeling in my family of restlessness. Everyone wishing to be someplace else. The journey endless.

Another imagination, way of living, on the edges of Salem. Older culture, a people for whom community and nature are not on separate poles. So that the fabric of the forest is the same as the fabric of the family, and of the village, the nation.

· · ·

I am reminded of the influence on the American Constitution of the Iroquois nation.[2]

Now though the knowledge was given freely, that history reads like a kind of theft. The land was stolen. And the gift of democratic tradition never recognized. Is this why in our minds we have been forced to chase an ever ineluctable freedom, not knowing, never comprehending?

At seven years old I am not without the imagery of my culture. Blondie and Dagwood. Dick Tracy. I have a toy six-shooter that fits in a black holster. My grandfather drives the car. I am bored. The land outside has become one great brown unrelieved field again. I have played all the games my grandmother has brought for me. Connected all the dots. Discovered all the figures hidden in the drawings. The silence in the car is old. It goes back many generations. I am not the only one who finds the air too stale. We are all uncomfortable.

The artist as the poor cousin of the medicine woman/man. Forging a link between one world and another, one generation and the next. Embedded in that continuity between nature and art, which European culture has tried to sever.

Memory, loss, requiem; record of endangered culture, imagination of what it is possible to retrieve in the work of Leslie Marmon Silko, Joy Harjo, Michelle Cliff, Alice Walker, Jamaica Kincaid, Ursula Le Guin, John Berger, Buchi Emecheta, Chinua Achebe, Cherie Moraja, and many others.

The land we long to possess but cannot though it is as if part of our own bodies.

---

[2] See Jerry Mander, *In the Absence of the Sacred* (San Francisco: Sierra Club Books, 1991), on the role of the Great Binding Law of Iroquois Confederacy as a model for the Articles of Confederation and the Constitution.

. . .

For to reach it we must walk through the history which has permeated the soil.

Back, and to the south, below me, behind me, the time and place of my childhood. That land drenched with those sorrows.

But there also, burying ground of my father, my grandparents, geography of my soul, which partakes, through the story, of everything.

Inside the Door

Oftentimes, beginning a new work, I feel imprisoned within myself. I am not supposed to say this or that. I am expected to write about such and such. Political expectations, expectations of style or character. And these are suffocating. But the line of the poem makes its way to consciousness despite this suffocation. Usually I hear the first line spoken in my mind. And the language strikes me. I am not taken with the analytical meaning. Rather, its appeal is more direct.

These lines occurred to me this morning:

> *I do not like*
> *the star*
> *put on my hand*
> *last night.*

At a concert last night, a star was stamped on my hand, as a sign of admission, and I do not like it. Very simple, and literal. But in the poem, more than literal. This is what one means when one says the language of poetry resonates. It leads somewhere. And not somewhere obvious.

For example, if I were to continue the poem with an obvious intent such as:

> *A tattoo*
> *reminding me of*

motorcycles and
violence

lines which are also literally true, the poem would begin to fall flat for me. Maybe it's true that the star looks like a Hell's Angel tattoo to me. But I feel disappointed with this outcome. "So what?" I say. This is nothing new. And I would either do away with these lines or abandon the poem altogether.

I often discover such a pattern in a student's work, three or four stunning lines, and then three or four very dead lines. It is as if the student had awakened from a dream prematurely and, quickly, before the images could exist, explained the dream away.

I like to dream, and I remember dreams. Like a series of poems, my dreams often have recurring images, and even a continuous narrative. Many times I have dreamed of a green place—a forest, wood, or park—and always, when I dream this place, I experience the same very deep feeling (for which even now I have no word). And just as I will write several poems about one theme, so too I dream thematically. All this month I have been dreaming about death, and my fear of dying.

What is it that makes poetry different than prose? It is said that poetry has rhyme, and rhythm, and line breaks, that it uses metaphor. But these distinctions have never seemed sufficient to me. They seem instead only to be symptomatic of a deeper-lying purpose. It is said that prose is rational and poetry is not. And yet, on one level, poetry is quite rational. The poem may seem irrational because, like a dream, it ignores the boundaries we accept as real. In a dream I can be several people at once—myself, my father, a child, a woman pregnant. And this is also true in a poem. In the poem one can have the direct experience of being in two places at once, feeling two opposite emotions, holding two contradictory opinions, at once. And of course, one *can*. This is the real nature of the mind. Poetry is closer to that nature than prose.

I love what is called "naive" painting, painting in which the artist does not know about, or does not care about, perspective.

In my kitchen I have a small water color by a woman in her nineties which depicts the kitchen of her childhood in Russia. The little girl, who is herself, floats next to the ground. Her hand is on a dreidel that is half the size of a chicken standing next to her. This chicken is almost as large as the child's mother, who holds out a plate of cookies to an identical, indeed, the same little girl who now stands next to her mother. She is very small in this second version. Near the hearth a goat floats in midair. Two men playing checkers and a third who reads the Talmud are all the same size as the little girl with her enormous dreidel. One might say the painter was mistaken about size and gravity, about time and space. But really she was not. She was precisely accurate about the size of things as she experienced them.

I do not think the painter decided beforehand to make the dreidel big because the little girl was preoccupied with it. I do not believe she premeditated at all. Instead she allowed herself to discover what the world looked like to her as a child. Robert Duncan has said about the poetry of H.D. that she was following image from image, word from word. I like to move this way through a poem, without premeditation.

I began "The Perfect Mother" when, driving home one day, the line came to me, "The perfect mother lets the cat sleep on her head." For some reason these words were a great relief to me. I had been worrying all season about my daughter and my mothering of her. These words made me laugh. They filled me with a kind of glee. And the line seemed crazy. Not really sane at all. So I kept on in that direction. Driving the car, I kept following this madcap feeling, tracing it like a nerve into the interior of a muscle.

In this way I came across buried memories of scenes from *McCall's* and the *Ladies' Home Journal,* my grandmother's magazines which I read as a child, pictures of emotionally balanced, ideal mothers in sunny remodeled kitchens giving Dixie Cups of juice to their healthy children. This was an archetypal kitchen, one I have never really inhabited. And at the same time I came across cartoon images of tortured cats.

What can one say about this poem? That it is a protest against the *Ladies' Home Journal* idea of motherhood? For some reason this prose statement offered as an "explanation" of my poem sets my teeth on edge. Makes me feel like that tortured cat, hair straight up. I agree with the new idea in criticism that there are many possible readings of one work, but even this begs the question.

I am saying of course that one cannot paraphrase a poem, or even a line of a poem, and in the same way, one cannot paraphrase an image. No symbol can really be made equivalent to another unit of meaning because it *is* the meaning.

For example, I am facing an aesthetic problem with the writing of a play (in poetry) about my childhood. I want certain configurations in the play to be subtle. But in the first version, I wrote them so subtly that they simply were not apparent at all. I could have decided to make these configurations a little less subtle. But another aesthetic possibility came to me. I suddenly saw an image of red ink sinking into the page with such intensity that it blurred the letters.

Now if you say, "Oh, of course you want to say those things in your play intensely," I would tell you that you missed the point. It is not intensity, I would say, it is letters blurred by red ink that I want.

One can describe a painting accurately, listing shapes, dimensions, and colors, but what one finds on the page finally is not a painting but an experience in and of *language*. The description does not equal (=) the thing. Poetry does not describe. It *is* the thing. It is an experience, not the secondhand record of an experience, but the experience itself.

And we forget that language *is* an experience.

The highwayman came riding, riding, riding.

My grandmother used to read me that poem when I was a child, and she read it to my mother too, when she was young. *Riding, riding, riding.* This is not a line about a robber who rides a horse; it is: *The highwayman came riding, riding, riding.*

Language is not only a way to speak with others; it is also an experience of oneself. I am going through a period of dissatisfaction with all that I have written except for my most recent work. Therefore it is particularly hard for me to write this essay. Or to write prose at all. Because I am changing. There is a movement, motion, emotion, which I don't yet understand. Prose would force me to "understand" in a language at a remove from the experience itself and hence untrustworthy. But poetry speaks directly. It gives me this motion in language. Through the poetic line I actually feel what I feel more intensely, and it is this that gives me knowledge of myself. My experience is not described or explained by language; it *is* language.

The healing power of speech . . . This is a particularly crucial question for women because circumstance has forced us to live inside a language which is false, and which therefore gives us a false experience of ourselves. To speak falsely, even with a false cadence, is to betray oneself. One aims for the language that resonates at exactly the same pitch that one feels. Perhaps whatever is said in this pitch is right.

The series of poems called "Our Mother" came to me, one after another, as I began to feel a certain way, at first mutely, and then, *in* language. For a long time I wanted to write poems addressed to a female God. (For some reason I do not like the term "Goddess.") I wrote some poems that had a thin, sickly feel. The voice was not convincing. I wanted an image of God as female, but I did not have such an image. The question is not, of course, whether there is or is not a God, or whether this God is male or female. Because, like it or not, I had an image of God in my mind and that image was male. All my conscious arguments could not change that image.

Then, in the late spring of this year, the voice of "Our

Mother'' came to me. It was not in the way that I expected. I was
not in a sanctuary or in any sacred place. I was not partaking of a
ceremony; I was not meditating or thinking seriously alone in my
study. I was in a hotel! It is true that I felt very good in this hotel,
an old walled house in the French countryside, favored by artists
who paid their bills with paintings and sculpture, the rooms filled
with the kind of furniture families handed down over generations,
worn with use. Wonderful food on pink and white tablecloths. I
had a sense of well-being here that women rarely feel because it is
usually we who create beneficent worlds, seeing that the tablecloths are ironed, the vegetables fresh.

This hotel bore the mark of a woman's hand too. But this was
not the familiar figure of the submissive or martyred, essentially
powerless wife and mother. Madame sat at the gate, sizing us up
as we walked in and out. One felt in her eyes that truth, for good
or bad, was mirrored. Here was no sentimental mother. She was
tough. Honest. We were required to bring a certain intelligence
to the way we lived in her eyes. To honor the food we ate with a
proper attitude toward the labors of growing and cooking. I began
to feel I wanted to entrust the world to this sensibility.

And then there were two events which occurred one after the
other. First, Kim and I took a walk through the country to the
next village. On the way we encountered one barking dog after
another, and I still have a child's fear of dogs. Because of these
dogs, I felt I would not be able to go back the way we had come.
But before we could reach the road a very nasty dog chased us
back down our path. I felt trapped, with no possible solution, and
so frightened and desolate was I that I burst into tears. But then,
as if from nowhere a French farm woman appeared, looking into
our faces with her own very kind face. Speaking slowly to us in
French we could understand, she said that she too was afraid of
the dog. She said she wanted so much to give us something, but
had nothing. Then she took us to the building where she stored
her lettuce and gave us cold water. She showed us a path through
her own farm by which we could reach the road. At the end of

this path, growing on the land guarded by the nasty dog, but out of the dog's reach, was a cherry tree, its branches full of fruit. All day we had walked past cherry trees wanting this fruit, and now we ate.

When we reached the next village, the newspapers on the street all announced the suicide of Romy Schneider. And I remember thinking, If only she had waited a few moments more . . .

Both Kim and I felt convinced that day that the universe is benevolent. But these poems are not an argument for a benevolent universe or for a female God. Rationally, even irrationally, I have in my mind many arguments against the existence of any God, or of a merciful universe. I worry that such belief may in fact serve to justify human indifference to human suffering. These poems are not part of that philosophical dialogue. They are instead an actual experience in language. I *did* hear this voice.

A friend telephones. She is losing her apartment, leaving her lover of many years, finishing her book. And she wonders why she has been weeping. Well, we joke, just a few details. "Now you have to get back to the serious things," I say, "like who does the shopping."

And we laugh again because everyone knows that who does the shopping is just a detail, and all that loss is the serious thing. But is this really so? For loss is experienced through detail, when, for instance, one shops alone if before one shopped for the night's food with a lover.

Thus, the presence of "Our Mother" came to me through many details, a pot of tea, a box of tissue, barking dogs, an unnecessary death, a woman sitting reading the newspaper. These details were my experience. They did not stand for it. They *were* it. And so was the voice of the poem "Our Mother."

Language is a state of being. It is real. But not in the way we are used to thinking of "reality." One acts on the world. Builds a road through a certain landscape. Prunes a tree in the backyard. And then one sees evidence of having acted. A road exists. A tree exists. But, having made a line of poetry which includes a tree or a landscape, one has put the tree and the land inside oneself. And at the same time one has stepped outside oneself to be with the tree and the road, or even to *be* the tree, in language.

What does it mean to change consciousness? Not just that one changes one's mind about this or that opinion. Rather, when consciousness alters, one exists in a different universe, differently charged, colored, felt. And can consciousness be separated from word or image, from the symbol?

I am not just saying that reality is subjective. No, because reality is not entirely subjective at all. We may at different times all have a different experience of reality. And yet the question of consciousness is not that simple. Among the utterances and pictures of others, one can recognize some images or words from one's own experience, and then there are those that one does not recognize. But it often happens that, years after I have read a line of a poem I did not understand, I will suddenly remember that line and say to myself, Oh, *this* is what it meant. States of consciousness exist within us and some we have entered and some not. But I have never experienced a state of consciousness within myself that was not shared somewhere by someone. And I am beginning to realize that when I encounter what is strange to me I am merely seeing the evidence for an unknown region of my own soul.

Walking daily in the mountains of Corfu, I pass the village idiot. He rests in a dark doorway; inside there is nothing but rags and old, unused machinery. He is covered with soot and filth. I don't want him near me. I don't want him to touch me. Although he is fed and allowed to stay, the villagers sit apart from him. In the next village, a mile away, a retarded boy is kindly accepted, included. But what is *this* man's history? Why is he kept apart? Is he mad? Is he hated? The next day, still afraid, I find myself entering his room in my imagination, thinking, How can such a life be endured? And at the same time I feel a murderous rage at him, because of his misery.

Now here, halfway around the world and months later, I can see him, his eyes, his face, his strange and awful smile.

And now at this point in my narrative I remember another vision I had last week. Standing before the sight of many different kinds of vegetables for sale in a market I frequent, I suddenly felt these different vegetables held the secret of life for me. And I laughed. Were there always eggplants? Didn't this particular species, which seems so right, so inevitable, which *is* so right, appear one day out of something else that may be gone now?

> *Inside that doorway is terror.*
> *I don't want him near me.*
> *I don't want him to touch me.*
> *The man who lives there.*

The play I've been writing is written in a child's language. And now I want to say everything in this language. Because this language is taking me someplace that I know exists, someplace I need to be.

And our friend Naomi Newman writes that she wants to get into the other rooms of her house, the rooms she always dreams. Lines leading somewhere. Outside expectation. Just that.

The Uncharted Body

The body. What body? The uncharted body.

The unexplored body.

And how can one describe what is unexplored?

Language contoured according to the lines of a map in which this territory is missing.

The map creating the fiction that every possibility is drawn there.

The uncharted never mentioned.

And yet.

Yet it is there in the borderlines, in cipher.

A memory: I am nine years old. I am going to the circus. It is sometime in the fifties, a time of repression, dullness, near sleep-walking. These are the last days of the traveling tents. I am very excited to be going. I have read about it, heard about it all my young life. And what draws me the most, more even than the lions or the clowns or the flying trapeze, all of which I love, is the freak show.

People with three arms, two heads, limbs petrified to wood. The man who can bend pipes with his mind; the bearded lady.

That sense of thrill, of amazement, when considering what lies outside the predicted, the expected.

Under those tents, people flying through space, ten clowns emerging from a tiny car.

In the earliest years of the first circuses there were no public zoos. People had not seen circus animals before. Elephants, tigers, gorillas then were all marvels, new discoveries.

At the turn of the century the circus was the most popular form of entertainment in the small towns of America.

All those confining assumptions about the nature of female sexuality and gender, abundant in this period, entrenched in rural America.

The classic dream of the small-town girl or boy: to run away with the circus.

Huck Finn, Madame Bovary, the desire to escape from a stultifying atmosphere into a wider world.

A body outside the defined body. The larger realm one dares to imagine only in secret.

Arm of the anatomical drawing. Of "standard" proportions. Classical proportions. The arm of a man with white skin who is young. A soldier's arm. The arm of a woman, a certain class, a certain weight, height, color of skin, bearing, stance.

The arm of function. That lifts. Or commands. Or carries. Or cooks.

Is my arm when I extend it, hover, slide over the breasts of another woman, my lover, a lesbian arm?

The arm neat in its outlines. A straight line, sharp edge, undeviating as the wooden ruler I inherited from my grandfather, border of skin defining where I begin in space.

And then I shut my eyes. And I let the idea of an arm drift away. I begin to explore what I feel in that area of my body I call an arm.

Energy. Moving out in every direction. Elongated sphere of radiance. No clear line. A pulsing motion even in stillness. Arm.

The idea of a limb as a tool, an instrument, almost as if designed for a purpose. Plotted and graphed. Convenient, the physiological placement of hands.

The idea of the sexual body as an implement of reproduction.

Vagina existing, then, for the insertion of the penis. Uterus for childbearing. Breasts for milk.

Homosexuality, according to this utilitarian vision, a waste of energy. Counterproductive. The body not used as "intended" in the design.

The author of the design anonymous. A god. God.

And the actual sacred experience of the body. The awe that can be felt, entering the experience of the body, which, by contrast to the restrictions of utility, is infinite.

Strict categories of sexuality. The man. The woman. The heterosexual. Homosexual. Bisexual.

Do these categories really exist? (Like arms, like breasts?)

Another memory: I am fifteen years old. I am invited to a party. I bring a boy from my geometry class with me. I like the olive color of his skin. His black hair. His kind face. We quickly become friends in class; I help him to pass his tests by letting him see my answers. At the party I drink two or three glasses of wine. I am exhilarated, by the wine, the party, the other guests. A group of students on vacation from college have come, and they read us poetry from the Beat generation. This seems to me to be what I have been looking for, seeking. A door. An opening. My friend and I go to his car. He touches me below my belly and moves his hand downward. I love the feeling. I am happy. I have never been touched in this way before. It is an adventure. My body grows in size and starts to swirl about me. The utter largeness of sexual feeling. We return to the party. Drift apart, even then. The next day we see each other in geometry class. Still friends. But I did fall in love that night. She is one year older. Sixteen. The party was at her house. I do not call myself a lesbian. She never touches me on my breasts, below my belly. I never touch her.

By what category or name does one label one's feelings, the sensations in the body, mingled with ideas, memories, emotions?

The words used for definitions not like numbers but like natural objects, whales covered with barnacles, trees with moss, altered by context, surroundings, history.

Memory: I am sixteen. The girl I met becomes my best friend. We talk about the boys who are our lovers. Laugh. Weep in each other's arms. It is our way of making love to each other.

The construction of the question, If I do this, or think that, then am I really a lesbian?

The idea that many girls pass through a lesbian "stage." And this stage is not "real."

Her real life beginning when she is married. Which is when the story ends. Happily ever after.

The power of the word "lesbian" deriving from silence.

A phenomenon at the periphery of vision. Exogenous. Outside (yet also inside) oneself.

Memory: the implication in the words of a well-meaning adult that my friend and I were in some kind of danger. That our friendship was not healthy.

Charts on the wall representing three kinds of food one should have on one's plate in order to be healthy.

The power of the word "lesbian" deriving from speech.

The power of words which through delineation makes visible, and palpable, what has always been present. Present and yet unrealized. Nascent. Half born.

The real substance of any human life is experience itself.

But an experience which is unnamed and unrecognized is not only invisible, it is also truncated.

Human experience is so intricately woven with consciousness, with knowledge and self-knowledge.

Like any kind of organic life, an experience develops. Perhaps it begins as a wish, or as something imagined. A hunch. Or perhaps it begins with a touch and then proceeds to a wish, and an intimation of the future.

She touches me.

She touches my breast. Then I feel desire.

Memory: I am twenty-two. For the past several months I have

shared a bed with a friend. It began innocently, I would have said then. Though, looking back now, I see in myself the force of desire from almost the moment I met her. It must have been many times before that, turning in bed, she brushed against my breasts. But this time the possibility of intention occurred to me. And I wanted her with an intensity I could not ignore.

Ringed by an alliance of institutional and cultural prohibitions, silence or, rather, the muting of speech, it is a miracle every time the desire of one woman for another is pronounced.

Memory: after the first few times we made love, I look into the mirror to see a different face. As if I have returned to myself. I find a wholeness.

The history of the word "whole" meaning wholesome, meaning what has been described by authority as good.

The idea that someone is or is not "one of our kind," belonging to the whole, an exclusive "whole."

A prohibition against "unnatural acts."

A man's hand against a woman's vulva "natural."

A woman's hand against her lover's vulva "unnatural."

That common sentence spoken by so many women just after their first experience of making love with another woman, said with a tone of surprise, "But it felt so natural."

Nature like a ferocious beast kept under the tent, and behind bars.

To ask once again, What is sexuality? What do I feel? Where does my desire take me? To ask in a field of perception that has been opened.

This in itself would be an event. For in sexual experience perception is an activity. Perception of one's own feelings, of what transpires between two lovers, the meeting, the penetration, the knowledge.

Year after year approaching and retreating from freedom within myself. Certain states of mind and body entering me as if by grace, old presuppositions falling away, transmutations.

The ignorance of certain definitions. Thinking I knew the parameters of my body's capabilities, and then a door is nudged open, and a whole new world appears, for which there ought to be a new vocabulary, a new dictionary.

Moving beyond the old anatomical drawings, the old ideas of who we are. The wholeness which exists beyond what is charted.

The ideas of the masculine, the idea of the feminine. Barriers to knowledge. Boundaries beyond which lie uncharted lands.

Not only knowledge of the body but intimacy itself.

The first real intimacy with a lover found with another woman.

Not that intimacy is impossible between men and women. But that the roles men and women play truncate being and thus militate against a real meeting.

Lesbians, gay men as explorers. Opening up new worlds for a civilization grown tired of itself.

The avarice for the land of other people's being perhaps a misplaced longing for a wider range of being.

Violence an expression of imprisonment.

The shaman, the berdache, the poet, artist, heterodox, androgynous, lesbian, gay, slipping out of the prescribed role and, in this slippage, learning the secrets.

That secret knowledge.

Whispered. Dreamed. Glimpsed in a moment of waking.

The whole body. That mansion with many houses.

Where, nevertheless, we dwell all of our lives.

Note

I owe a great deal in my thinking for this piece to Emily Conrad Da'Oud and her work with movement, "Continuum."

Canaries in the Mine

It is early in the morning. Perhaps five o'clock. I don't want to sit up to see the clock. Any unnecessary move may mean I will never get back to sleep. For anyone with this illness, to lose sleep is disastrous. And yet insomnia is one of the symptoms. I am almost always awake at this hour. I fall back to sleep at six or seven. And in between I think. The wind is dashing the trees into the windows. Howling. Banging. Creating a great feeling of crisis. Clamor. Trouble. Like a character from *Wuthering Heights,* I feel comforted by this. The wind echoes my feelings, though I have learned to detach myself, to say, summoning up all my nerve, this is just biochemistry, this harrowing desperation, this is just the mood of the night.

To become interested in the physical states and the states of mind this illness creates has become one of my saving graces. Now I am remembering an old term of literary criticism I learned in school years ago. Or at least I remember the concept. It is an idea critical of the Romantics, suggesting that any resemblance between human emotions and natural phenomena such as the weather is misleading. The "raging" wind does not feel rage, so goes the argument. A few weeks later the words "sympathetic fallacy" return to my mind. Even on the days when I am at my best, there are things I can't remember. This is, I say with relief and trepidation, just a temporary forgetting. The word, name, or location of an object will eventually return. Just not when asked for, not by me, or anyone.

At this hour it feels more ominous to me that I cannot remember the term. It is not only that this puts me at a distinct disadvantage whenever there is any disagreement. Question: Where did you read that? Answer: I can't remember right now. Ask me in two weeks! No, it is the loss of texture that bothers me, texture that allows language to move beyond mere reference and enter experience.

And then of course I know immediately that I am grieving for a quite literal loss. Before this last most severe relapse, while sitting in a chair talking with a student, I realized that whole parts of myself were disappearing. At first I could no longer feel my hands and feet. They were muffled in a seminumbness, screened by an odd tingling. Then, over time, legs, arms, parts of my face, head, shoulders vanished, replaced by the sensation of needles which grew strong as the rest of me grew weak. I became conscious of the enormous effort I seemed to be making to keep myself from fading like a faint signal on a screen into oblivion.

One night in Germany after I finally collapsed I dream that I am put to bed in a room with a brick wall. I try to sleep. But the wall is crumbling. (The crumbling wall is an accurate symbol for my bodily state.) Just outside the wall a couple of menacing-looking young hoods of the skinhead variety are standing, listening to hard rock. I can't bear this music, especially now. It is as if I have no skin. Loud music, loud noises pass right into me. There is no protection. The illness affects the nervous system, at times causing a kind of stripping of the outer layer that protects the nerves.

In my dream, no one else seems to notice the crumbling wall. Certainly those around me know I am ill and treat me with kindness. But the inner state that this virus produces is nearly impossible for others to grasp. What a relief when a few of us among the afflicted gather. As each of us tries to bend language around and through this strange experience the look of recognition lights up the other faces in the room. We allude to the awful paradoxes, entrapments which could well fit into Dante's *Inferno* —a ceaselessly restless feeling accompanying exhaustion; a terrifying sense of isolation together with an intolerance for too much conversation, too many people, too much presence; the magnification of every event and yet at the same time that sensation of fading away, of existing somewhere between the worlds of life and death.

Five-thirty in the morning. Is it a sympathetic fallacy to imagine that I am experiencing the morbidity of biology itself, the end of the life cycle on earth, thrown into confusion, a matrix, in opposition to itself, disharmonized by all the strange phenomena that human beings have created: plutonium, carbon fuels, DDT?

A series of intense dreams began just before I left for Germany. Over time they grew more dramatic. One day my friend read a story to me from the German newspaper. Thousands of seals were dying in the North Sea, perhaps from an immune disorder. She showed me a photograph of their bodies stacked high on the beach. That night I dreamed I was on that beach, standing in front of the dead seals delivering an oration to the still healthy sunbathers who lay on the sand. "Don't you see," I plead with them, "if you don't act, this will be your future."

Now, at this early hour, I have the same feeling again. For me it is unique to this illness. Others with immune disorders have spoken of it. That the world is dying within one's own skin. That we are the canaries in the mine. Why this disease? Is it a kind of metaphorical layering, apocalyptic thinking, environmental disaster simply related by coincidence in my mind? No, there is more here, I am convinced. Not only in the many indications that the immune systems of, at least, mammals are under assault (the seals in the North Sea, the whales in the St. Lawrence Seaway, the dolphins of Santa Monica Bay, the koala bears of Australia) but also in the eerie experience of the illness itself. The slow disappearance of capacities, sensations, energy. The grief which seems to well up from the very material of cells. The feeling of having been poisoned, of toxicity, of which so many with the illness speak.

In my journal I begin a series of meditations on these various states of feeling, not ascribing symbolic value to them, but simply recording them, both physical and mental states—though often, since the illness affects brain chemistry, they cannot be separated. To lend these phenomena attention brings about a profound reconciliation with my body. Poised on the edge of survival, I have been forced to pay these symptoms respect. I have turned my gaze in this direction. I have entered the world of physical being.

Whatever state of irreconciliation or disrespect toward the body I had been in before was not mine alone. It is a habit born of a culture that denigrates all that is earthly or "mundane." The mind shaped thus does not value material existence for itself and prefers not to dwell there for too long. Out of a new respect for the material of my own existence, I do not immediately subject my body to analysis. Rather I allow the terrain to become familiar. I am like a peasant who has lived and worked on the same land for years and knows that there is a meaning here unto itself, and mysteries. When I begin to measure it is not with a ruler but with footsteps, and odors and chills, hungers and angles of light.

At the end of August, after reading John Berger's account of peasant life in France, *Pig Earth,* I write in my journal:

To be reduced to the mere tasks of survival, the conventional thinking goes, is a kind of degradation. Part and parcel of this thought is the mistaken idea that life's meaning transcends physical survival, and is not derived from it. But a peasant derives significance from the tasks themselves. (And our "holy days" come from these tasks—the harvest, the sowing.) . . . There are those who reject illness, preferring to continue as if bodily sensations and necessities did not exist.

Western medicine is tailored to such a predisposition, with interventions that fail to respect bodily processes. . . . I am interested in the consistency with which this culture rejects actual three dimensional material experience.

Submerged entirely in the body of oneself, the body of the earth, through intense suffering, or through the intense and unremitting intimacy with the stuff of life that comes from physical labor, one can grasp the immanent meaning. The connection is not abstract. This disease enters the brain, makes one sensitive to the least fluctuations in barometric pressure. My friend Jan experiences the Alaskan cold front as a seizure. One is aware then of how the wind howling outside this night is part of oneself.

Perhaps this is why denial can be so excruciating. If there is dignity in suffering and illness it is in the simple recognition that these exist. Yet the disease can be invisible. Up half the night with a sudden unexpected bout of pain, the next day, in a state of near exhaustion, I go out anyway. A passing acquaintance asks after me. "Better but still ill," I say. "Well, you *look* very good," she says. How I understand the impulse. To emphasize the best, to make words perform miracles of transformation—if I say it it must be so. But I am left isolated, oddly disconnected in this body on its weak legs, with its failing balance and the sudden blankness in my mind when I try to remember for two infinite minutes where I am and why.

Why should this console me: the howling wind and then silence, as if the planet were in a fluctuating state, looking so lovely in the near spring, pollution making an exquisite display at sunset over the bay, small deaths occurring at the edges, in peripheral vision, or out of sight? If only for this reason, that to know is a form of intimacy, *in sickness and in health;* and a conversation takes place, a call and response, and the earth speaks, and listens, within me.

The Internal Athlete

It is 1992 and I am watching the winter Olympics. As the first skiers in a cross-country event near the end of the course, the announcer speculates that their legs must be burning now, almost giving way beneath them. Then, while the first three cross the line, and each in turn falls, I watch with rapt attention as their heads turn into the snow, eyes shut, and except for a momentary gasping effort to take in air, their bodies lie still and limp. It is that human need to see whatever we have experienced depicted in some way outside ourselves. This image serves for me as a mirror of what I have suffered.

I can still remember the feeling. My whole body in pain, deep in muscle and bone. Legs too weak to hold me upright. What we call ''energy''—it seemed like life itself—so drained from me that even the simplest task, turning or sitting up in bed, became monumental.

I was not told (as others have been told about this condition) that I was not ill. I had had a life-threatening infection, and my doctors felt I was simply making a slow recovery. As new symptoms arose, new diagnoses accompanied them. Stomach ulcer, arthritis in the spine, a minor heart condition.

And then there were the symptoms accounted for by none of the diagnoses. (Some I could not even describe. As I learned long ago from Wittgenstein, what one has no language for is often not even perceived.) I had observed one symptom before, in a friend recovering from a concussion. As if the central switchboard of her brain were jammed, she could focus on only one event at a time. Suddenly I would be unable to decipher a passage from a book that would have come easily to me before. Waiting at a traffic signal, for an instant I could not remember whether the green light meant to stop or to go. Yet I needed to know that my nervous system was impaired before I could describe what was happening to me with any more clarity than the word "exhaustion."

When my doctor suggested I might have chronic fatigue immune dysfunction syndrome (CFIDS), I rejected the idea. I did not want to have a disease with no clear prognosis or cure. Months later, after an attack that had sent me to bed for weeks, I ran into a friend whose partner was very ill with CFIDS. As she questioned me about my symptoms, I began to suspect I might really have this disease. And then she told me how serious it can be. Her partner was in the hospital; she was having seizures, and had been in a coma.

I felt shock, then rage and depression, but finally a sense of relief to have a name and some recognition for what I felt. Yet this definition was double-edged as I began to understand I was facing another battle in addition to the one raging in my body: a battle I and countless other women had fought before. Like survivors of rape, sexual abuse, or harassment, women were again being told that what we suffered was trivial, or even unreal.

It began with the name "Yuppie Flu." Though I can count at least six women of color with CFIDS among my own friends, in the first articles the disease was described as striking mainly white professionals, predominantly middle-aged women. One can see how the idea must have evolved. To reach a diagnosis can often require travel from doctor to doctor and a battery of tests—which take money, entitlement, the leverage to fight an entrenched medical system. What followed from these skewed demographics was the suggestion that women who suffer from CFIDS are over-ambitious, stressed, neurotic. The fact that most women of every class are chronically overworked did not enter this picture. Instead, the tone of the analysis echoed certain earlier admonitions to women in the nineteenth century, that to seek a higher education would result in damage to the ovaries. Then there is the name itself, centering as it does on the word "fatigue," with connotations of a more gracious age, a leisured recovery, sunning on a chaise under a lap blanket. On hearing I had CFIDS, a casual acquaintance suggested that she too would welcome a rest, time to catch up on her reading. But, in the first months of my most severe attack, I could not read at all. Books were too heavy to hold. Moving my eyes across the page nauseated me. And far from being at leisure, I felt I was in the most titanic struggle of my life.

It was almost four years ago, in the midst of a conference in Germany, that I collapsed. Most of my body had gone into a state of partial numbness. I had a pins-and-needles tingling over my arms, legs, head, face. Moments of clarity alternated with minor blackouts of memory. I was weary, weak, nauseated, but somehow able to fake my way through the speeches and panels. By the next evening I was sagging, leaning on a friend's arm as we made our way to the adjacent hotel. Each step was a herculean effort. And when we found that the path through a garden was closed off by a locked gate, at the thought of redoubling my steps to walk one extra block to my room, I began to weep. My legs gave way underneath me.

For nearly two years I was forced to let go the mandates of my work, my life. At first I felt a kind of peace. I can give in now to the complaints of my body, I told myself, I can rest. But I was to get worse before I began an agonizingly slow recovery, moving by hardly detectable increments. And there was no rest. There were headaches as severe as the worst migraines; a constant heavy-headed feeling; vertigo; vomiting; heart palpitations; the cold that had migrated to the core of me so that nothing could make me warm; excruciating pain in my joints; parts of my body quivering involuntarily; and a biochemical depression so terrifying that one can understand why it is listed as the major cause of death from CFIDS.

What a triumph when, after two or three months, I was able to sit up and read a bit! I set myself the monumental goal of ten pages a day. It took me over a month to read the 106 pages of Gabriel García Márquez's *The Story of a Shipwrecked Sailor*. But what a joy, to read about someone else fighting for his life! The comradeship I felt with that sailor was a crucial respite from the continual loneliness that is a side effect of this syndrome. Aloneness is an existential state endemic to all illness. The ill experience intense feelings within the boundaries of skin and bone that the healthy do not. But with CFIDS this isolation is more alienating than usual. Broken bones, surgeries, even head colds are easier to see and understand than the suffering that comes from disorders of the immune and central nervous systems, which disturb every bodily function and even trouble the waters of consciousness.

Then there is the shattering isolation of those who are unpartnered, without a family. No social services exist to meet the needs. I was single when my first severe attack occurred, rendered unable to shop or prepare meals, balance my checkbook, earn money to pay my bills, or even think clearly about these problems. Friends came to my aid with loving and generous care. But there were the moments when, panicked and sobbing, I called out or even demanded help, times inevitably followed by a sense of shame. And fear—if I overburdened my friends, I would be left even more alone.

But, in a terrible way, no one who has CFIDS is truly alone. Sadly, we are all part of this global process, those who are ill, like canaries in a mine; our sickness a signal of the sickness of the planet. An epidemic of breast cancer, the rising rate of lupus, MS, a plethora of lesser-known new disorders of the immune system. Pollution. Radiation waste. The loss of the ozone layer. Acid rain. The diminishing of species. On the simplest, most practical level we are in this together.

I watch as the athletes rise from the snow. They have traveled not only over this wintry landscape but through the extreme internal territories of physical endurance and capacity. We stand on common ground. I too have explored the life of the body in a manner more precise and profound than usual. And as certainly as the skier must feel the subtle contours of the land as she skis, I know in every cell that the life of my body is connected to the life of this earth.

Steadily my health has improved. But at least once a week I am forced to return to bed in the middle of the day. Most of the time I have subtle, ghost symptoms, and there is a continual fear of relapse. Except for the days when I feel as if I had never been sick. Then, it is like what those who have recovered from serious illness always say: the air is exquisite, the light enchanting, and to walk a few blocks in a crowded city a marvel.

Walking Through
Amsterdam

A woman is walking through the streets of Amsterdam. She is thinking of the passage of time. This is the second time she has been in this city. She was here before her daughter was born. Now her daughter is a young woman. As she walks she thinks, It has been twenty years.

Can I remember exactly what I felt the moment I heard about the accident at Chernobyl? A kind of dread. And this laced with the usual skepticism about the news. No one tells the truth. Not the Soviets. Not our own government. Among my circle of friends, we exchange telephone calls. There are rumors. Speculations. Someone tells me Fritjof has canceled his trip to Europe. Because of the new baby. Should I change my plans too? Fritjof must know more than I do. He is a physicist.

The woman who walks in this city is just recovered from an illness. She feels like a bird let out of a cage, a bird who had forgotten the smell of the outside world. This and the passage of time give an edge to the beauty around her. The water of the canals reflects the trees with their luminous spring color. All that she sees is so much at hand, so close, even inside her. Perhaps she is becoming someone different. The day has been very long, the light stretching and stretching. As it grows later, she feels as if she is stealing time.

For two days I think about canceling my own trip. I know there is some danger. The radiation is not in the air any longer. But it will be in the food. Then I decide I will go. Why? It is only because I cannot bear not to go. Later I hear Fritjof will go too. Now in my imagination I locate the disaster on the streets of Amsterdam. And I watch myself as I walk through catastrophe.

She has walked to this neighborhood of canals and narrow streets from South Amsterdam. She was there an hour before, in the late afternoon, to search for a particular address, 6 Gabriel Metsustraat. A small apartment in an attic with windows facing out toward the Rijksmuseum.

Before I leave I write down several addresses. A restaurant. A café. Two friends. And the address, 6 Gabriel Metsustraat, that I find in the preface to *An Interrupted Life*. This is the diary which Etty Hillesum, a Dutch Jew, kept in the years from 1941 until 1943. During a time of convalescence, I read this book. I had just been forced to confront my own mortality. The diary made a deep mark on me, speaking as it does with such astonishing clarity of how or even why one ought to live. I want to see the place where she wrote

She stood on the street staring up at the outside of a building. She was trying to find the right apartment. It was at the top. The woman who once lived there died in Auschwitz. There was no plaque commemorating the building. From the window below the attic a woman and a man stared down at her. Did they know the history of this place? she wondered. They smiled and waved at her. There was no way to speak with them. She smiled back.

The day I leave I meet a friend who has just returned from Italy. "They have confiscated vegetables," she tells me, "and the milk, the government has warned us not to drink the milk. You didn't know?" she asks me. The newspapers have become useless.

Facing away from the attic window, she walked across a vast square. There was a very cold wind, stronger and colder in that open space, and she did her best to protect herself from it. As she walked, she tried to imagine what that square had looked like during the occupation, when the city was occupied, under siege.

What a strange choice for me, to locate the disaster in Amsterdam. What must it be in the Ukraine? But this is a new age. An accident in Chernobyl occurs at the same time in Berlin, in Tokyo, in New York. This modern mind that believes it can understand creation has not yet grasped the simple nature of space. All boundaries have disappeared. The boundaries are in our minds.

Then, as she walked out of the square and through the arcade of the great museum, she felt as if she had passed into another atmosphere. The wind had subsided on this other side, and the sun was warmer. In her mind she felt she was walking out of history.

For the last two months I have been very happy. At the beginning of this year I was frail, and in a depression, one of a familiar kind that I have suffered many other times in my life, when slowly I could see the faint signs of a different frame of mind growing in me. I knew the depression well. It was a trusted structure of meaning through which I could always make sense of fate. But I was in the process of dismantling this structure.

As she walks beside the canals she feels a kind of ecstasy take hold of her. This is different from the happiness she had when she was younger. She is different. Even the city that has hardly changed since she saw it last is different to her. She was filled then with all the plans that the young make. Now she feels as if brushed by the giant wings of movement. She could come to live here in one of these houses by the canal, or she could not. And she does not know what the rest of her life will be.

As the old structure left me, besides bewilderment, I began to feel a very quiet, simple happiness. And at the same time I was witnessing many calamities take place around me. American planes bombed Libya, and near the same date a fire was set by an arsonist in the apartment building next door to me. The building nearly exploded. I had to leave my house in my pajamas at dawn. And then, Chernobyl. Each event shared a certain similarity— each had the nightmare quality of the unforeseen. And yet this was not the first fire the arsonist had set. Didn't imaginary fires take place in his mind? Each disaster had a predictable side, as if the bare bones of fate had been laid into the ground, the way bones do lie just under the paving of certain roads.

As she walks she looks into the windows of each café. It is as if she were looking into other lives. And now she finds a café that draws her into it, by the force of its vividness, a brightness. The place is crowded. The conversation is full of humor and sails around the room from one end of the bar to the door, even reaches her. She takes in the sound of another language as she enters. Then for an instant she wonders, Is this a world that is vanishing?

The day I leave for Amsterdam my friend who has returned from Italy tells me a rumor she has heard in Europe. The story is that radiation ventilated from the site of the one of the underground atomic tests in the last weeks has equaled the radiation from Chernobyl. While I am in Europe I search the newspapers for any word of such a disaster. When I return my friend tells me that she has written several letters to various officials. She is trying to find out what actually happened. She has received no replies.

She stands at the bar next to two women who are close to her own age. They are friends and she is fascinated by the animation of the conversation between them. She does not understand the words they say, but so much is said between them in another language, the language of gesture, of expression, of presence, of silence.

Silence stretches out all around us in every direction. Still searching for some word about the underground test in Nevada, I read a letter in my local newspaper. It has been reprinted from an Italian newspaper. The letter is written by a woman who lived in Chernobyl. It is full of speculation, full of questions. Why was the news delayed for two days? When can we return home? And rumors. That bizarre mushrooms are growing in the fields now. That the tallest trees are dying.

She begins to watch one of the women. Something draws her. The way she smokes. The way she gestures. The way she speaks and does not speak. There are no polite smiles. There is no pretense in her appearance. No apparent veil drawn over her face. Each of her expressions is authentic. What would it be like to be this woman? she asks herself. To live her life?

This weekend I attend a large meeting of men and women who have survived exposure to nuclear radiation—those who have

worked in the industry, veterans exposed to tests, citizens living
in the track of a cloud or a wind laden with radioactivity, those
who lived through Hiroshima. The atmosphere is electric with a
certain quality. How can I describe it? Authenticity? Awareness.
There are those in wheelchairs, those who are clearly very ill, and
those who are in grief, and everyone is telling a story that bears
somehow on the essential.

Then suddenly a certain tiredness swept over her. She felt the limita-
tions of her body. She had been ill. She was supposed to rest. The day
would not be endless.

Then from the speakers' rostrum one more story is told. It is
about Mighty Oak, the name for an underground test at Nevada
which took place around the time of the Chernobyl disaster.
There was an accident. The explosion blew through two safety
shields under Ranier Mesa. It caused millions of dollars in damage. And it released xenon gas into the atmosphere. Xenon gas,
we learn, breaks down into radioactive iodine. The accident was
not reported to the public for three weeks. From the audience a
man who worked for years supervising cleanup at the sites of the
tests asks a rhetorical question. "Do you know why they delayed
the announcement for three weeks?" His answer of course is
speculation. But it is a speculation educated by years of grief. In
his briefcase he carries a list of men he has worked with who have
died of various kinds of cancer. There are 212 names on his list.
"They delayed the announcement," he said, "so there would be
no independent measurements of radioactivity just after the accident."

She left the bar and walked what now seemed a long walk back to South
Amsterdam and her hotel. It would be night. The light would leave the sky
just the way her courage had left her body.

It was not an American nor a Russian who wrote these words
which I reach for now that seem to describe this man and the
manner of his questions. It is a Dutch woman, Etty Hillesum,
writing just before her own death in the Holocaust:

*I am not the slightest bit concerned about cutting a fine figure in the
eyes of this persecutor or that. Let them see my utter sadness and my
utter defenselessness, too. There is no need to put on a show, I have
my inner strength and that is enough, the rest doesn't matter.*

*She had learned this. To let the tiredness come over her, without
resisting it, to give in, to yield to it, and found that each time she did this
there was a certain comfort, a sweetness even, in knowing the truth. The
limits of her flesh forced her to change direction into another dimension,
one of greater slowness, or stillness, or, even, of dreams.*

I hear that in Chernobyl many years ago, centuries ago, there
was a famous rabbi. People would travel miles to see him because
he had that indefinable quality we sometimes call wisdom. Were
he alive today, I would go to speak with him. He might tell me
what I cannot decipher from all these facts and figures.

*She goes to sleep in a room far above the city. It is a room that could be
anywhere. She has been in one like it in Berlin. In Tokyo. In New York.
There is no mark of the human anywhere. We all know what these rooms
are like. They have become familiar to us.*

From my hotel room in Amsterdam I can see the whole city.
After visiting Etty Hillesum's apartment, I imagine I can feel the
presence of the German occupiers. What would it be like, I ask,
to see an SS man standing in uniform in this square? But the truth
is more subtle. Often as not you would not see the SS man. But
you would know he was there. As I look over the city I can see no
trace of radiation. But I know, one knows, every minute, every
hour, that it is there.

*But even in that room she could take refuge in her body, in her own
skin, in the feel of her face against the sheet, her hand against her own
hair, she could breathe, and make that journey into blackness from which
mysteries take place.*

There are many thoughts, many intense feelings I have about
the accident at Chernobyl. I looked out over Amsterdam and
thought, *This place, this landscape can never be the same.* I thought of
the Ukraine, vast region of imagination, of dreams. It too is

forever changed. And here, where I am now in California, looking out over the Pacific Ocean, toward Japan, toward the Marshall Islands? In the beginning I had a moment of hope. Perhaps this accident would bring awareness. Then, when awareness did not come, I despaired. And, as I write now? There is just this: a moment of suspension.

In the Path of the Ideal

Not the male body but the masculine idea of the body.

Or perhaps one should say masculine ideal.

Because this is a theoretical body. And a body which by implication includes the feminine body. How that body is supposed to be.

It is an ideal from which I suffer directly.

That woman I saw walking past my kitchen window. It was obvious to me she felt uncomfortable with herself. Was it because her hair was not looking the way she wanted it to look, because she had put on weight, because she didn't like the clothes she had chosen to wear? I recognize the look.

A certain gaze directed to a woman's body.

Those young men watching pornographic videos. Trying to do what the men on the screen do to women. Tying women up, pulling their breasts, slapping them, raping them. Those young men watching the feminine body suffer.

The young men who watched pornographic films just before they flew over Iraq and the battlefields of the Persian Gulf to drop bombs.

> The male body, the female body
> innocent
> helpless when faced with certain kinds of attack.

That woman walking past my kitchen window, preoccupied with a gaze that exists outside herself. A gaze belonging to no one in particular. Where are her own thoughts? What would she be thinking without this preoccupation?

> *Preoccupation / occupation*
> *Occupied territories.*
> *Colonized bodies / countries.*

That group of young men I saw standing on the corner. Skinheads. They look so much like a photograph I have of skinheads and Fascos in Germany. An international fashion. Only the clothing is new. But the posture, the attitude is older. It belongs to the aesthetic of strength. Violence stripped of any justification. Existing here in its purest form, for its own sake. The quintessence of the masculine ideal.

Not very far removed after all from the gangster film, the spy story in which the plot hardly matters, and every other reality dissolves into insignificance before the central motif of violence.

Warfare as the apotheosis of violence.

There is of course the man who feels he isn't who he is supposed to be. His body is too soft. Perhaps he is a coward. He is preoccupied with this thought. Who would he be, what would he think if he were not so preoccupied?

The feminine man as the object of derision. The ridicule of homosexuals, a ritual of male bonding.

Pornography as psychological violence.

The story in the newspapers. She said that he used pornographic imagery to humiliate her. He said he did not. That nothing took place.

The idea that she fantasized what she said had happened to her. The violence of the lie that preoccupies my mind. Neither the crime nor the denial of the crime, but how these two fit together, making me feel it is no use to speak. Especially I who am a lesbian.

• • •

Despair as an effect of violence.

The mesmerized state through which a nation goes to war, wages war, and celebrates victory. As if no one had suffered. No one had pulled a trigger.

No one had killed or been killed.

As if there were no one at the core.

Bombs simply mathematical coordinates on a screen. Virtual reality. Manufactured to replace what is given.

The body that is given. This female body. The male body. Innocent, helpless, in the path of the ideal.

Ideologies of Madness

Nuclear war has been described as a form of madness. Yet rarely does one take this insight seriously when contemplating the dilemma of war and peace. I wish to describe here the state of mind that has produced nuclear weaponry as a species of socially accepted insanity. This is a state of mind born of that philosophical assumption of our civilization which attempts to divide human consciousness from nature. Exploring the terrain of this state of mind, one will find in this geography, in the subterranean and unseen region that is part of its foundation and history, the hatred of the other in the quite literal forms of misogyny (the hatred of women), racism and anti-Semitism.

If one approaches the explosion of a nuclear weapon as if this were symptomatic of an underlying mental condition, certain facets begin to take on metaphorical meaning. Even the simplest physical aspects of a nuclear chain reaction carry a psychological significance. In order for a chain reaction to be created, the atom must be split apart. The fabric of matter has to be torn asunder. In a different vein, it is important to realize that the first atomic weapons were dropped over a people regarded in the demonology of our civilization as racially inferior. Tangentially, and carrying a similar significance, the first nuclear device exploded over Bikini atoll had a pinup of Rita Hayworth pasted to its surface. And then,

This is a revised version of Susan Griffin's Schumacher Lecture delivered in London in November 1983.

speaking of a history that has largely been forgotten or ignored, the prototype of the first missiles capable of carrying nuclear warheads was invented and designed in the Third Reich. And those first rockets, the German V-2 rockets, were produced in underground tunnels by prisoners of concentration camps who were worked to death in this production.

These facets of the existence of nuclear weaponry can lead us to a deeper understanding of the troubled mind that has created our current nuclear crisis. To begin at one particular kind of beginning, with the history of thought, one can see the philosophical roots of our current crisis in the splitting of the atom. In the most basic terms, what occurs when the atom is split is a division between energy and matter. Until this century, modern science assumed matter and energy to be separate. This assumption began not with scientific observation but out of a religious bias. Examining the early history of science, one discovers that the first scientists were associated with and supported by the Church (as was most scholarship at that time) and that they asked questions derived from Christian theology. "What is the nature of light?" A question intimately bound up with the theory of relativity and quantum physics began as a religious question. And the guiding paradigm of the religion that posed this question has been a fundamental dualism between matter and spirit. Matter, or body and earth, were the degraded regions, belonging to the devil and corruption. Spirit, or the realm of pure intellect and heavenly influence, belonged to God, and was, in human experience, won only at the expense of flesh.

Of course, science does not recognize the categories of spirit and matter any longer, except through a process of translation. In the new vocabulary, though, the old dualism has been preserved. Now, matter was conceived of as earthbound and thus subject to gravity, and energy, the equivalent of spirit, was described as a free agent, inspiring and enlivening. Newtonian physics continued the old dualism, but Einsteinian physics does not.

When Einstein discovered the formula that eventually led to the development of the atomic bomb, what he saw was a continuum between matter and energy, instead of a separation. What we call solid matter is not solid, nor is it static. Matter is, instead, a process of continual change. There is no way to divide the energy of this motion from the physical property of matter. What is more, energy has mass. And not only is there no division between matter and energy as such, but to divide any single entity from any other single entity becomes an impossibility. No particular point exists where my skin definitely ends and the air in the atmosphere begins and this atmosphere ends and your skin begins. We are all in a kind of field together. And finally, with the new physics, the old line between subject and object has also disappeared. According to Heisenberg's Principle of Uncertainty, whatever we observe we change through our participation. Objectivity with its implied superiority and control has also vanished.

One might imagine that, with the disappearance of a scientific basis for dualism and the appearance of a physical view that is unified and whole, a different philosophy might arise, one which might help us make peace with nature. But instead what this civilization chose to do with this new insight was to find a way to separate matter from energy (it is spoken of as "liberating" the energy from the atom). And this separation has in turn produced a technology of violence which has divided the world into two separate camps who regard each other as enemies.

The real enemy, however, in dualistic thinking, is hidden: the real enemy is ourselves. The same dualism which imagines matter and energy to be separate also divides human nature, separating what we call our material existence from consciousness. This dualism is difficult to describe without using dualistic language. Actually, the mind cannot be separated from the body. The brain is part of the body and is affected by blood flow, temperature, nourishment, muscular movement. The order and rhythm of the body, bodily metaphors, are reflected in the medium of thought, in our patterns of speech. Yet we conceive of the mind as separate from and above the body. And through a subtle process of socialization since birth, we learn to regard the body and our natural existence as something inferior and without intelligence. Most of the rules of polite behavior are designed to conceal the demands of the body. We excuse ourselves, and refer to our bodily functions through euphemism.

From this dualistic frame of mind two selves are born: one acknowledged and one hidden. The acknowledged self identifies with spirit, with intellect, with what we imagine is free of the influence of natural law. The hidden self is part of nature, earthbound, inextricable from the matrix of physical existence. We have become very seriously alienated from this denied self. So seriously that our alienation has become a kind of self-hatred, and this self-hatred is leading us today toward the suicidal notion of nuclear combat.

Of course, the body and mind are not separate. And, ironically, the warfare incipient between our ideas of who we are and who we really are is made more intense through this unity. Consciousness cannot exclude bodily knowledge. We are inseparable from nature, dependent on the biosphere, vulnerable to the processes of natural law. We cannot destroy the air we breathe without destroying ourselves. We are reliant on one another for our survival. We are all mortal. And this knowledge comes to us, whether we want to receive it or not, with every breath.

The dominant philosophies of this civilization have attempted to posit a different order of being over and against this bodily knowledge. According to this order of being, we are separate from nature and hence above natural process. In the logic of this order, we are meant to dominate nature, control life, and, in some sense felt largely unconsciously, avoid the natural event of death.

Yet in order to maintain a belief in this hierarchy one must repress bodily knowledge. And this is no easy task. Our own knowledge of our own natural existence comes to us not only with every breath but with hunger, with intimacy, with dreams, with all the unpredictable eventualities of life. Our imagined superiority over nature is constantly challenged by consciousness itself.

Consciousness emerges from and is immersed in material experience. Consciousness is not separable from perception, which is to say sensuality, and as such cannot be separated from matter. Even through the process of the most abstract thought we cannot entirely forget that we are part of nature. In the biosphere nothing is ever entirely lost. Death itself is not an absolute end but rather a transformation. What appears to be lost in a fire becomes heat and ash. So, too, no knowledge can ever really be lost to consciousness. It must remain, even if disguised as a mere symbol of itself.

If I choose to bury a part of myself, what I bury will come back to haunt me in another form, as dream, or fear, or projection. This civilization, which has buried part of the human self, has created many projections. Out of the material of self-hatred several categories of otherness have been fashioned. Existing on a mass scale and by social agreement, these categories form a repository for our hidden selves.

The misogynist's idea of women is a fundamental category of otherness for this civilization. In the ideology of misogyny, a woman is a lesser being than a man. And the root cause of her inferiority is that she is closer to the earth, more animal, and hence material in her nature. She is thus described as more susceptible to temptations of the flesh (or devils, or serpents), more emotional and hence less capable of abstract thought than a man. Similarly, in the ideology of racism, those who are perceived as other are, at one and the same time, more sensual and erotic and less intelligent.

During the rise of fascism in Europe a fictitious document was created called the *Protocols of the Elders of Zion*. In this "document" Jewish elders plan to corrupt and eventually seize Aryan bloodlines through the rape and seduction of Aryan women. If one has projected a part of the self upon another, one must always be afraid that this self will return, perhaps even entering one's own bloodstream. But what is equally significant about this myth, and the symbolic life of the racist and anti-Semitic imagination, is that a sexual act, and especially rape, lies at the heart of its mythos.

It was in writing a book on pornography that I first began to understand the ideology of misogynist projection. Since so much in pornography is violent, I began to ask myself why sexual experience is associated with violence. This is a question which poses itself again in the context of nuclear weaponry, not only because Rita Hayworth's image happened to adorn an experimental nuclear bomb, nor simply because of the phallic shape of the missile, nor the language employed to describe the weapons—the first atomic bomb called "little boy," the next "big boy"—but also because of the sexualization of warfare itself, the eroticization of violence in war, the supposed virility of the soldier, the test of virility which is supposed to take place on the battlefield, and the general equivalency between masculine virtues and prowess in battle.

Over time in my study of pornography I began to understand pornographic imagery as an expression of the fear of sexual experience itself. Sexual experience takes one back to a direct knowledge of nature, including mortality, and of one's own body before culture has intervened to create the delusion of dominance. It is part of the nature of sexual pleasure and of orgasm to lose control. And finally the feel of a woman's breast, or of human skin against bare skin at all, must recall infancy and the powerlessness of infancy.

As infants we all experience an understanding of dependence and vulnerability. Our first experience of a natural, material power outside ourselves was through the bodies of our mothers. In this way we have all come to associate nature with the body of a woman. It was our mother who could feed us, give us warmth and comfort, or withhold these things. She had the power of life and death over us as natural process does now.

It was also as infants that we confronted what we have come to know as death. What we call death—coldness, isolation, fear, darkness, despair, trembling—is really the experience of an infant. What death really is lies in the dimension of the unknown. But, from the infantile experience of what we call death, one can see the psychological derivation of civilization's association between women and death. (One sees this clearly in the creation myth from Genesis, as Eve the seductress brings death into the world.) In this sense, too, sexual experience returns one to a primal fear of death. And through this understanding one can begin to see that at the center of the impulse to rape is the desire to dominate the power of sexual experience itself and to deny the power of nature, including mortality, as this is felt through sexual experience.

The connection between sexuality and violence exists as a kind of subterranean theme in the fascist and authoritarian mentality. In several places in Jacobo Timerman's book, *Prisoner Without a Name, Cell Without a Number,* he points out a relationship between the violence of the dictator and a pornographic attitude toward sexuality. Imprisoned and tortured himself, he recalls that those who did not do "a good scrubbing job" when ordered to clean the prison floors were forced to "undress, lean over with their index finger on the ground and have them rotate round and round dragging their finger on the ground without lifting it. You felt," he writes, "as if your kidneys were bursting." Another punishment was to force prisoners to run naked along the passageway, "reciting aloud sayings dictated" to them, such as "My mother is a whore, I masturbate, I respect the guard, the police love me."

That, to the fascist mind, "the other" represents a denied part of the self becomes clear in the following story about Adolf Hitler. In a famous passage in *Mein Kampf* he describes the moment when he decided to devote his life's work to anti-Semitism. He recounts that while walking through the streets of Vienna he happened to see an old man dressed in the traditional clothes of Jewish men in that city at that time, i.e., in a caftan. The first question he asked was, "Is this man Jewish?" and then he corrected himself and replaced that question with another, "Is this man German?"

If one is to project a denied self onto another, one must first establish that this other is different from oneself. Were one to notice any similarity, one would be endangered by the perception that what one projects may belong to oneself. The question that Hitler asked himself became a standard part of German textbooks in the Third Reich. A stereotypical portrait of a Jewish man's face was shown under the question, "Is this man German?" and the correct answer the students were taught was, of course, "No." In fact, Germany became a nation rather late. For centuries it existed as a collection of separate tribes, and one of the oldest tribes in that nation was Jewish.

Hitler's story of the man in the caftan became a standard part of his orations. He would become nearly hysterical at times telling the story, and is said to have even vomited once. In the light of this history, a seemingly trivial story from Hitler's early life becomes significant. As a young art student he bought his clothes secondhand because, like many students, he was poor. In this period most of those selling secondhand clothing were Jewish and Hitler bought from a Jewish clothes seller one item of clothing that he wore so often that he began to be identified with this apparel. And that was a caftan.

What is also interesting historically is that the caftan was a form of medieval German dress. Exiled from Germany during a period of persecution, many Jews, who then lived in ghettos, continued to wear this traditional German dress and were still wearing it when they returned to Germany centuries later. Not only did Hitler fail to recognize an image of himself encountered in the streets of Vienna, but so did an entire generation of Germans. And an entire civilization, that to which we all belong, is in conflict with a part of human nature, which we try to bury and eventually even destroy.

The weapons that now threaten to destroy the earth and life as we know it were developed because the Allied nations feared that the fascist powers were making them. And the missiles which are now part and parcel of nuclear weaponry were first developed in the Third Reich. It is crucial now in our understanding of ourselves and what it is in us that has led to the nuclear crisis that we begin to look at the Nazi Holocaust as a mirror, finding a self-portrait in "the other" who is persecuted and denied, and seeing a part of ourselves too in the fascist dictator who would destroy that denied self.

The illusion this civilization retains, that we are somehow above nature, is so severe that in a sense we have come to believe that we can end material existence without dying. The absurdity of nuclear weaponry as a strategy for defense, when the use of those weapons would annihilate us, would in itself argue this. But if you look closely at the particulars of certain strategies within the overall nuclear strategy you encounter again the same estranged relationship with reality.

An official who was part of Reagan's administration, T. K. Jones, actually proposed that a viable method of civil defense would be to issue each citizen a shovel. It took an eight-year-old boy to point out that this plan cannot work because, after you dig a hole and get into it for protection, someone else must stand outside the hole and shovel dirt on top. The Pentagon refers to its strategies for waging nuclear war as SIOP. One year the Pentagon actually went through the paces of an SIOP plan. As a literary scholar I found the scenario which the Pentagon wrote for this dramatization very disturbing. The Pentagon was free to write this play in any way that they wished; yet they wrote that the President was killed with a direct hit to Washington, D.C. Any student of tragic drama will tell you that what happens to the king, or the President, is symbolic of what happens to the self. But symbolically this death is not treated as real. Though the earthly self dies, in the Pentagon's version the sky self does not die: the Vice-President goes up in an airplane fully equipped to wage nuclear war by computer. There is such a plane flying above us now, and at every hour of the day and night.

The division that we experience from the natural self, the self that is material and embedded in nature, impairs our perceptions of reality. As Timerman writes:

The devices are recurrent in all totalitarian ideology, to ignore the complexities of reality, or even eliminate reality, and instead establish a simple goal and a simple means of attaining that goal.

Through maintaining the supremacy of the idea, one creates a delusion of a supernatural power over nature. Proceeding from an alienation from nature and an estrangement from the natural self, our civilization has replaced reality with an idea of reality.

In the development of this alienation as a state of mind, the delusion of well-being and safety eventually becomes more important than the realistic considerations which will actually effect well-being or safety. Hannah Arendt writes of an illusionary world created by totalitarian movements ". . . in which through sheer imagination uprooted masses can feel at home, and are spared the never-ending shocks which real life and real experience deal to human beings. . . ." Later, in *The Origins of Totalitarianism,* she speaks of the state of mass mind under the Third Reich in which people ceased to believe in what they perceived with their own eyes and ears, preferring the conflicting reports issued by the Führer.

One encounters the same failure to confront reality in Stalin's psychology as it is described by Isaac Deutscher in his biography:

He [Stalin] was now completely possessed by the idea that he could achieve a miraculous transformation of the whole of Russia by a single *tour de force.* He seemed to live in a half-real and half-dreamy world of statistical figures and indices of industrial orders and instructions, a world in which no target and no objective seemed beyond his and the party's grasp.[1]

During the period of forced collectivization of farms, Stalin destroyed actual farms before the collectivized farms were created.

---

[1] Isaac Deutscher, *Stalin: A Political Biography* (Oxford, 1961).

As Deutscher writes, it was as if a whole nation destroyed its real houses and moved "lock, stock and barrel into some illusory buildings."

We are, in fact, now living in such an illusory building. The entire manner in which plans for a nuclear war are discussed, rehearsed, and envisioned partakes of a kind of unreality, an anesthetized and nearly automatic functioning, in which cerebration is strangely unrelated to experience or feeling. The generals imagine themselves conducting nuclear war from a room without windows, with no natural light, choosing strategies and targets by looking at enormous computerized maps. The language they use to communicate their decisions is all in code. No one uses the word "war," the word "bomb," the word "death," or the words "blood," "pain," "loss," "grief," "shock," or "horror." In Siegfried Sassoon's[2] recollection of World War I, he remembers encountering a man, a soldier like himself, who has just learned that his brother was killed. The man is half crazy, tearing his clothes off and cursing at war. As Sassoon passed beyond this man into the dark of the war, he could still hear "his uncouth howlings." It is those "uncouth howlings" that those who are planning nuclear war have managed to mute in their imagination.

But of course that howling is not entirely lost. In the shared imagination of our civilization, it is the "other" who carries emotion, the women who howl. And, far from wishing to protect the vulnerable and the innocent, it is the secret desire of this civilization to destroy those who feel, and to silence feeling. This hidden desire becomes apparent in pornography where women are pictured in a traditional way as weaker than men and needing protection, and yet where erotic feeling is freely mixed with the desire to brutalize and even murder women.

One can find a grim picture of the insane logic of the alienated

---

[2] Siegfried Sassoon, "The Complete Memoirs of George Sherston," as collected in *Sassoon's Long Journey*, ed. Paul Fussell (London, 1983).

mind of our civilization in the pornographic film *Peeping Tom*. The hero of this movie is a pornographic film maker. He has a camera armed with a spear. As he photographs a woman's naked body the camera releases the weapon and he makes a record of her death agonies. The final victory of the alienated mind over reality is to destroy that reality (and one's experience of it) and replace reality with a record of that destruction. One finds the same pattern in the history of actual atrocities. In California a man lured women into the desert with a promise of work as pornographic models. There, while he tortured and murdered them, he made a photographic record of the event. The Nazis themselves kept the best documentation of atrocities committed in the concentration camps. And the most complete records of the destruction of Native Americans have been kept by the United States military.

Now, the state of conflict in which this civilization finds itself has worsened. The enemy is not simply "the other" but life itself. And it is in keeping with the insane logic of alienation that the Pentagon has found a way that it believes we can win nuclear war. We have situated satellites in space that will record the process of annihilation of life. The Pentagon counts as a future victor that nation which has gathered the best documentation of the destruction.

There is, however, another form of reflection available to us by virtue of our human nature. We are our own witnesses. We can see ourselves. We are part of nature. And nature is not divided. Matter is intelligent. Feeling, sense, the needs of the body, all that has been consigned to the "other," made the province of women, of darkness, contains a deeper and a sustaining wisdom. It remains for us to empower that knowledge and carry it into the world. In insanity and madness, one is lost to oneself. It is only by coming home to ourselves that we can survive.

Inheritance of Absence

There are stretches of land scattered throughout the United States that have become so desolate they are the stuff of legends. Chain-link fences and signs warning trespassers away set them apart from the rest of the countryside—deserts in California, Nevada, and New Mexico; pastures, fields, forested land along creek beds or rivers in Tennessee, South Carolina, and Washington State.

It is as if these patches of earth have been erased from existence, or at least existence as it is configured in the public mind of the last half century of this nation. These are the dumping grounds for the United States military, places where the unintended excrescences of wars real and imagined have been hidden, shed, stored.

There are shell casings, live bullets, unexploded mines and grenades, countless chemicals, and radioactive waste. Toxic substances bubble to the surface, destroying vegetation, turning it brown or fluorescent. Underneath, subterranean waters are fouled and carry their poisons unobserved past the gates and sentries into the surrounding countryside, towns, cities.

The effects where they have been observed are devastating. Cancers, childhood leukemias, whole communities uprooted, farms abandoned, unworkable. Armies are supposed to defend the people against early, untimely death from unseen enemies. Over centuries the most sophisticated equipment has been devised for this task. Heat-sensitive photographs taken from satellites, every kind of radar, computerized projections made from the slightest evidence. How is it then that these visible marks on the land, and the countless less visible traces of danger, escaped notice?

I am thinking of the military body. The body of a good soldier. Trained to respond quickly to danger. And yet at the same time educated away from fear and other more subtle responses. Toughened, of course, against discomfort, pain, fatigue, cold. Tuned to the highest possible pitch of aggression, mastery, control. This is the masculine ideal. Ramrod straight and orderly.

But there are losses. The posture does not allow for peripheral interest. Whatever is in the background disappears in the focus of a gunsight. And the quick reactions necessary in battle make the soldier speed past so much texture, detail. To identify the enemy in time one must not be looking at minute variations, only the uniform.

Of course, these habits of perception would not prepare the mind to see the intricate levels of existence in a field, valley, stretch of desert, forest, at the edge of the stream. Each of hundreds of species of birds, insects, grasses, cacti, fade into what is called background. If there is learning to be had from the land, from the ancient texts of rock, tree, or "layers of pollen in a swamp"—as Gary Snyder names them—these are books unread, lessons ignored.

So this mind would not be prone to detect the path of a watershed. Not even know that water is running underground, much less that it will reappear thirty, or a hundred, or even several hundred miles later, and enter the life cycles of plants, the mouths of animals, or other people.

And as for the death of an owl, a coyote, a species of small insect that might be a harbinger of danger, how can one expect the soldier to observe these with grief? Everything in his training tells him it is his life or the life of the enemy. The other. Everywhere he looks he must make this distinction. One or the other.

Since birth he has been taught another attitude. An approach going back centuries to at least the Roman Empire where whole forests were destroyed to build the ships and palaces of expansion.

Perhaps armies are the most intense evocation of this state of mind. Initiated early in life, the soldier has already learned to think of what he calls nature not only as background but also as other, and even enemy, or prey.

And he has been raised with the belief that other life forms are without spirit or souls. The life or death then of a small ecosystem, a pond, a hundred square miles of hot sand, red rock, inhabited by lizards, snakes, mice, has no cosmic significance and means nothing to him.

Or so he believes.

And if the meaning of these deaths is somewhere in him, he has learned to bury this in an unconscious region. Unclaimed as the lands set off by sign and fence.

I am remembering G. He was the lover of a friend in our last year of high school. Just returned from Korea, he still wore a khaki uniform. Our circle was a group of rebels and no one could quite understand our friend's attraction to him. Nor his to her. He gave the appearance of a leathery skin, thick neck, imperviousness to any delicacy. Talked to us for hours about the Japanese women he had had as lovers. How attentive they had been to his needs. How obedient they were to his demands. They would cook elaborate meals for him, give him massages, walk on his back, and make love to him exotically, passionately, all with no demands of their own, no complaints. None of these women had names or histories he could tell us. They fell into the background as part of a general category: Japanese women.

But at the same time he was obsessed and in love with Japan. And we all liked this in him. He took us all to Japanese restaurants. Introduced us to new ways of eating fish, a different beer; showed us poetry, water colors. Nothing in California pleased him as much as this more delicately sensual world. Because of the quality of intense presence he had whenever he spoke of Japan, one was drawn to him in these moments.

It is certainly possible to be someplace, any place, and not be present in this way. By the time I was born, my mother's father had become a kind of emptiness in himself. Most of the time he seemed scarcely present, adding little to family conversations. He had a sweet side, though, through which he seemed to come alive solely for me. At these times he would tell me about his childhood or watch the Westerns with me and joke and laugh.

The unclaimed regions of a man, which military training walls off more effectively. To reveal hesitation, sensitivity, fear—above all fear—occasions ridicule. He is likened to a woman. Or a faggot. There is a subtle heritage that connects the military repression of homosexuality with negligent pollution. The inheritance of absence.

So much of modern warfare is not present to itself, takes place in the mind as if nowhere. Almost hypothetically. On a computer screen in an airplane miles above the target. Or in a room with computerized controls set to launch rockets. But this only mirrors a much older divide by which the soldier walls himself off from his own compassion, remorse, terror.

And if there is evidence? Trace deposits, toxins, the as yet unkindled fire of all that has been avoided. It is best to ignore it, he reasons with himself.

But the logic is circular. Ignoring place, earth, his own knowledge, the fear in his body, the delicacy of his own perceptions. He is oddly dislocated. He is like a computer screen floating in air. Where is the ground of his being? What is his purpose? Only a marching band with a strong martial rhythm and the sound of his feet indistinguishable from the lockstep of a battalion which follows the clipped, familiar shouts of a commander, can give him back some sense of direction.

And if the parade is marching off to war, some war which he can hardly understand, which means nothing to him, he already has a sense of loss. And grief and rage because of it which will now be useful while he fights over possession of some small stretch of land, two or three acres, over which the victor will one day draw a boundary.

Something Wants to Be Seen: on the Art of Lenke Rothman

We are in the mountains. The ocean cuts the sky like a great blue belt. But we have wandered away from this sight, into the closer world of detail. An owl has died in a field of grass. A soft circle of feathers floats around this place of emptiness. The feathers are white. Lenke Rothman takes up as many of them as she can. Her hands are already full. She carries laurel leaves, many kinds of moss, strands of a red-barked vine, an unnamed plant that is yellow, long and segmented like bamboo. In her hands these small entities begin to speak like beasts in a fable. I walk carefully back into our view of the ocean. My hands too are filled. I am carrying magic.

Do all the materials of art have their own histories? Tarnish. A worn look. Marks. The color blue. Calling up the sea or sky. One cannot look at the blue in a painting by Yves Klein, as Lenke Rothman says, without recalling that he leapt to his death through an open window. But one need not know that story to catch a scent of sadness as it arises from that particular tone. The strange alchemy by which in art the personal begins to speak for everyone is still a mystery to me.

The color red, for instance, thread and the red chain that

crosses over one of Lenke Rothman's canvases. In Hungary her mother tied a red thread around Lenke's wrist to keep her safe. And I am told this is also a Tibetan custom, red thread, worn for years around the wrist, until it breaks, for protection. But as I gaze at the chain of red painted from a memory that is not my own, I do not need to know this story. Instead, when I hear this story it merely proves to me that what I felt when I saw this image was right.

And then again, even more mysterious, certain materials have a will of their own. They gravitate toward expression. They arrive as if (by some means we have failed to understand) they have arranged to be placed in the right hands at the right time. Lenke is in Budapest. She is walking down the street. She sees a sign reading DOLL CLINIC. And she cannot resist entering the door. The woman inside this door tells Lenke her life story. And then she gives her a parcel. This parcel is filled with old doll clothes. They have been collected here for years. The woman had considered discarding them, but instead she decided to wait, she tells Lenke, until she could find the right place for them.

These doll clothes are not alone. A Hebrew prayer book, many different kinds of buttons, umbrellas, string, all these have migrated into Lenke Rothman's hands, as if, through these humble things, the desire to reverse the diaspora were being expressed.

Once, climbing a hill for a better view of the sea, I asked, "How do you begin?" Some sense I had from her made me feel we shared a process. But now I have forgotten what she said, and what I said in return. So I ask again. I am in Berkeley. She is in Stockholm. After three attempts, we succeed in establishing a clear connection, and after a minute, I am no longer marveling at modern technology for it is as if our first conversation had never stopped. And this is a much more ancient human skill I am witnessing, to remember, and to speak in dialogue as if speech had never stopped. She does not decide, she tells me, what she will do. It is rather that things begin to talk to her. A piece of thread, a in a way that reveals the brush stroke, so that we can see the approximate motion of her arm as it goes in a certain direction and then stops, in a kind of dance. And it is this, this dance, which is made up of food and table and cloth and wine and prayer and memory, that sustains.

It is a ritual dance. The images manifested in the process are sacred. Yet they have not been refashioned to be holy. Rather, their essential sacredness has been recognized in the work. In Lenke Rothman's vision the external reveals itself, and by this revelation, echoes an inner world. Longing, loss, solace, terror, beauty, a white tablecloth, white paint, all this in the hand's dance over the canvas.

One feels in her work that the creation is being continued. This is perhaps true with all art. The poet Osip Mandelshtam believed that the poems he wrote existed in finished form before he wrote them, and that his task was simply to bring them into apparent being. But each is an astonishment. Lenke tells me she is always surprised, with each new work, that it arrives finally in spite of the fact that she does not know how to do it. Because it is necessary, she says, somehow you do it. The technique is always different, always being discovered and learned. Yet the beginning point is the same. One opens oneself to a new kind of listening and seeing.

Lenke is on a street in Stockholm. A man, a stranger, approaches her to ask, "Where is the central station?" She lets this question work its way inside her; it begins to unravel. Where is the center from which we can go away and reach different places? it says to her. And from this question, she paints several pictures.

This openness depends on a particular attitude toward the world. One does not pretend to know except as one can comprehend with empathy. So that the work finally contains many levels of experience. The wealth of the inner world that is in the outer world (or evoked or echoed by it), a record of an approach to life: the dance, and evidence of an attitude that is compassionate.

You may notice that Lenke Rothman's work is replete with the

numbers eight and ten, that the black box she paints over and over
has a quality of dread which threatens to wash out over her
canvases, that the stitches she uses sometimes resemble surgical
stitches.

I am in Lenke's studio again, and she has brought me to stand in
a corner in back of the door. There I discover eight creatures, a
wild, defiant family, made of wood. Of her family of ten, she and
one brother were the only survivors. She lost her mother and
brothers and sister on the platform at Auschwitz, where they were
sent in two separate directions. "The entire time of the six
months that I remained in Auschwitz," she writes, "I was forever
walking toward the electrified barbed wire bent forward in my
sorrow, where I was sure we had become separated. I walked that
way in order to catch a glimpse of my small brothers, my sister
and mother. After never finding them where they should have
been, I lost my sense of direction forever."

She does not like to be known as an artist of the Holocaust, and
this I can understand. By such a category one diminishes both the
artist and the event. The category seals away the experience of the
Holocaust so that one is neither touched nor taught by it. Yet in
fact one cannot help but be touched by the Holocaust. That it
happened is a fact in all our lives. It is a fact we must let in, to our
innermost souls, a history that continues and will continue until
we are able to claim the grief that the world, were it not for fear
and denial, shares with those who survived.

The Holocaust is there, in all of Lenke Rothman's work, as
foreground or background, shadow, light, mood or assumption,
detail. It is not nor can it be circumscribed in any single place.
And at the same time, all of Lenke Rothman's work, including
those pieces in which the Holocaust stands at the center, is about
something else. This something else cannot be stated simply. It is
not in that sense a subject. It is born out by the statement Lenke
has made elsewhere: that there were "many ways to eat bread at
Auschwitz." Of this other element in Rothman's work one can
say that it leads one to believe there is always a margin of choice in

the world, even if this margin occurs in the midst of the greatest suffering, at the point of death, or even dying, or terrible loss. And it is perhaps only an infinitesimally small space. But it is also a door, it is a window.

"Behind a brow/ a knife point of morning light/ has become ecstatic." Lenke Rothman's work does not illustrate these lines by Nelly Sachs so much as embody them. Noting that in Lenke's work where a black square is attached to paper, light shines through the perforations, the writer Sivar Arnér reminds us that in the world of mysticism, "darkness does not stand for evil, it is on a par with light."

How moving the friendship between Lenke and Nelly. They met when Lenke emerged at twenty-two years of age from years of hospitalizations, surgery and recovery. Nelly Sachs was sixty years old. The younger who had been through the terrors of the Holocaust, the older who did not protect her soul from knowledge of this suffering. The older who reached out to the mysticism of the Kaballah as an adult. The younger for whom such understandings were familiar. Her father was a religious teacher who asked Lenke to tell him her dreams. Who told her that as a boy, on his way to *cheder,* a bird spoke to him, telling him, "Go and learn, little boy."

Is it only those who listen for the speech of birds who know that we have all come from the dark, and that darkness, as Rilke writes, "pulls in everything"? There is a sense in which Lenke Rothman is truly an artist of the Holocaust. As Nelly Sachs is. As I am. As any artist or writer is. To understand this we need to pronounce a word from the daily language of those who perished, the Yiddish word for the Nazi genocide, *hurbn.* This is a word that connotes "the violation of the sanctified life within the community"; its etymology returns us to the destruction of the temple. Understanding this word is to know that it is the work of the artist to rebuild the temple, to again sanctify life.

Is there any hope? We are on the eve of a destruction once more. It is perhaps only this. The Polish poet Tadeusz Rozewicz writes that he makes his poems "out of remnants of words, salvaged words . . . words from . . . the great cemetery." Lenke Rothman, too, remakes the temple, the place of the beginning time, of the creation which came from the dark, the place of sheltering power, where the *Shekinah* lights up the tabernacle, from the remnants of destruction, and all that has been lost, discarded, left temporarily invisible to us though it is all sacred. "The Holocaust," Lenke tells me, "is too vast. I can only handle a fragment of it." And it is true. It is vast like a great sea that moves infinitely beyond the horizon. Vast as a single life is vast, filled with moments that expand infinitely. Or as a single detail that can speak to us of everything.

Acknowledgments

I would like to acknowledge the late Diane Cleaver for her work with this book and her able and graceful representation of my work for the last twelve years. Among those of us who write and edit and publish, her presence will be greatly missed.

The title essay of this book, on the subject of ecology and social justice, could not have been written without the help of many writers and thinkers among my friends and colleagues, for whose counsel, teaching, writing, or work in the world I am grateful. Among them are Helena Norberg Hodge, Vandana Shiva, Joanna Macy, Grazia Borini, Jerry Mander, Wendell Berry, Jeremy Rifkin, Fritjof Capra, Andy Kimbrell, Chellis Glendinning, Stephanie Mills, Ty Cashman, Lee Swenson, Vijaya Nagarajan, Carolyn Merchant, Charlene Spretnak, Ynestra King, Martin Khor, Benina Berger Gould, Claire Greensfelder, Mayumi Oda, Annie Prutzman, Sheldon Margin, Elle Marit Gaupt Dunjifeld, and Joan Halifax. I am especially grateful to the Foundation for Deep Ecology, which contributed materially to the writing of this work and also invited me to a continuing seminar on ecology, technology, and development that strongly influenced this work. The same is true for a similar seminar held almost a decade ago in the Department of Public Health at the University of California, Berkeley. And I am equally grateful for the many seminars, forums, and meetings held by the Elmwood Institute. I would also like to thank Nan Fink for her intelligent and perceptive reading of the manuscript of the title essay; Edith Sorel, Odette Meyers, Joanna Macy, Ronnie Gilbert, Karin Carrington, and Donna Korones for their early reading and support of the work, including many elucidating discussions; and Dorian Ross, Jan Montgomery, and Lenore Friedman for reading portions of the manuscript and the important discussions I had with them. And last but certainly not least I want to thank Roger Scholl for his sensitive, intelligent editing and his kind and steady support.

"Red Shoes" first appeared in *The Politics of the Essay: Feminist Perspectives,* edited by Ruth-Ellen Boetcher Joeres and Elizabeth Mittman, published by Indiana University Press in 1993. "Where No One Dwells" appeared in *The Ohio Review,* No. 49, "Art and Nature," edited by Wayne Dodd. "Inside the Door" appeared in *19 New American Poets of the Golden Gate,* edited by Philip Dow, published by Harcourt Brace Jovanovich in 1984. "The Uncharted Body" appeared in *Same-Sex Love and the Path to Wholeness,* edited by Robert H. Hopcke, Karin Lofhus Carrington, and Scoot Wirth, published by Shambhala Publications in 1993. "Canaries in the Mine" appeared in the *CFIDS Chronicles* and in *The Inquiring Mind.* "The Internal Athlete" appeared in *Ms.* magazine, Vol. 2, No. 6. "In the Path of the Ideal" appeared in the *City Lights Review,* No. 5 (1992), "War After War," edited by Nancy J. Peter. "Ideologies of Madness" appeared in *Exposing Nuclear Phallacies,* edited by Diana E. H. Russell, published by Pergamon Press in 1989. "Inheritance of Absence" appeared in *The New Internationalist,*" No. 261 (November 1994). "Something Wants to Be Seen: on the Art of Lanke Rothman" appeared in the catalog for an exhibit of her work at the Judah Magnes Museum in Berkeley, the Jewish Museum in New York, and the Goldman Fine Arts Gallery at the Jewish Community Center in Washington, D.C.

About the Author

A well-known and respected writer, poet, essayist, lecturer, teacher, playwright, and filmmaker, **Susan Griffin** is the author of several critically acclaimed books—including *Women and Nature* and *Pornography and Silence*—and is the recipient of numerous grants and awards. Her previous book *A Chorus of Stones* was the winner of the Bay Area Reviewers Association Award for Nonfiction, and a finalist for the Pulitzer Prize for Nonfiction and the National Book Critics Circle Award for Criticism. She lives in Berkeley, California.